ADVENTURES IN NATURE

HONDURAS

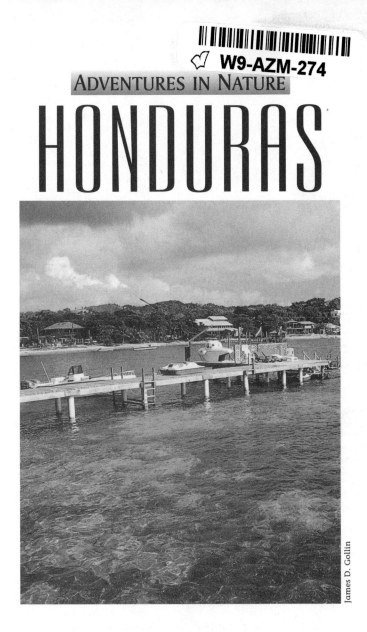

James D. Gollin

**AVALON
TRAVEL**
publishing

Adventures in Nature: Honduras
2nd EDITION

James D. Gollin

Published by
Avalon Travel Publishing, Inc.
5855 Beaudry St.
Emeryville, CA 94608, USA

Printing History
2nd edition—February 2001
5 4 3 2 1

© Text and photos copyright James D.
Gollin, 2001.
All rights reserved.
© Maps copyright Avalon Travel Publish-
ing, 2001.
All rights reserved.
Some photos are used by permission
and are the property of the original copyright owners.

Please send all comments, corrections,
additions, amendments, and critiques to:

Adventures in Nature: Honduras
AVALON TRAVEL PUBLISHING
5855 BEAUDRY ST.
EMERYVILLE, CA 94608, USA
e-mail: info@travelmatters.com
www.travelmatters.com

ISBN: 1-56691-241-5
ISSN: Pending

Editors: Gregor Krause, Marisa Solís
Copy Editor: Nancy Gillan
Index: Ellen Cavalli
Graphics Coordinator: Erika Howsare
Production: Darren Alessi
Cartography: Kathleen Sparkes, White Hart Design — Albuquerque, NM, USA;
  Mike Morgenfeld
Map Editor: Mike Balsbaugh

Front cover photo: © Tim Brown/Index Stock, Inc.—Kayaking on Honduras Coast
Back cover photo: © Jodi Jacobson/Peter Arnold, Inc.—Scuba diving, Honduras

Distributed in the United States and Canada by Publishers Group West

Printed in the United States by Publishers Press

*Although every effort was made to ensure that the information was correct at the time
of going to press, the author and publisher do not assume and hereby disclaim any
liability to any party for any loss or damage caused by errors, omissions, or any
potential travel disruption due to labor or financial difficulty, whether such errors or
omissions result from negligence, accident, or any other cause.*

CONTENTS

CONTENTS

ACKNOWLEDGMENTS

On my first trip to Honduras, nearly a decade ago, I attended a board meeting of the "Environmental Air Force" Lighthawk, and my life was enriched by meetings with such wonderful Hondurans as eco-entrepreneur Pepe Herrero, indigenous leader Osvaldo Munguia, and biologist Gustavo Cruz. They quickly convinced me that Honduras is one of the most underrated and misunderstood nations in the hemisphere. They also made me promise to return. It has been my great pleasure to fulfill that promise. I have returned many times to write articles, shoot photographs and videos, interview representatives of NGOs on behalf of the foundations that support them, to research this book and its second edition and, of course, simply to enjoy the beautiful land and people.

In many ways, this book is a cooperative effort. The first edition was co-written by the illustrious Ron Mader, author of Mexico: Adventures in Nature and publisher of the award-winning and always fascinating Eco-Travels in Latin America website (www.planeta.com). And even before he and I began to write this book, my Honduran friends have been asking to have their story told. During the writing process, not only Pepe and Osvaldo but members of many of the environmental groups discussed herein, government leaders, tourism promoters, Peace Corps volunteers, and Catrachos proud of their country have been generous in their support and meticulous in their offering of relevant details that, we hope, will make this book invaluable to the reader. Special thanks to expatriates such as Tony Brand, Kent Forte, Chet Thomas, Guillermo Yuscaran, and others who, like me, have succumbed to the spell of Honduras, as well as to dedicated Hondurans such as and Max Elvir, Fito Steiner, Julio Galindo, and Jorge Betancourt.

I want to praise Avalon Travel Publishing for having the courage to publish a book that is more than simple travel-fluff, a book that attempts to tell the true story of a threatened paradise and those fighting to save it.

And I want to thank Suzanne once again, for her support during the research and writing of this edition, and our son Noah Benjamin, who was born during the writing of this book.

Traveler, if you find something worthy of mention in Honduras, or that some of the information in this book has become outdated, please send an email to jgollin@aol.com.

— James D. Gollin

ABOUT THIS BOOK

Adventures in Nature: Honduras is a guide to Honduras's most exciting destination for active travelers who are interested in exploring the country's natural wonders. Along with the best places for hiking and mountain biking and prime spots for bird-watching and white-water rafting, author James Gollin recommends outfitters and local guides who can provide gear and lead you to the more remote parts of the country. He also points out places to eat and stay that will help you enjoy local cultures and cuisine. All prices are given in Honduran lempiras.

ACRONYMS USED IN THIS BOOK

AHE—Honduras Ecological Association
AMARAS—Environmental and Wildlife Rehabilitation Center
AMITIGRA—Amigos de la Tigra (La Tigra National Park)
APROECOH—Honduras Ecotourism Promoters Association
ASCONA—Associación Surena para la Conservación de la
  Naturaleza
BCIE—Central American Bank for Economic Integration
BICA—Bay Islands Conservation Association
CENCA—Center for Environmental Education
COCESNA—(Central American Air Traffic Control
CODDEFFAGOLF—Committee for the Defense and Development
  of the Flora and Fauna of the Gulf of Fonseca
COHDEFOR—Honduran Forestry Development Corporation
COVITUDENA—"A grass-roots non-lucrative organization exclusively
  formed by the Native Indians of the Reserve of the Río Plátano,
  whose purpose is to defend their ancestral rights and the natural
  beauty of the biosphere against ambition and greed from ousiders."
  (quote from Cecilio Colindres, owner/operator of COVITUDENA)
DIGEPESCA—Ministry of Natural Resources Fisheries Department
EIS—Environmental Impact Studies
ENEE—National Electric Company of Honduras
ESNACIFOR—managing agency for Lancetilla Botanical Gardens
EU—European Union
FHIS—Honduran Social Development Fund
FIDE—Foundation for Investment and the Development of Exports
FMLN—Frente Farabundo Movimiento para la Liberación Nacional

FUCAGUA—Foundation for Capiro and Calentura National Park and the Guaimoreto Lagoon
FUPNAPIB—Pico Bonito National Park Foundation
FUCSA—Cuero y Salado Foundation
FUSEP—Public Security Force
GEO—Ecological Group of Olancho
HRPF—Fundación Ecologista Hector Rodrigo Pastor Fasquelle
IDB—Inter-American Development Bank
IHT—Honduran Institute of Tourism
INA—National Agrarian Institute
INAH—Honduran National Institute of Anthropology and History
MOPAWI—Mosquitia Pawisi (Development of La Mosquitia)
NAFTA—North American Free Trade Agreement
NGO—non-governmental organization
PAG—Proyecto Aldea Global
PANACAM—Parque Nacional Cerro Azul Meambar
PNJK—Parque Nacional Jeannette Kawas
PROLANSATE—Foundation for the Protection of Lancetilla, Punta Sal, and Texiguat
RIMS—Roatán Institute for Marine Science
SAEC—South American Explorer's Club
SANAA—the Honduran governmental agency in charge of water resources
SEDA—Environmental Secretariat
SERNA—Secretariat of Natural Resources and Energy
UNAH—Universidad Nacional Autonoma de Honduras
USAID—U.S. Aid for International Development
WATA—environmental group formed by the Pech tribe
WTO—World Tourism Organization
WWF—World Wildlife Fund

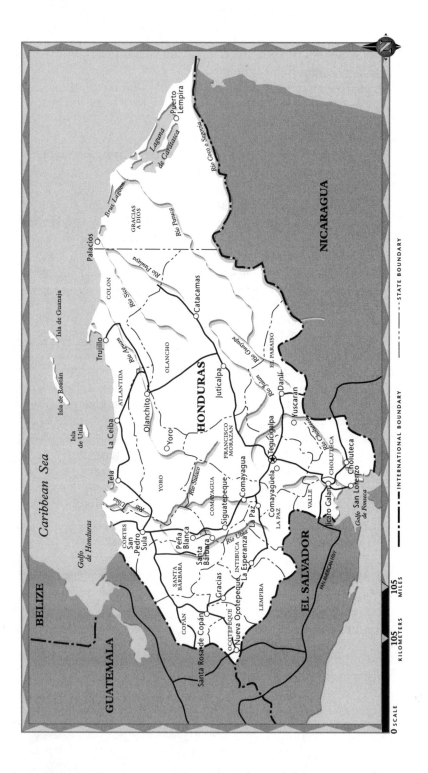

CHAPTER 1

Honduras:
An Adventure Awaits

Why visit Honduras? Because it is the most underrated tourist destination in Central America. Honduras has more accessible and beautiful reefs than Belize or the Yucatán, more extensive rain forests and cloud forests than Costa Rica, Mayan ruins comparable to those of Guatemala, better beaches than Nicaragua, a more peaceful political climate than El Salvador, safer cities than those of Panama, and the greatest undeveloped wilderness area in all of Central America. For environmentally oriented travelers, especially for those who like to get off the beaten path, Honduras is a dream come true.

With all these attractions, why does Honduras not enjoy a bigger presence in the international tourism market? Honduras is largely undiscovered because it is widely misunderstood. Try telling friends that you are thinking of going to Honduras. They will probably comment on Hurricane Mitch and ask, "Isn't it dangerous there?" Yes, Honduras was badly mauled by a hurricane in 1998, but it has recovered. And Honduras is no more dangerous than many parts of the United States. Yes, there were wars all around Honduras. There was a civil war in Nicaragua, and the counterrevolutionary Contras found sanctuary on the Nicaragua–Honduras border, a fact that still taints Honduras in the eyes of some North American leftists. At the same time, there was a civil war in El Salvador, and leftist FMLN (Frente

Farabundo Movimiento para la Liberación Nacional) guerrillas found sanctuary along their border with Honduras. And to the north, there has been a vicious genocidal civil war in Guatemala. But in the 1980s, a time of turmoil in Central America, Honduras didn't have a civil war. It has chosen to resolve its issues peacefully—and to open its borders to refugees in need.

Your friends might then ask, "Isn't Honduras a banana republic run by a bunch of corrupt generals?" The answer again is no. For decades Honduras has been a well-functioning democracy with a free press and regular rotation of power between the political parties. Of course there is some corruption. Sure, money plays a role in Honduran politics—just as it does in the United States and other flawed democracies. And yes, the military still plays an important role in society, but less and less each year. Honduras has changed from its "banana republic" days of the past.

Honduras is still a poor country, and the fledgling tourism industry is not a well-oiled machine. Honduras lacks the resort-hotel infrastructure of Costa Rica or the Yucatán. Except for the Bay Islands and Copán, its roadless forests and simple beach resorts are unrefined and even, to be polite, a bit funky. It is a land of "soft adventure." But many who come for the adventure return several times, and in doing so are helping Hondurans (or Catrachos, as they call themselves) to build both a tourism industry and an environmental movement.

In Honduras, environmental tourism is more than a way for foreign travelers to have fun while spending hard currency. Tourism is an integral part of environmental preservation. Honduran environmentalists have thrown themselves into the tourism business, seeing tourist money as the key to convincing their countrymen that their forests are worth more standing than cut to make way for cattle, that their beaches are worth more as tourist sites than as gravel supply dumps. They recognize that tourism is an animal not easily tamed, but they see no significant economic alternatives. They are facing the challenge and hoping for the best, strategizing ways to develop tourism without destroying fragile habitat or traditional cultures. While it may be imperfect, tourism is better than slash-and-burn farming, cattle ranching, or clear-cutting tropical timber.

Visit Honduras now. Go now because you want to visit a country to which few people you know have been. Go back because you find

Honduras irresistible. Return yet again, later, because Honduras is big enough and varied enough to handle the crowds and still maintain its wilderness. And each time that you visit, know that the judicious use of your tourist dollars is helping to preserve this slice of paradise.

For the moment, relatively few tourists visit Honduras—approximately 405,000 in 1998, less than half the number who visit Costa Rica. There is very little doubt that these numbers will soon explode. Hotels are opening or expanding, travel agencies are publishing glossy flyers, and American Airlines has joined Continental in offering nonstop flights from the United States.

LAY OF THE LAND

With a land area of 112,492 square kilometers (43,433 square miles), Honduras is the second-largest country in Central America (only Nicaragua is bigger).

It is a land of mountains and forests, of beaches and coral, of mangroves and wilderness. It is the most mountainous country in Central America. Indeed, two-thirds of the national territory is mountainous (the cities and agricultural fields lie primarily in the valleys that make up the remaining third). The average altitude of the Honduran mainland is roughly 300 meters (1,000 feet) above sea level, with the highest peaks, in Celaque National Park, rising to 2,827 meters (9,275 feet). The volcanic cordillera that runs down the backbone of the Central American isthmus divides Honduras into contrasting coastal ecosystems on the Pacific and the Caribbean. The

Virgin rain forest in Olancho

James D. Gollin

3

lowlands are divided by three major mountain ranges. The southern cordillera runs along the Nicaraguan border; the central cordillera divides the eastern department of Olancho from the Caribbean; and the northern cordillera follows the north coast. The mountain range that begins in the northwestern quadrant (El Merendon, home to Cusuco National Park) disappears under the Caribbean Sea and emerges as the Bay Islands.

The country encompasses the largest tract of remaining forest in all of Central America—about 40 percent of the total land area. The Holdridge System of biological classification shows eight distinct ecosystems present in Honduras: humid tropical forest, dry tropical forest, very dry tropical forest, very humid subtropical forest, humid subtropical forest, dry subtropical forest, humid low montane forest, and very humid low montane forest. In layman's terms, we call the humid and very humid lowland forests "rain forests" while the montane forests, those above 3,600 meters (11,800 feet), are referred to as "cloud forests."

Tropical rain forest covers the warm, wet lowlands of the Caribbean coast. The Pacific lowlands are drier than their Caribbean counterparts and support tropical dry forests. Trade winds from the northeast get stopped by the mountains that run parallel to the coast. La Ceiba and Tela receive more than 3 meters (10 feet) of rain each year. You'll also find the most active rivers draining into the Caribbean. As the elevation increases in the interior of the country, the climate becomes drier and cooler in the tropical highlands and valleys.

If you love beaches, Honduras offers more than any other Central American country, and much of it is within easy access to some of the country's most interesting national parks. The country has 820 kilometers (about 509 miles) of exceptional coastline, much of it blanketed with mangroves—the nurseries of the country's productive marine fisheries. The mangroves are threatened with urban development as well as commercial shrimp fishing. The distribution of mangroves on the Caribbean extends from Puerto Cortés to Cabo Gracias a Dios. All of the Bay Islands have extensive mangroves as well. On the Pacific side, mangroves are found throughout the Golfo de Fonseca (Gulf of Fonseca), from the Río Goascoran to the Nicaraguan border.

The Caribbean coast boasts white-sand beaches and the well-developed tourist towns of Tela, La Ceiba, and Trujillo (as well as the underwater paradise of the longest coral reef in the Northern Hemisphere, paralleling the coast and easily accessible from the Bay Islands). The Pacific coast has black-sand beaches and the less-frequented towns of San Lorenzo and Ampala. The beach resorts of Cedeño, Punta Ratón, and the volcanic island of El Tigre are frequented primarily by Hondurans and Salvadorans.

On the Pacific, the rainy season begins in May and lasts until October. Clouds build up in the late afternoon until torrential rains pour down 'til dusk. It usually rains for a few hours each day, leaving mornings clear. On the northern coast, heavy rains occur from September to February, again in the afternoon, while hurricanes threaten the coast and the Bay Islands from late summer through October or November. December and January are the coolest months in Honduras.

Given the combination of high rainfall and the country's status as the most mountainous in Central America, it should be no surprise that Honduras has a large number of spectacular waterfalls and raging rivers, many of them ideal for white-water rafting and kayaking, an activity discussed in Chapter 4: The Lenca Trail. The rivers are beautiful but, when combined with poor environmental policies that allow deforestation, they are dangerous. When Hurricane Fifi struck the Caribbean coast in 1974, deforested hillsides slid into rivers forming temporary dams that burst and destroyed entire villages, leaving 15,000 dead.

The longest rivers—Coco, Patuca, Sico, Aguán, Chamelecón, and Ulúa—drain the north coast and La Mosquitia. They form numerous wide, flat, terraced plains, the only flat land in Honduras except for the coastal plains. Rafting and outboard *pipantes,* or small dugout canoes, are ideal methods of travel on the larger, easternmost rivers.

CULTURE

About 90 percent of the Honduran population is mestizo, a mixture of indigenous, African, and Spanish races also referred to as Ladino.

There also are small minorities of European, African, Asian, and Arabic peoples, and six main indigenous Indian groups: the Miskito, Pech or Paya, Chorti Maya, Lenca, Jicaque or Tolupan, and Tawahka. Yet another group in this diverse mix is the Garífuna people.

The Garífunas' story began to unfold a thousand years ago when the Arawak, a South American tribe of hunters and farmers, moved up the Orinoco River to the Caribbean Sea, where they traded with the Caribs. The mixture of Carib and Arawak created a new people who came to be called the "Island Carib."

In the 1500s Europeans brought African slaves to the Caribbean Islands. The Island Caribs defended their islands but lost much of their territory. In 1635 two Spanish ships bringing slaves to the West Indies were shipwrecked near St. Vincent; the slaves on board escaped and took refuge with the Island Caribs. The Africans adopted the language and culture of their hosts, and intermarriages brought a new hybrid mixture of African and Indian Caribs, known today as the Garífuna (or Garinagu or Black Caribs).

In the 1700s Britain took over St. Vincent after a long and bloody war, and exiled the Garífuna to the island off Roatán. They arrived at Port Royal on April 12, 1797, and from there dispersed along the mainland coast from Belize to Nicaragua. Two hundred years later, in 1997, the Garífuna celebrated their bicentennial in Honduras.

Most Hondurans are Roman Catholic, but Protestant proselytizing has resulted in significant numbers of converts. Miskito Indians are usually Moravians. Spanish is the predominant language, although some English is spoken along the north coast and is the dominant language on the Caribbean Bay Islands.

THE EARLIEST INHABITANTS

Human occupation of what is now Honduras began sometime between 9000 and 7000 b.c., during the final stage of the last major ice age. The first peoples of Central America, like the first peoples everywhere, were nomadic hunters and gatherers. About 6,000 years ago, clever pre-Catrachos threw down some seeds on a muddy riverbank and agriculture was born in the region. Once plants were cultivated, people could settle in a particular place and begin building more permanent shelters. Scientists call the period from 4000 to 1000 b.c. the "Formative Period" in which societies became more complex and people began to create villages. As agriculture improved, surpluses allowed for the development of a priestly class and the construction of temples.

Honduras appears to have been a major center of activity for a variety of civilizations that predate the Maya by thousands of years. Glimpses into this early history are offered by new discoveries from excavations at the Talgua caves in Sierra de Agalta, at Las Naranjos on the north shore of Lake Yojoa, and at dozens of archaeological sites deep within the wilderness of the Mosquito Coast. Very little of the information gathered has been released yet, but the next decade is sure to be an exciting one for Honduran archaeology.

"We have found the first evidence of Early Formative Period people in the heartland of Honduras," says Dr. Rosemary Joyce of the University of California, "and those people are in contact, unexpectedly, with the Olmec civilization."

Her findings at Puerto Escondido (in the suburbs of San Pedro Sula) reveal a new society taking shape between about 1200 and 900 b.c. across a region stretching from Mexico to Honduras. For the first time, people widely separated by geography—particularly a new, elite class—were developing long-distance contacts and sharing luxury goods, religious ideas, and customs.

The Olmec lived on the distant Gulf Coast of Mexico, but Olmec-style vases have been uncovered near Lake Yojoa, in the department of Olancho, and near Trujillo. The Trujillo Museum has stone carvings of baby-faced twins that may represent the Olmecs' "Morning Star and Evening Star." It is not clear if the Olmecs traveled to Honduras or if the Honduran Indians traveled to present-day Mexico. Further, it is unknown whether the pottery itself or the skills to make it were transferred south from the Olmec territory.

What did the early Hondurans have to trade? Some gold, jade, and, not to be discounted, cacao beans, the source of chocolate. Not only were the beans themselves used as currency, the chocolate drink made from them was the exclusive privilege of the aristocratic class, used for special ceremonies. Native to Central America, the plant became popular in Mexico, and cacao delicacies were even served to the Spanish conquistadors.

The mysterious pre-Mayan civilizations of Honduras are often referred to collectively as "the Lencas." In fact, the Lenca Indians were the dominant civilization at the time of the arrival of the Europeans, and Lencan culture lives on today in remote parts of Western Honduras. The use of the name "Lenca" to describe the earlier civilization or civilizations shows how little is actually known about them. As new information is published by the archaeologists now at work, ancient history will be rewritten.

The Maya Indians settled in western Honduras around 1000 b.c. and developed an important network of cities centered at Copán, the ceremonial hub, sometimes called the Athens of the New World. The well-studied archaeological remains tell the story of a civilization that grew slowly from 2,000 b.c. to a.d. 800, expanded wildly in a flowering of art, then collapsed around a.d. 900. What caused the downfall of the Mayan civilization? Skeletal remains provide evidence that the people were not getting enough nourishment. Other evidence indicates that the nearby forests were ravaged. Deforestation probably resulted in less-productive hunting, soil erosion, and inadequate rains. Ecological collapse is assumed to be the cause of the demise of the Mayas.

In an era before hardwood exports and cattle ranching, what caused the deforestation? Was it solely the result of gathering firewood for cooking or clearing land for farming? Current theories postulate that the Mayas' increasingly large temples were the culprits. Plastering the temples required lye, which was produced by burning limestone, which in turn required a tremendous amount of fuelwood. Archaeologists at Pennsylvania State University maintain that the Copán Maya would have used oak, not pine, for firewood. The lime kilns never use pine. So, these archaeologists assert, the pine forests disappeared for other reasons, such as to provide timber for construction. Either way, though, temple construction and maintenance may well have resulted in deforestation, soil degradation, and poorer harvests.

As conditions worsened, one can imagine the people of Copán turning increasingly to religion, building bigger temples to appease the gods, which, ironically, hastened the demise of their civilization. By a.d. 900, the Copán Maya abandoned the city; their descendants, the Chorti Maya, inhabit the region today. (At the beginning of a new millennium, the Chorti Maya are still struggling for the return of some ancestral lands usurped centuries ago by European conquest. In a hard-won accord, the government promised to investigate more thoroughly the 1997 assassination of Chorti leader Candido Amador and to turn over 2,000 hectares in Ocotepeque and 500 hectares in Copán, with a promise of more land later.)

THE ENCOUNTER: EUROPE COMES KNOCKING

The European invasion of Honduras started in 1502 with the fourth and final voyage of Christopher Columbus. That summer, Columbus sailed along the coast looking for refuge in the deep waters; historians suggest this is the origin of the name "Honduras," which means "depths." He landed on the island of Guanaja, which he called Isla de los Piños (Pine Island), at the site of present-day Trujillo. There he celebrated the first Catholic mass on the American continent. Things would never be the same.

Prior to the Encounter, Honduras was heavily populated. Estimates run from 500,000 to 1 million people. However, slavery and diseases such as smallpox ravaged the population, and in just 100 years the indigenous population was decimated, plunging to 15,000 to 20,000—a 95-percent reduction. It was not until the 19th century that the population reached pre-conquest levels; in the second half of this century it exceeded them, with environmental destruction following close behind.

Three Spanish expeditions arrived in 1524, and in 1525 Hernán Cortés led an overland exhibition from Mexico to Honduras. A governor was appointed the following year, but the native population of Lenca Indians did not accept colonialism without a battle. Lempira, the chief of the Lencas, led 30,000 Indians against the Spanish and repeatedly repulsed their invasions. During peace talks in 1536 Lempira was betrayed and assassinated. Without his leadership, resistance was quickly crushed by the Spaniards.

The colonization of Honduras by the Spaniards brought not only new kinds of people, from the Spaniards themselves to African slaves, but also new species of plants and animals. The Spanish introduced cattle, horses, and other livestock to the New World, taking tobacco, coffee, maize, squash, potatoes, and many other species back to the Old. Gold- and silver-mining techniques were brought up to 16th-century standards, large cattle ranches and plantations were developed, and the landscape itself began to change as new towns and fields were carved out of the forests on the valley floors and coastal plains.

Central America gained its independence from Spain in 1821, and the great debate began: Should Central America be one nation or many? Factions fought bitterly as the country was briefly annexed to the Mexican Republic, then withdrew to join the newly formed United Provinces of Central America. Conservatives from the Central American government invaded Honduras in 1826. At that time Francisco Morazán, a Liberal, repelled the invasion and then in turn took control of the Central American federation. Efforts to maintain the union were unsuccessful.

In 1838 the Central American countries decided to go their separate ways. Honduras signed its new constitution in 1839. The capital of the country alternated between the twin towns of Tegucigalpa and Comayagua until taking root in the former (known affectionately as "Teguz" in Honduras) in 1880 after the high society in Comayagua reportedly snubbed President Marco Aurelio Soto's Guatemalan Indian wife. The rise of Tegucigalpa was also due to the massive mineral wealth, in the form of gold and silver, that was then being mined at Rosario, under what is now La Tigra National Park.

Since independence, Honduras has been plagued with nearly 300 internal rebellions, civil wars, and changes of government, more than half occurring during the 20th century. The country has also been the repeated target of foreign intervention. The most infamous example was the intervention by U.S. soldier of fortune William Walker, who appointed himself President of Nicaragua and attempted to take over the rest of Central America in 1860. His campaign ended in defeat and he was executed in Trujillo.

The British occupied Tigre Island in the Gulf of Fonseca in 1849. This action set off panic in the United States, and led to the binational 1850 Clayton–Bulwer Treaty in which the United States and Great Britain pledged to leave Honduras alone. The Americans were concerned about British influence in what they considered to be their own backyard, and were particularly nervous about British plans to build a canal across Central America. The Clayton–Bulwer Treaty was violated in 1852 when Britain declared the Bay Islands a crown colony, though it withdrew that claim seven years later in exchange for recognition of its rights in British Honduras (now Belize).

THE ECONOMY: BANANAS AND BEYOND

The history of Honduras in the first half of the 20th century is a tale of banana companies, banana wars, and the establishment of a banana republic. The fruit was selling fast in the United States, and New Orleans banana traders saw Honduras as an excellent location to build up production and diversify supply away from Costa Rica. The resulting boom would transform both the economies and the ecosystems along the north coast.

In 1911 the Cuyamel Fruit Company (the predecessor of the United Fruit Company) was organized by Sam Zemurray and began operations on Honduras's north coast. In 1913 the Standard Fruit Company followed. Eventually these companies owned 75 percent of

Celaque National Park, as seen from San Cristobal Castle in Gracias

11

the nation's banana plantations and nearly 100 percent of its politicians—hence the term "banana republic." The companies allied themselves with political factions, and because bananas dominated the economy, the companies had great influence in local politics. The banana companies built railroads and seaports, and the banana industry dominated the national economy, but very little of this wealth remained in Honduras.

Since 1912 Chiquita Brands International—formerly the United Fruit Company—has dominated the north coast of Honduras. In 1987, one of Chiquita's best years in Honduras, banana exports topped 32 million 40-pound boxes. In 1990, then-President Rafael Callejas sought to put a positive spin on the country's derisive "banana republic" nickname by announcing plans to nearly double banana exports by the end of the year 2000. Demand had been growing, especially in Europe. But in 1993 the European Union (EU) slapped tariffs and later country-by-country quotas on Latin America in order to favor bananas from their former colonies in the Caribbean. The United States appealed to the World Trade Organization, which handed down a verdict favorable to Honduras, but the Europeans have so far refused to accept additional Honduran bananas.

In the 1930s the Honduran economy diversified, after silatoka, known as "the Panama disease," devastated large portions of the banana plantations. There was new impetus for investments in mining, ranching, and coffee farming. Coffee now actually tops bananas as an export crop.

Bananas have been good to Honduras, but apparently not good enough. The nation ranks among the least-developed countries in the Western Hemisphere. According to the World Bank, per-capita gross national product (GNP) remains low, at an estimated $600. Twenty-seven percent of the adult population is illiterate, and almost 19 percent of children under age five suffer from moderate to severe undernutrition. An estimated 60 percent of the population is inadequately housed.

The country's economy is still primarily based on agriculture. Mainstays coffee and bananas contribute more than 50 percent to Honduran export revenues, though these have been joined by "nontraditional" exports such as farmed shrimp and dive-caught lobster.

Hoping to diversify away from agricultural products, the Honduran government embarked on a program of bringing *maquiladora* plants (factories that assemble imported items for re-export, usually clothing or electronics) to the country in 1990. The main selling point was the country's low wages. In 1991, wages were 48 cents per hour, the lowest in Central America. Over the last decade, the country's Foundation for Investment and the Development of Exports (FIDE) has been working to attract foreign investment in tourism and environmental tourism, allowing for tax incentives and free trade zones for *maquiladoras* and duty-free importation of tourism-related capital equipment (such as rental cars or hotel fixtures) in areas named, rather oddly, "Tourist Free Zones."

The Honduran *maquilas* have a bad reputation in the United States, largely because of adverse publicity relating to the production of a line of Kathie Lee Gifford clothing at a factory that used child labor. While true child labor is indefensible, it is important to distinguish between North American and Central American concepts of childhood. In the United States it is quite acceptable for a young person to enter the workforce at 18, after high school, or at 22, after college. In poorer countries, most kids start to work as soon as they are physically able, tending animals or working in the fields to bring in a bit more money for a bit more food for the family. The idea of a 15-year-old working full time in a factory is not shocking to most Hondurans.

In fact, most *maquila* workers are women in their 20s, many of them unmarried mothers who support their families on their meager but sufficient wages. The alternative to *maquila* work, for most of them, is agricultural work, which pays less and is harder on the body. Many *maquilas* are owned by Korean and Taiwanese entrepreneurs who have emigrated to Honduras, a land of comparative opportunity due to its ease of access into the United States. Many Hong Kong Chinese have also emigrated to Honduras, purchased citizenship under a plan that allows immigrants with capital to become Hondurans, then re-emigrated to the United States under the Honduran quota, an easier path than applying directly from Hong Kong. It turns out that corrupt officials in the Callejas administration, aided by an ally in the U.S. Embassy, orchestrated this scheme to line their pockets with the capital that was supposed to help build the

Honduran economy. Years later, this "Chinazo" scandal is still under investigation.

During the 1980s the economy was propped up with massive amounts of U.S. aid, an unofficial quid pro quo for letting the Contras' and Ollie North's secret army fight the Sandinistas from Honduran soil. The nation's access to bilateral and multilateral credit expanded rapidly, along with the external debt that nearly tripled to more than $3.6 billion by 1990. However, much of this loan money was spent on military hardware, military base expansion, and aid to the Contras. As a result, the "assistance" did not address the country's social or infrastructure needs.

In the same go-go atmosphere, the Honduran government began to spend far more than it could bring in through taxation, running huge fiscal deficits. External credit eventually became scarce as peace talks made progress in the region. By 1989 Honduras, unable to cut its fiscal deficit, went into arrears with multilateral banks and was cut off by the international finance banks.

The Reina administration came into office in 1994 and instituted fiscal measures to enable Honduras to comply with international banking requirements. These measures reduced the 1994 deficit to 6.9 percent of GDP, down from 11.6 percent in 1993 under the Callejas administration. The next year the Reina administration was able to reduce the fiscal deficit to 3.6 percent of GDP. Reina's economic reform plan was hampered by the 1994 drought, which caused tremendous economic and environmental problems. Because there was insufficient rainfall to fill the El Cajón reservoir, the government began rationing power. Businesses and homes were without electricity for six to 14 hours a day. This power shortage was largely responsible for the country's negative 1.4 economic growth rate.

In 1995 the rainy season replenished El Cajón and, with the addition of used diesel power plants purchased from Mexico, the Honduran energy company (ENEE) has been able to meet demands. A second thermoelectric plant has been inaugurated, adding to the nation's electricity supply, and a number of new dams are under construction or in early planning stages, many of them opposed by environmentalists. With electricity flowing, the Honduran economy grew by nearly 4 percent in 1995 and 1996 and by more than 5 percent in

1997. In 1998 the Honduran economy was impacted by a tariff squabble with the United States, which was irritated that Honduran cable and satellite television distributors were engaging in "intellectual property piracy," charging Honduran customers for the services but not paying royalties to the U.S. networks. Of course, many nations, including giants like China, regularly pirate the intellectual property of Hollywood, but Honduras was chosen as an example and punished with restrictions on exports to the United States.

On October 26, 1998, disaster struck Honduras when Hurricane Mitch soaked and wind-whipped the unlucky nation nonstop for a solid week, destroying crops, factories, bridges, and homes, and killing an estimated 7,000 to 12,000 people. Eighty percent of the nation's agriculture was destroyed, as were 94 important bridges, and 20 percent of the Honduran people were left homeless. Mitch was the fourth most powerful hurricane ever measured, and the most deadly in 200 years. At the time, pundits declared that Honduras would become a basket case, dependent on handouts for survival for at least a decade. In fact, emergency relief efforts reopened roads and airports rapidly and widespread starvation and disease were avoided. Most lives were lost in semi-urban *"colonias,"* poor neighborhoods outside of major cities where people built ramshackle homes on unstabilized, hilly soil, and cut down the trees for timber and fuel. With the rains, entire hillsides collapsed, creating a tremendous human tragedy. In less-populated, more natural areas, the wind blew down a good many trees but the rainforest ecosystem was able to soak up the excess water like a sponge, averting disaster. Mitch was a lesson to all Honduras: deforestation endangers lives.

Ninety percent of Honduran lodging capacity was up and running just one week after Mitch passed through, but the tourists stayed away that season, causing further hardship to the 45,000 people who earn their livings from the tourist trade. In certain areas there was a short boom as hotels filled with aid workers and media, but most vanished in a matter of weeks, heading on to the next big disaster story. A number of guides and outfitters, unable to handle a year without significant income, went under. By 1999, however, tourism was back to pre-Mitch levels, though still far below what the nation would like to see. The Honduras Institute of Tourism began a massive advertising campaign in 1999, spending almost a million dollars on ads in U.S. and European magazines to support post-Mitch tourism recovery.

GOVERNMENT AND POLITICS

Honduras's 1982 constitution provides for a strong executive branch, a unicameral National Congress, and a judiciary appointed by the National Congress. The president is directly elected to a four-year term by popular vote, and political parties tend to hand off power to each other with a minimum of fuss and no violence.

Members of the 128-seat legislature also serve four-year terms; congressional seats are assigned the parties' candidates in proportion to the number of votes each party receives.

The judiciary includes a Supreme Court of Justice, courts of appeal, and several courts of original jurisdiction, such as labor, tax, and criminal courts. Honduras is divided into 18 *departamentos* ("departments," similar to states), each with its own *cabecera* ("capital"); officials are elected for two-year terms.

James D. Gollin

Traditional architecture in Tegucigalpa

With a population of 5.5 million people, Honduras has the second-lowest population density in the region (after Nicaragua), with one person per 5.5 acres, according to the World Resources Institute. This low density has resulted in land ownership patterns more equitable than those of its neighbors. More than anything else, this sense of unending wilderness has eased social tensions and allowed Honduras to avoid the violent civil wars that have raged all around it.

Unlike Costa Rica, Honduras has no pretensions to being the Switzerland of Central America. Poverty, while not desperate, is widespread. Because the land is rich, the people are rarely hungry, but most live lives of simplicity by necessity. Besides, Hondurans wouldn't want to be Swiss or North Americans. They are proud of being Catrachos.

National pride is a major force behind the growth of the Honduran environmental movement. While Costa Rica and Belize host 747s filled with wealthy tourists coming to marvel at the rain forests and reefs, Honduras is regularly visited by executives of multinational corporations who believe that they can dupe the Catrachos into underselling their natural resources. Stone Container Corp., for example, received permission in the early 1990s to pulp a million hectares of the forests of the Mosquito Coast and turn them into cardboard boxes. Hondurans of all regions and classes rose up against the plan, forcing government officials to retract permission. In 1997 a Kuwaiti concern received permission to build a giant oil refinery on Trujillo Bay, an incomparably beautiful bay that contains the best undeveloped deepwater port in the Americas. Once again, popular opposition forced the cancellation of this ill-conceived plan, at least for now.

The government of Honduras has not traditionally been a leading force for environmental protection. It wasn't until 1980 that the nation celebrated the creation of its first national park, La Tigra, outside of Tegucigalpa. Also in 1980, the Río Plátano Biosphere Reserve was created on the Mosquito Coast and soon thereafter named a World Heritage Site by the United Nations. While the government has dithered, local Hondurans have banded together to protect their local environment, whether it be a mountainous forest that provides water for cities like San Pedro Sula or a mangrove swamp that acts as a nursery for marine life and, in turn, provides sustenance to fishermen. Recently, the government has climbed on the bandwagon, declaring 107 areas as "protected." Although the declaration of protection and actual protection are two different things, the Honduran government has laid the groundwork for what may prove to be the most innovative and ambitious park management program in the Americas.

The violence that engulfed all of Honduras's neighbors during the 1980s was due in large part not to ideology but to a struggle over scarce land. An earlier example of a similar crisis was the infamous

"Soccer War" waged between Honduras and El Salvador in 1969. The population of El Salvador, far denser than that of Honduras, had effectively deforested most of its land by the 1960s. Landless campesinos (peasants), seeing unused jungle fit for burning right across the border, began to migrate into Honduran territory, straining relations. Hondurans felt abused by the quiet invasion while Salvadorans were outraged at the alleged mistreatment their nationals were receiving at the hands of the Honduran authorities. A disputed decision in the 1969 World Cup qualifying match led to a short but bloody war in which 2,000 people were killed. The dispute also prompted Honduras to withdraw from the Central American Common Market, which soon dissolved. Hopes for regional economic unity were dashed, to be revived again only in the 1990s with the passage of the North American Free Trade Agreement (NAFTA).

The military held onto power in Honduras, not only by force of arms but also by a shrewd application of land reform; it supported the land tenure rights of campesinos and developed various schemes to encourage landless citizens from crowded regions such as the south to migrate to the areas around Trujillo, Olancho, and toward the Mosquito Coast. This type of land reform, while popular with the voters, is leading to the destruction of rain forests and the creation of nonsustainable farms on hillsides and other barely arable land that is subject to erosion. Why don't the campesinos farm the valleys? In 1988, the Central Bank of Honduras estimated that 48 percent of the valley lands in Honduras had been converted to cattle pasture, with much of the rest given over to plantation crops destined for export. Although the military has had no formal role in the civilian government since 1981, U.S. influence and money have allowed it to exert continued influence beyond its constitutional role.

During the 1980s the Honduran army received more than $500 million, hosted 5,000 American soldiers, and opened a number of new military bases. Meanwhile, the Honduran secret police and their Contra allies kidnapped and murdered suspected leftists and communist sympathizers in a CIA-aided operation that is only now being brought fully to light. It is estimated that approximately 183 enemies of the military "disappeared" during this dark time. While the injustice of those acts should not be downplayed, it is also important to remember that during that era 183 deaths would occur on a bad weekend in El Salvador or in a single afternoon in Guatemala.

As the Reina administration ended in 1997, its reputation was one of weakness due to a faltering economy, but the lasting legacy of President Reina will likely be his final reining in of the military's power. Previously, the Honduran police were supervised by the military. Reina created an independent police system accountable to civilians, disbanded the military's secret police, and established an independent judiciary. None of this is working very well at present, with former secret-police thugs implicated in a string of bank robberies and the civilian police not yet capable of taking on the challenge. But in the long term, this change will be critical to the establishment of some form of just and civil society in Honduras.

Prior to the Reina administration, the military filled their ranks via a crude form of conscription. Press gangs would raid villages or urban street corners, grab any young men they could find, drive them away in trucks, and put them in uniforms. Under Reina, the military have been forced to adopt a system of voluntary enlistment, reward the recruits with better pay and treatment, and, in an era of limited budgets, get by with a much smaller number of armed men. After Reina, it seems unlikely that the military will ever again seize power in a coup, as it so often did earlier in the century.

President Reina, of the Liberal Party, stepped down at the end of 1997, replaced by fellow Liberal Carlos Flores Faucusse, the former President of Congress. Flores, a graduate of Louisiana State University who is married to an American, is the nephew of one of Honduras's wealthiest industrialists, Miguel Faucusse. He has been in power in the National Assembly during the three administrations and was chief of staff to President Suazo Cordova during the Contra war. There is little evidence that he understands the importance of environmental issues and sustainable economic development. Whatever his intentions might have been, President Flores was plunged into the daunting task of helping his country survive Hurricane Mitch, and then repair and rebuild after the storm's devastation. Throughout the land, temporary "Bailey" bridges still cross many rivers. The foreign relief workers have left, leaving many to wonder what happened to funds earmarked for the building of permanent replacement bridges. Flores seems not to have learned the basic lesson of the storm, that intact forests save lives, and has sped up timber sales and resource exploitation in the name of getting the economy moving again. Ordez Turcios, his head of the forestry agency COHDEFOR (Honduran Forestry Development Corporation), is a throwback to pre-Reina days of massive chop.

Much as in the United States, it seems that the next presidential campaign begins scarcely after the last one was over. Potential candidates hoping to replace Flores after his single term include former Central Bank President Ricardo Maduro, who looks a bit like actor Richard Gere and is unofficially campaigning hard already to be the National Party candidate. If you see a bumper sticker announcing "Maduro," it does not mean "ripe." At least one Honduran friend, reacting to the plethora of Maduro bumper stickers, is planning to distribute others saying "Verde" meaning "green" or "unripe." On the Liberal Party Side, industrialist and media mogul Jaime Rosenthal is ever hopeful.

President Flores is also the owner of the middle-of-the-road pro-Liberal newspaper *La Tribuna*. Other papers include the nationalist-leaning establishment paper *La Prensa;* the left-of-center El Tiempo, owned by Liberal leader Jaime Rosenthal; the independent El Nuevo Día; and the sensationalist *El Heraldo.* While journalism in Honduras is not always of the highest standard, the press is generally free of government censorship. If you read any Spanish, buy a local paper and catch up on the latest scandal.

FLORA AND FAUNA

Due largely to its complex topography, Honduras boasts a veritable cornucopia of habitats, with everything from coral reefs to steamy rain forests to misty cloud forests, and pine forests, grasslands, mangroves, and much more in between. Each ecosystem, of course, supports a diverse array of plants and animals, birds and insects, reptiles and amphibians. With less than 1 percent of the world's surface area, Honduras harbors 10 percent of the world's biodiversity. There are nearly 50,000 species of insect, and 2,000 freshwater fish species.

Visitors will be surprised to find not only tropical environments but also forests of pine and oak reminiscent of North America.

Reminiscent, yes, but not identical. In these pine forests you can see troops of monkeys, families of toucans, and other exotic creatures.

In addition to the diverse habitat in Honduras, the country benefits from its location at the intersection of the Nearctic and Neotropical regions of the world. For millions of years, these regions were physically separated and each developed its own unique species. This changed when a land bridge emerged connecting North and South America. In Honduras and its neighbors, South and North American flora and fauna have all found a home.

Finally, what sets Honduras apart from some of its neighbors is the relatively pristine quality of much of the Honduran environment. Yes, the quetzal is the national bird of Guatemala, but the bird is almost extinct in the denuded cloud forests of that country while it can still be seen flitting among the trees in literally dozens of cloud-forest locations in Honduras.

These facts aside, information about Honduras's natural diversity is scattered and hard to find. While the relatively deforested nation of Costa Rica is thick with research zoologists from around the world and each remaining wild area is being carefully combed by "parataxonomists," the wilds of Honduras have been all but ignored by the international scientific community. Local biologists, including Dr. Gustavo Cruz, labor mightily with short funds, discovering new species and coming to understand the complex interrelationships between those already known. And U.S.-based professors such as Oliver Komar, editor of the biology and conservation bulletin Mesoamericana, are doing their best to fill in the gaps.

Sadly, the general level of ignorance about Honduran flora and fauna has an effect: It is a truism that people will not pro-

James D. Gollin

The web of life in the rain forest

21

tect what they don't understand or don't know exists. For that reason, we salute the likes of Gustavo Cruz and his colleagues, including Sherry Thorn, Saul Flores, Cirilo Nelson, and Sixto Aguilar, as well as North Americans such as Kent Forte. It is our hope, in future editions of this book, to provide improved, user-friendly lists of the non-human inhabitants of Honduras. Like the science of conservation biology itself, this is a work in progress.

Birds

Honduras is home to more than 710 species of birds (8 percent of the 9,000 bird species in the world), including birds that live in Honduras year-round and approximately 200 species that, like the tourists, come down to escape the winters of the north. Fifty-nine bird species are threatened and five are in imminent danger of extinction. For a more complete list of where you might find which birds, get the *Field Checklist of the Birds of Honduras* compiled by Dennis Beall (Chukar Publications, 1997). Some of the more dramatic birds to be found in Honduras include the following.

The largest eagle in the New World, the harpy is found in intact lowland broadleaf forests. The harpy navigates dexterously through the forest understory, hunting for its prey (monkeys, other birds, and small mammals) beneath the upper canopy. With a 7-foot-plus wingspan, this is no mean feat. Once thought to be extinct north of Panama, the harpy has been repeatedly sighted in the large, undisturbed areas of Honduras such as the Mosquito Coast. Other birds of prey in Honduras include ospreys; swallow-tailed and black-shouldered kites; various hawks, eagles, and falcons; caracaras; and four species of vulture, including the magnificent king vulture.

The quetzal, the sacred bird of the Maya—whose plumage was once traded like currency and used to adorn the crowns of kings and queens—is all but extinct in Guatemala but thrives in Honduran cloud forests from an altitude of 1,400 to 3,000 meters (4,593 to 9,842 feet). In spring, quetzals breed in dead tree stumps, and this is the best time to see them in places such as La Muralla, La Tigra, Cerro Azul Meambar, and anywhere else altitude and human absence allow. The quetzal's resplendent tail feathers, up to 1.2 meters (4 feet) long, curl under its iridescent green, red, and blue body in a question-mark shape.

The motmot, like the quetzal, has a tail that looks like it was invented by Dr. Seuss. In the case of the motmot, the long thin tail ends in two brightly colored, silver dollar–sized circles that it drapes through the foliage and waves around like a natural pendulum. The bird takes its name from its hooting cry.

The keel-billed toucan, a popular bird among those of us who grew up eating Froot Loops cereal, is easily recognizable due to its huge, brightly colored beak that seems to weigh it down as it flies through the forests in search of ripe fruit. This very social bird is rarely found alone. The toucan is abundant in Honduran forests despite being a traditional source of food for hunters. The smaller emerald toucanet can be found in higher elevations, especially around coffee plantations, while the rarer yellow-eared toucanet flits about middle elevations along the north coast and thrives in La Mosquitia. The large chestnut-mandibled toucan is present only in La Mosquitia, while the collared aracari, a type of small toucan, can be found in many Honduran forests.

The giant jabiru stork, with a wingspan of up to 3 meters (about 10 feet), can be found in wet lowland environments such as the Mosquito Coast and the Gulf of Fonseca. The black-headed jabiru has an inflatable crimson ring around the base of its neck, nests in the top of trees, and feeds primarily on small fish, snakes, and frogs.

Seven species of parrot and parakeet flit through the tropical forests of Honduras, but many are being hunted mercilessly to supply the pet market in the United States and Europe. Favored species include the yellow-naped and red-lored parrots, both of which are easily trained to "talk."

Scarlet macaws, brilliant-colored giant cousins to the parrot,

James D. Gollin

Parrots are often kept as pets in Honduras.

threatened, both by hunters and by the campesino tradition of keeping a bird with clipped wings as a family pet. Scarlet and military macaws were originally found throughout most of the country but now, due to loss of lowland forest habitat, just the type of territory that ranchers and campesinos like to cut and burn, their range has decreased. Presently, the greatest remaining macaw populations are in La Mosquitia. There are hopes that advances in captive breeding of macaws will one day satisfy the international pet market without recourse to hunting these magnificent and increasingly endangered birds.

Mammals

One hundred and ninety-five species of mammal have been recorded in Honduras, 5 percent of the total global mammal biodiversity. Nineteen of these, or nearly 10 percent, are classified as threatened, while another eight are in danger of extinction. Nearly half of all local mammals are bats, including 70 insect-eaters and two blood-drinkers.

The tapir, generally weighing between 350 and 650 pounds, is the largest indigenous land mammal in Central America. Distant relatives of horses and rhinos, tapirs require large areas of lowland forest to satisfy their 100-percent-vegetarian diet. The mammal lives primarily in La Mosquitia, though it once inhabited a larger portion of eastern Honduras and as far west as Comayagua Valley. The meat is considered quite tasty, so the tapir is particularly threatened by the intrusion of humans into its remaining habitat.

The West Indian manatee, a tuskless, walrus-like sea cow weighing up to 1,000 pounds, loves to loll just below the water's surface munching sea grasses. Manatees are terribly endangered, not just because their flesh tastes like pork and their lolling activity makes them the unintentional victims of motorboat propellers but also because their prime habitat zones, where freshwater streams and rivers meet the ocean, are being degraded by upstream deforestation and agrochemical use. Manatees are still plentiful in the Cuero y Salado refuge near La Ceiba, in Jeannette Kawas National Park near Tela, and throughout the lagoon system of the Mosquito Coast.

Bottlenose dolphins are common in the coastal waters around Jeannette Kawas National Park and in the Bay Islands. They frequently leap in the bow wakes of motorboats and will occasionally check out snorkelers or scuba divers. At Anthony's Key Resort on Roatán, dolphins in luxurious captivity perform for tourists and swim out in the open ocean to frolic with divers.

The jaguar *(el tigre)*, sacred symbol of the Maya, still stalks the forests of Honduras, though it is nearly extinct in neighboring Guatemala. Approximately the same size as a human, the jaguar is so stealthy that you will probably never see one unless you are a trained observer who sets up an observation blind in a likely location and sits still for days. *Panthera onca,* the largest Central American cat, rarely roars. The jaguar once ranged from Uruguay to the American Southwest, but now its territory has shrunk to the zone from Mexico to Argentina. Each cat requires several hundred square kilometers of "home range," a fact that helps explain its endangered status—along with a largely mistaken sense that the beasts are dangerous to humans. Still, if you do see a jaguar, don't run, as that can stimulate its instinct to give chase. Smaller cousins of the *tigre* include the jaguarundi, ocelot, margay, and puma.

Monkeys inhabiting the forests throughout Honduras include howler, white-faced, and spider monkeys. If you hear a bone-chilling roar in the forest near dusk or around dawn, don't worry. It's probably a howler monkey rather than a jaguar.

Anteaters, sloths, and armadillos together make up the order *Edentata* (literally, "without teeth"). Sadly, slow-moving sloths are already nearly extinct in much of their original Honduran range. The most common anteater is the tamandua, a beast at home in trees and on the earth, with a pronounced prehensile tail; its strong front claws and long tongue are suitable for extracting ants and termites from rotting trees. The rarer giant anteater weighs up to 65 pounds, lives on the ground, and feeds on soil-nesting insects.

Collared and white-lipped peccaries, ungulates resembling wild pigs, are quite common in Honduras. The collared runs in family groups of three to 30, while the larger white-lipped peccary is much more aggressive and moves in herds of up to 300.

The agouti, known locally as a *guatusa* (pronounced "gwah-TOO-sah") looks somewhat like a cross between a large rabbit and a rat. A close relative is the larger paca, identifiable by the white spots along its sides. Both are prized prey for hunters throughout the country.

Divers and swimmers should beware of crocodiles.

James D. Gollin

Reptiles and Amphibians

Green and spiny-tailed iguanas are still fairly common throughout Honduras, but hunting has endangered them in heavily populated areas. Iguana nurseries in Tegucigalpa and near La Ceiba have been established to raise public awareness about these Jurassic Park look-alikes. Their tasty tail meat has earned them the nickname "jungle chicken." During mating season, when these creatures are high on hormones and completely fearless, they make easy prey. They are also widely hunted during their incubating season, as their eggs are reputed to have aphrodisiacal properties. Other iguana species, on the Bay Islands and in the Mosquitia, are now under official protection.

Crocodiles inhabit the secluded riverways of areas such as the Mosquito Coast. Always ask a local before diving into a slow-moving river; rapid-flowing streams are safe.

The fer-de-lance *(Bothrops atrox)*, known locally as the *barba amarilla,* is the snake that you don't want to run into. The fer-de-lance and its pit-viper cousins are extremely well camouflaged in the litter of the forest floor. Always step carefully, especially if you are the first in line on a jungle walk, and watch where you place your hands. On the other hand, a Honduran saying is that the second person in line is the most likely to get bit because the first one will just wake the snake up. Most Honduran snakes are not poisonous, but if you see an arrow-shaped head or a diamond-patterned body, freeze. Then slowly, slowly back away. If you are walking through remote areas at night, consider wearing high rubber boots. These snakes hunt at night, using their infrared sensitivity to find small rodents and birds. They will bite humans only in what they believe is self-defense. So don't step on them or grab a tree trunk where one is sleeping. It's also a *very* bad idea to poke one with a stick.

If you are bitten, try to remain calm and to move as little as possible. Do not run, as that will spread the venom throughout your bloodstream. If possible, get to a hospital for an antivenin shot, and consider placing a tourniquet around the affected limb to slow the spread of venom. In fact, the snake will probably inject only a small bit of poison, enough to make you back off, as it prefers to conserve killing doses for its actual prey. But if it truly is a fer-de-lance that has bitten you, and if it has chosen to give you a full dose, you will probably die long before you get to a hospital. So remain calm and pray hard.

Sea turtles, including loggerheads, hawksbills, green ridleys, and leatherbacks, crawl up the beaches near Cedeño on the Pacific coast and along the Mosquito Coast on the Caribbean. These prehistoric beasts were being decimated until recent egg-protection programs and a ban on hunting reversed the decline in population. When diving off the Bay Islands, keep an eye out for these wonderful creatures, who will sometimes allow you to swim quite close as long as you make no threatening moves.

Flora

Honduras is home to more than 8,000 species of vascular plants, including 1,000 known to have medicinal properties and 148 found nowhere else in the world.

Bromeliads, principally from the epiphytic family, are uniquely a New World phenomenon, reaching the greatest abundance in misty cloud forests. The pineapple is a rare form of terrestrial bromeliad. Most epiphytes are not directly parasitic in that they do not prosper at the expense of their host tree. Indeed, many live happily on rocks. Some bromeliads, called "tank" or "cistern" bromeliads, can hold as much as 2 to 3 gallons of rainwater, providing a venue for an entire ecosystem of insects, amphibians, and even small mammals. However, with all this water weight, a significant epiphytic community on a single tree can bring about disaster simply by their sheer weight, causing a tree to come crashing to the forest floor. Some trees have adopted protective measures, such as rapidly peeling bark, chemical defenses, or weak branch connections that allow a limb to drop off easily without damaging the main trunk of the tree.

There are more than 700 species of orchids in Honduras, including a few commercially important species. In fact, along the forest floor, you will see many plants that look familiar, such as philodendrons, begonias, wandering Jews, coleus, and various species of ferns that are cultivated as houseplants.

Water vine *(bejuco de uva)* is filled with fresh, naturally purified water. When cut, the vine pours water out like a faucet and can save your life. Epizote, or wormseed, is used for its distinctive flavor in preparing the traditional dish of pinto or black beans. It is also used to eliminate parasitic worms.

James D. Gollin

Aloe plant

Aloe's cooling gel can relieve burns, and mixed with water and lemon juice can be used as a tonic that improves digestion. Aloe is originally from Africa. Red hibiscus, originally from China, is high in vitamin C and can produce a tea or tonic that helps fight colds. Papaya is high in vitamins A and C and lysine. It's used for digestive "cleansing" and can be an effective remedy for stomach problems. The flowers from banana plants are used to alleviate symptoms of bronchitis and dysentery.

Honduras has a wide variety of tree species, from the mangroves and palms on the coast to the figs and tropical hardwoods of the rain forest to the oak and pine covering the cooler highlands. In fact, only 12 percent of Honduras is flat and therefore appropriate for traditional agriculture. The other 88 percent has pronounced slopes that make it ideal for forestry. Despite this, about half of Honduras's forests have been converted from their original state to other uses, but there are now 37 protected cloud forests in the country. In fact, Honduras has more forest (over 40 percent, of which 50 percent is broadleaf, 49 percent pine, and 1 percent mangrove) left than any other Central American country. Deforestation continues at around 3,000 square kilometers (1,158 square miles) a year. If this rate continues, all broadleaf forest will be cut down within 20 years.

There are seven species of pine in Honduras, dominated by the Caribbean pine *(Pinus caribea)* along the north coast and in La Mosquitia, and the ocote pine *(Pinus oscarpa),* the principal commercial species found throughout the high elevation areas of the country's interior.

Sapodilla *(chico zapote* or *sapote)* exudes a sticky resin known as chicle that was used as the main source for chewing gum (remember Chiclets?) until synthetics were developed. The fruit, known as zapote, is orange-brown and quite sweet, while the wood of the tree is extremely durable even in the tropics and so is frequently used for beams and fence posts.

Actually a vine, the strangler fig produces a fruit that is eaten by birds, which then drop the seeds, which lodge in the crannies of other trees. The strangler fig then pulls water and nutrition from the environment, drops roots to the ground, creating its own root system, and eventually completely engulfs the host tree, shading its foliage and killing it. Fast-growing trees like palms can actually be "strangled." Soft-wooded victims rot quickly, leaving a giant hollow surrounded by the fig. The long, thin tendrils of the strangler fig and other similar trees can be cut for rattan, a renewable rain-forest resource.

If you hike into the rain forest with a well-trained naturalist (such as Kent Forte of Bosques Atlántida) and randomly point at a tree, asking "What is that?" he will probably shrug and say, "Some kind of fig." There are an extraordinary number of subspecies of these trees, some of them resembling the ficus commonly domesticated in North

James D. Gollin

Visiting a Honduran nursery

American homes and shopping malls. In fact, there are so many subspecies that almost no one knows them all. So if someone asks you to identify a particular rain-forest tree and you don't know what it is, you'll sound like an expert if you just shrug and say, "Probably some kind of a fig."

Mahogany *(caoba)* is a hardwood valued for its beauty and durability. Unfortunately, its popularity has led to its wholesale exploitation, and mahogany will probably be listed as an endangered species during the next meeting of the Conference on International Trade in Endangered Species. These slow-growing trees take about 50 years to reach a height of 30 meters (100 feet), and until recently have not been grown in plantations. Other tropical hardwoods include guayacan, or ironwood (already listed as endangered), reputedly the hardest of all woods known. Other hardwoods of importance include rosewood, Spanish cedar (a close relative of mahogany), cortes, gunacaste, and redondo, a native magnolia. Teak, increasingly grown on Central American plantations, is a native of Southeast Asia.

Naked Indian *(palo de turista)* has a red, easy-to-peel bark that reminds Hondurans of the skin of tourists who have forgotten their sunblock, hence the Spanish name. This tree is most commonly found along riverbanks. The peeling bark is a form of defense against epiphytes and parasitic plants such as strangler figs. Because it is difficult for predators to climb the trees, they are a favorite nesting spot for wasps and for the oropendula *(Psarocolius montexuma),* a gregarious and highly social bird that nests in large colonies.

The copa is a tall tree with an aromatic resin (copal) that is extracted from living trees and burned as a kind of incense. The tree is related to frankincense and myrrh.

Ceiba trees put out a seed pod filled with a cotton-like substance known as kapok, which was used in life preservers until the advent of synthetics and is still used in pillows, furniture stuffing, and the like. The ceiba was a sacred tree to the Maya and can be seen to this day presiding over many a ruin mound at Copán. The Caribbean town of La Ceiba takes its name from this tree. The cohune palm is a versatile plant with dozens of uses. The fronds are used for roofing, the heart of a young tree can be eaten as "heart of palm," the meat of the nut is edible or is boiled to make an edible oil, and the shell is used as fuel and is an ingredient in NASA's activated charcoal filtering systems. The hard shell is also used for jewelry and buttons. Taller palmetto palms are used in construction, while nonnative coconut palms are prized for their delicious and edible nuts (not to mention coconut milk). African palms are the backbone of the palm oil industry.

Tall, straight, liquidambar trees are distant relatives of the maple, a fact hinted at by the shape of the leaves, which resemble elongated maple leaves. In addition, like the maple, sap can be drawn from the liquidambar. The liquid is not sweet, but it can be used to sterilize wounds or relieve stomach distress.

Black, white, and red mangroves cover parts of the shores of both Pacific and Caribbean Honduras, as well as the Bay Islands. The interlaced network of roots provides a protected environment for small fish and crustaceans and protects shorelines from erosion, while the tangle of branches and leaves provides shelter for water birds such as egrets, herons, ibises, roseate spoonbills, pelicans, frigate birds, and raptors.

Nance trees grow to a height of about 9 meters (30 feet) and produce a yellow fruit that is very popular with Hondurans (less so with foreigners). The tree is found throughout Central America and in Mexico's Yucatán. Among its medicinal uses is the prevention of diarrhea.

OUTDOOR ACTIVITIES IN HONDURAS

Honduras is not the kind of place to experience in an air-conditioned tour bus, shuttling from monument to museum to well-marked mountain vista. But it is heaven for fans of a kind of travel known as "soft adventure." To sample the greatness of the country, that which sets it apart from other tropical destinations and from your home town, you'll have to put on hiking boots, fins, or water sandals. You can gaze at the birdlife through binoculars or peer at the living rainbow of the coral reefs through a diving mask. You can pole a cart along a banana-company railway, paddle a high-tech kayak to uninhabited isles, or climb the rock face of a rain-forest waterfall. And when you've had enough of that, you can contemplate an archaeological site built long before the birth of Christ, watch the sun set through the palms, or listen quietly to the hoots, calls, trills, and buzzing of rain-forest life.

In Honduras today, scuba diving is probably the single biggest draw for environmentally oriented tourism. Diving is not always considered an ecotourism activity, like hiking in the rain forest is. But this distinction should fade over time, especially as divers develop a more sophisticated environmental consciousness. Quite rightly, the reefs are called "the rain forests of the sea," home to over 4,000 different types of fish and thousands of species of plants and other life forms. Fully 2 percent of all marine life depends on coral reefs for survival. The flora and fauna of reef systems contain countless as-yet-

James D. Gollin

Mayan totem at Copán

unstudied chemicals that have tremendous potential for medicinal use, while the physical mass of reefs protect beaches and shorelines from erosion. Throughout the world, however, reefs are being degraded and destroyed. Some estimates indicate that up to 70 percent of the world's coral may be gone in 20 to 40 years.

In Honduras, however, the reefs are pristine, the water is crystalline, and the biodiversity and beauty of the flora and fauna are unsurpassed. Swim through canyons of brain coral and elkhorn, lettuce, star, and pillar coral. Float past barrel, finger, rope, and vase sponges; sea fans; and fish species too numerous to mention. While you'll find some coral all along the long mainland coastlines and quite pleasant diving opportunities off Tela and other spots, there is little reason to dive anywhere other than the Bay Islands.

Anyone can learn to dive, and Honduras is one of the best places in the world to learn. If you are short of travel time, go ahead and get certified at home. But why learn to dive in a chlorine-filled pool? You can do it for a fraction of the price in the turquoise waters of the Caribbean, surrounded by multicolored fish. Safe, high-quality equipment is available for rental at many locations. If you have your own gear, do bring it, but leave the heavy stuff behind. First-class instruction in various languages has made the Bay Islands a "certification destination" for divers from throughout the world. For advanced divers, course work in underwater photography, cave diving, and instructor certification is available.

For those who want to experience the fish and the coral but do not want to get certified, "resort dives" allow a taste of the experience, diving with an instructor one-on-one in shallow but still beautiful water. Snorkeling on the surface is fun, too.

If you've always wanted to learn to dive, don't put it off. It's easy. Like driving a car, you can kill yourself if you don't know what you are doing, but the rules are simple to follow. Don't dive on the day you fly in or the day you fly out, don't go too deep for too long, and make sure to descend and ascend slowly. Always review the safety precautions before a dive. While the chance of getting decompression sickness, "the bends," is extremely remote, there is a NOAA-certified recompression chamber on Roatán just in case.

More likely than the bends is the possibility of getting an earache. It is sometimes difficult to equalize your inner ear pressure to the changing pressure of progressively deep water, especially if your nose is stuffed with the remnants of a cold you brought down from colder climes. If you think your sinuses might be stuffy, make sure to use a long-lasting decongestant such as 12 Hour Sudafed. Short-term decongestants can wear off in the middle of a dive.

All three Bay Islands (Roatán, Utila, and Guanaja) are near-perfect dive destinations. Head to almost any section of the coast off any of the islands. You can't go wrong.

Less than ten years ago, kayaking in Honduras was extremely rare and its rivers had never been explored by white-water rafters. By the year 2000, however, Honduras may well take its rightful place as a Mecca of white-water destinations. As the most mountainous country in Central America, with major rainfall in the mountains, it doesn't take a rocket scientist to figure out that Honduras is blessed with a lot of water moving downhill toward the sea. Crystal-clear water pours out of the cloud forests, shooting down through more than a dozen river systems, most of which empty into the Caribbean Sea.

In 1992 Ríos Honduras out of La Ceiba pioneered the rafting industry, importing equipment and crews from Colorado and running day trips on the Cangrejal River. Ríos now runs trips on rivers throughout Honduras, from day trips to weeklong adventures, and their success has spawned a host of competitors. Kayaking trips are also available, with some trips appropriate for novices and others survivable only by the extremely skilled.

Former Ríos white-water guide Andrew Hubbard has written an excellent guidebook to white-water opportunities entitled *Honduras: The Undiscovered Country*. For a copy, send $15 to 1191 Sunnycrest

Rios Honduras runs white-water rafting trips throughout Honduras.

Ave., Ventura, CA 93003, or call 805/654-1294. The book not only provides maps and clearly explains how to access 13 rivers, it also gives detailed descriptions of the beauties and challenges of each river. White-water rapids are designated by class, with Class I and II being appropriate for beginners, Class III appropriate for intermediates, and so on, all the way up to Class VI, rapids that are not runnable without probable loss of life. Some of the river journeys available in Honduras are briefly summarized below.

Río Cangrejal: Just minutes east of La Ceiba, this is the most rafted river in Honduras, and for good reason. The river drops 240 meters (787 feet) over 18.5 kilometers (11.5 miles), running through a narrow canyon cloaked on both sides with lush rain forest. The river forms the boundary of Pico Bonito National Park and has rapids suitable to every skill level, with the more technical stretches furthest upriver, the easiest closest to town.

Río Papaloteca: Some 48 kilometers (30 miles) east of La Ceiba is the put-in for the Papaloteca, which flows from the eastern edge of the Nombre de Dios range into the Caribbean. Roughly 9.5 kilometers (6 miles) of Class III rapids are separated by three Class Vs, all of which can easily be portaged (walked around).

Río Mame: The Mame flows from the mountains of Olancho and empties into the Aguán and is easily accessible from La Ceiba, Trujillo, or Olanchito. Some 46 kilometers of rapids are divided into three sections, with the lower section appropriate only for rafts.

Río Sico: Flowing down from the mountains of Olancho and into the border area of the Mosquito Coast, passing through cowboy territory and into pristine rain forest wilderness, through Class II and III and one Class IV rapids, the Sico is ideal for a four-day supported expedition.

Río Yaguala: The Yaguala flows into the Aguán behind La Muralla National Park, between Yoro and Olanchito. The 38.5-kilometer (24-mile) route passes through a deep, V-shaped canyon highlighted by a descent to a 200-meter (656-foot)-long white-water journey through a cave known as La Ventana.

Río Guaimas: The Guaimas flows northwest from the western edge of the Nombre de Dios and empties into the Ulúa between Pico Pijol National Park and San Pedro Sula. The 22.5-kilometer (14-mile) stretch is a narrow, challenging, continuous Class IV-plus, appropriate for advanced kayakers.

Río Sulaco: South of Yoro, the Sulaco flows into the man-made reservoir of El Cajón dam. The roughly 19-kilometer (12-mile) journey through a beautiful canyon culminates in four consecutive Class IV rapids after 3 hours of calmer waters.

Río Humuya: From a put-in just below the El Cajón dam, the Humuya flows through green canyons cloaked in tropical vegetation and wider valleys, lightly populated by campesinos who travel this Class II and III river in their dugout canoes.

Río Ulúa: From northwest of Santa Bárbara National Park, the Ulúa runs down to the fertile fields and banana plantations around San Pedro. The white-water section, closer to Santa Bárbara, has about 19 kilometers of Class II rapids that are perfect for beginners.

Río Chamelecón: The put-in for the Chamelecón is about halfway between San Pedro Sula and the ruins of Copán. This Class I river rapidly twists and turns though Class III and IV-plus stretches for about 16 kilometers (10 miles). A natural calcium carbonate coating on the banks and rocks makes them feel like sandpaper.

Río Jicatuyo: Flowing northward from Gracias toward La Entrada, the Jicatuyo passes through three distinct canyons and is suitable for a three-day trip. There are hot springs on the riverbank and a limestone canyon with several caves.

Río Higuito: Between Nueva Ocotepeque and Santa Rosa de Copán, the Higuito is a wide-open intermediate river flowing through a wilderness area and emptying into the Jicatuyo.

Río Copán: The Río Copán runs past the ruins at Copán and on into Guatemala. The put-in is near the Hacienda El Jaral hotel and takes a few tricky turns past hazards such as pin boulders, strainers, and sieves. The 12-kilometer (7.5-mile) route runs right through the archaeological park that contains the ancient Mayan ruins.

Most of the organized rafting and kayaking in outfitters in Honduras are centered in or near La Ceiba on the Caribbean Coast.

Fisherfolk from around the world come to Honduras for its legendary snook fishing in the rivers and lagoons of the Mosquito Coast. Snook up to 40 pounds and tarpon up to 200 pounds are regularly taken, using catch-and-release techniques. According to the fish stories, anglers can land ten to 20 snook per day, with an average weight of 10 to 15 pounds. They can also "jump" 20 tarpon and perhaps catch four of them. (Dick Thomas runs a relatively luxurious fishing camp on Cannon Key in the Mosquitia's Brus Lagoon; see Chapter 10: The Final Frontier, for details.)

Tim Muery of Palacios is known as Honduras's number-one fishing guide and can be contacted at Expatriates Bar and Grill in La Ceiba. In addition to La Mosquitia, he fishes along the Pacific coast, where snook and orange corvina congregate around the shrimp farm canal outlets. Fishing is still the principal source of nourishment and income for the coastal people of the South.

In Honduras's many rivers, there are trout-like species including the cuyamel, weighing up to 10 pounds; the guapote, at 5 to 8 pounds; and the tepemechin, at around 3 pounds. Fish in most mountain streams are threatened by spear fishers and by deforestation and siltation caused by dam construction. Overfishing almost destroyed the black-bass fishing in the calm waters of Lake Yojoa, described in Chapter 3: Forests in the Sky, but the efforts of environmentalists and local fishermen have brought the population back.

The entire coastlines and the surrounding coral seas are now protected as an extensive marine sanctuary. Come and see the fish, but don't attempt to spear them. Offshore, you can catch sailfish, marlin, and wahoo from July to November, and grouper and snapper all year long.

Honduras boasts Central America's most extensive wilderness areas in the roadless expanse of the Mosquito Coast region, described in Chapter 10: The Final Frontier. Outfitters take adventurers on expeditions up the Río Plátano into a biosphere reserve named a World Heritage Site by the United Nations. Most of these trips involve extensive travel by dugout canoe. If you have the

Hikers in Cusuco National Park

37

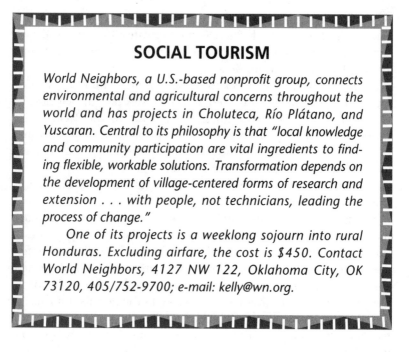

SOCIAL TOURISM

World Neighbors, a U.S.-based nonprofit group, connects environmental and agricultural concerns throughout the world and has projects in Choluteca, Río Plátano, and Yuscaran. Central to its philosophy is that "local knowledge and community participation are vital ingredients to finding flexible, workable solutions. Transformation depends on the development of village-centered forms of research and extension . . . with people, not technicians, leading the process of change."

One of its projects is a weeklong sojourn into rural Honduras. Excluding airfare, the cost is $450. Contact World Neighbors, 4127 NW 122, Oklahoma City, OK 73120, 405/752-9700; e-mail: kelly@wn.org.

experience and the will, you can outfit your own expedition, heading up rivers, crossing mountains, and traversing tropical savannas filled with wildlife.

Honduras is an ideal spot for hikers, with trails suitable to every skill and motivational level. Well-marked educational trails in parks such as Lancetilla, Cusuco, La Tigra, and La Muralla can be strolled in street shoes. Adventurers in peak condition can attempt multiday ascents of unclimbed summits, bushwhacking through thick tropical forests. In between are literally thousands of opportunities for challenging day hikes through virgin rain forests. For those who have never been to a rain forest, it is important to note something that is not obvious from the Discovery Channel and National Geographic Society documentaries: It rains in the rain forest. It's a good idea to carry a light poncho for yourself and a waterproof bag for your camera and anything else that you don't want to get wet.

Another point: When it rains in the forest, the floor of which is made of earth, the ground becomes wet and muddy. Light hiking boots with good tread will help keep you from slipping, but you may well get soaked if you cross rivers, wade up streams, or climb water-falls. On day hikes this is not a serious problem, because when the sun comes out it will dry out your gear, but on overnights you should carry a spare pair of footgear. On the beaches and in the rivers, Teva-type water sandals are terrific, especially those with some tread. A great innovation is the water shoes put out by companies such as Nike and Adidas, shaped like sneakers and sporting a deep tread, but made with waterproof uppers. For difficult climbing these will pro-tect your feet from rocks and roots better than water sandals. Bring along a few pairs of thin synthetic socks or "gobi" sock liners. It may not be a great fashion statement, but you can wear them under your sandals to protect your feet from stings and scrapes, and they'll dry off in minutes once the sun reappears.

Trekking is an activity that is associated with the mountains of Nepal, but Honduras may soon become a major tropical trek desti-nation. In the Cerro Azul Meambar National Park, described in Chapter 3: Forests in the Sky, park managers are developing a net-work of simple "B&Bs," allowing individual hikers to spend many days and nights out in the cloud forests without having to carry camping equipment or food. In Western Honduras, discussed in Chapter 4: The Lenca Trail, many groups offer trekking trips through remote mountains and traditional villages far from roads, electricity, or auto-mobiles.

Honduras is ideal mountain-biking terrain, with thousands of miles of dirt road and hiking path, free of traffic and surrounded by breathtaking scenery. Unfortunately, though bikes can be rented in many cities, there are few opportunities for "catered" bike trips sup-ported by four-wheel-drive vehicles carrying gear and food. If you are a serious biker, bring your own equipment and take day trips.

Honduras is a bird-watcher's paradise, with hundreds of species of exotic birds such as the quetzal, motmot, and toucan, as well as, in the winter months, all those birds that have flown south for the sea-son. That bird pecking at worms in your back yard in June may well be pecking at insects in the Honduran rain forest in February, but it will be covered with a plumage that you have never seen.

Bird-watching opportunities abound, from the coastlines of the Caribbean and the Pacific and the riverways of La Mosquitia to the cloud forests of the mountainous center, and from the ancient forests around Copán to the verdant rain forests that still cover huge parts of the lowlands, providing habitat for an amazing variety of birdlife. Although professional bird-watching guides such as Jorge Barrazo in Copán do provide binoculars to their clients, it is better to bring your own. If they are inexpensive binoculars, consider leaving them with a guide in one of the parks as a tip. Such a gift will mean more to him than you can imagine.

For archaeology buffs, Honduras is currently one of the world's hottest spots. The Mayan ruins of Copán, discussed in Chapter 4: The Lenca Trail, are a marvel on the scale of Tikal, Palenque, and Chichén-Itzá. Archaeologists are in the process of unearthing evidence of an ancient culture or cultures that flourished and died away two to three thousand years ago, long before the Maya. At Los Naranjos (described in Chapter 3: Forests in the Sky) or at the "cave of the glowing skulls" (discussed in Chapter 9: The Wild East), archaeologists are only now piecing together recently discovered evidence of the people known as the "ancient Lencas."

Camping

There are formal campgrounds in places like Lago de Yojoa and some of the national parks, but most Hondurans don't camp unless they have to. In extremely rural areas, this is your only choice. Make sure you notify the landowner or the local COHDEFOR office before pitching a tent on what might be private property.

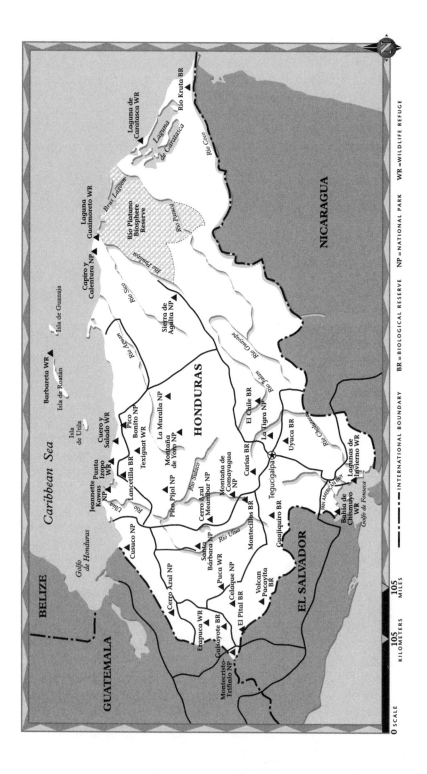

BELIZE

GUATEMALA

Caribbean Sea

Golfo de Honduras

Gulf of Honduras

Isla de Guanaja

Barbareta WR

Isla de Roatán

Isla de Utila

Cusuco NP

Jeannette Punta
Kawas Izopo
NP WR

Lancetilla BR

Pico
Bonito NP

Texiguat WR

Pico Pijol NP

Montaña
de Yoro NP

La Muralla NP

Sierra de
Agalta NP

Cuero y
Salado WR

Capiro y
Calentura NP

Laguna
Guaimoreto WR

Laguna de
Caratasca WR

Río Kruta BR

Laguna
de Caratasca

Brus Lagoon

Río Plátano
Biosphere
Reserve

Río Patuca

Río Coco

NICARAGUA

Río Aguan

Río Sico

Río Patuca

Río Guayape

Río Jalan

Río Sulaco

Cerro Azul
Meambar NP

Santa
Bárbara NP

Puca WR

Montecillos BR

Montaña de
Comayagua
NP

Guajiquiro BR

HONDURAS

Carías BR

El Chile BR

La Tigra NP

Tegucigalpa ★

Uyuca BR

Río Choluteca

PAN AMERICAN HWY

Laguna de Invierno WR

Bahía de
Chismuyo
WR

Golfo de Fonseca

EL SALVADOR

Cerro Azul NP

Erapuca WR

Guisayote BR

El Pital BR

Celaque NP

Volcán
Pacayita
BR

Montecristo-
Trifinio NP

Río Ulúa

BR = BIOLOGICAL RESERVE   NP = NATIONAL PARK   WR = WILDLIFE REFUGE

INTERNATIONAL BOUNDARY

0 SCALE

105
KILOMETERS

105
MILES

CHAPTER 2

Conservation and Responsible Tourism

At a conference on Ecotourism and Conservation, held in the town of La Ceiba on the Caribbean coast, eco-entrepreneur Pepe Herrero declared that Honduras would have "ecotourism in the watersheds or no watersheds at all." This statement recognizes the fact that in poorer countries the government has only a small budget for environmental protection and has trouble shutting down economic activity within protected areas, even if that activity will ultimately lead to deforestation and environmental degradation. Tourism is seen as the best compromise, a way to maintain necessary economic activity while protecting biodiversity and wilderness.

The Central American Alliance for Sustainable Development promotes "tourism that improves the quality of life for residents of Central America." Since 1996, various Summits of Central American Presidents have declared tourism a priority for regional and national development. This sounds great in theory. But this type of "sustainable development" is an unlikely marriage between the forces of conservation and those of development. There are risks involved. But the risks of not attempting to develop sustainable economies that will support the protected areas are greater still.

At last, the Honduran government and private sector are at work improving infrastructure and services, knowing that travelers won't return to a country if they aren't treated well. After Hurricane Mitch, the international airports at Roatán, San Pedro Sula, and Tegucigalpa have been repaired and improved. The network of highways in Honduras is said to be the best in Central America (which, of course, is not saying much), and roads to selected tourist destinations such as Copán, Tela, La Ceiba, and the hill towns around Tegucigalpa are now all in good condition, though some of the bridges are still technically "temporary." Honduras has four ports that receive cruise ships and many more that receive yachts.

Despite tourism's position as the country's third-largest generator of foreign revenue, the industry has traditionally received little support from the government. Honduras's Office of Tourism was created in 1958 and the Honduran Institute of Tourism (IHT) in its present form dates back to 1970, but only recently has the government been willing to spend scarce funds on tourism promotion. In 1995 the IHT budget jumped to $700,000, far less than comparable budgets in Guatemala or Costa Rica but a sign of a shift in national priorities nevertheless. By 1999, the IHT was spending almost $1.7 million, advertising in magazines such as *Outside, Archaeology,* and *Scuba Diving,* developing domestic infrastructure and tourist information services, and promoting Honduras's natural wonders at tourism fairs around the world. They have established an in-country toll-free number (800/220-8687) for travelers in Honduras to ask for advice on hotels, sights, and travel, and a U.S. toll-free number for their Florida office (800/410-9608). By late in the year 2000, the IHT expects to unveil a new web-based reservation system that will allow tourists to reserve hotels throughout the country. E-mail ihturism@hodutel.hn or check www.hondurasinfo.hn for an update on their progress.

DEFINING ECOTOURISM

Like most buzzwords that pop in and out of the language, "ecotourism" is a confusing term used by different people to mean different things. Without a standard definition, anything involving tourism and the environment is sometimes referred to as ecotourism, even if the act of tourism diminishes or destroys that environment, even if there is no educational component, and even if no respect or fees are paid to the indigenous peoples living there.

At its best, ecotourism is a tool to channel the energies of the tourism market toward building sustainable economies. At worst, it is a marketing tool that sells environmentally destructive activities under nature's banner.

The purpose of this book, in addition to providing useful information about hotels, restaurants, and destinations, is to help readers refine their travel sensibilities by shedding light on issues that are sometimes hidden beneath the lure of the luxuriant rain forests. There are real campesinos attempting to feed their children by burning the forest and planting corn, there are real environmentalists who sometimes give their lives in service to their beliefs, and there are real decisions that caring and educated travelers can make to either improve or degrade the delicate environments through which they pass.

As you travel through Honduras, and through other countries, including your own, ask yourself the following questions:

• To what degree does the introduction of tourism encourage members of the local community to preserve and protect their natural surroundings?

• Are poor local people being displaced to make way for a resort that will profit a wealthy owner? You might not want to see a milpa, a campesino's cornfield, in the buffer zone of a national park, but remember that he and his family were probably born here and you are a guest who is just passing through. In the best circumstances, locals are hired as guards and guides and let their fields go fallow.

• Who owns the resort or hotel? Does the travel agent I am paying support local conservation efforts? Ask around. In Costa Rica, almost all the rain-forest lodges are owned by foreigners. In

Pepe Herrero stops a bulldozer by the Congrejal River.

James D. Gollin

Honduras, the owners tend to be wealthy Catrachos. Community-owned hotels, while rare, do the most good to support the goals of ecotourism.

• What is the source of the food that is served, and does the demand for that food hasten environmental degradation? Some hotels serve iguana meat, or lobster out of season. The food might be tasty but the consequences of eating of it are bitter.

• Where does the sewage that I flush from my hotel bathroom go? If human waste washes out onto a coral reef, causing an algae bloom and killing the reef, how good do you feel about the waterfront location of your hotel?

What, then, is ecotourism? While there is no single strict definition, in this book we embrace the most common tenets of ecotourism, which hold that it is a form of tourism that assists local environmental conservation efforts, includes the active participation of local communities, and is sustainable over the long run.

By definition, ecotourism assures the traveler—and local leaders—that a portion of the financial resources spent on a vacation remains in the area to protect the environment and bolster the local economy. Ecotravelers don't necessarily expect air-conditioned suites; they want to immerse themselves in the adventure of getting to know a particular place.

Ecotourism serves as a catalyst to other services and practices important to sustainable development, such as environment-friendly lodging, organic agriculture, the promotion of local handicrafts, and development of environmental education. In Spanish this is called *un ciclo virtuoso,* "a virtuous cycle."

One of the advantages of ecotourism is that it has the potential to satisfy the desires of both large and small trips for travelers of all incomes. Some ecotourists take educational cruises and others backpack throughout the countryside. There is shoestring ecotourism and gold-card ecotourism. It is not about money. It is about intention and the effects of one's actions.

EXPLORING ECOTOURISM

An ecotourism boom is just around the corner, travel agents say. Although numbers are difficult to estimate, the World Tourism Organization (WTO) has estimated that all types of nature travel represent 10 percent of the travel market. If, according to estimates, the tourism market will top $4.4 trillion in the year 2000, well, you can do the math yourself. Nature tourism is expected to grow much faster than tourism as a whole, which is forecast to grow by around 4 percent annually over the next decade. These studies are subject to debate and standard criteria are lacking. Nevertheless, tourism industry leaders acknowledge a growing demand among their clients to search out environment-friendly destinations and are now catering to this growing market.

Even if those involved in the activity don't consider themselves ecotourists, nature-based tourism is increasingly popular in Honduras, from divers who plumb the reefs off Roatán to hikers who ascend the country's many cloud forest–covered mountains and rafters who shoot down the cool, clear rivers.

So far, the ecotourism organizations that do exist approach the subject either on a purely academic basis or on a commercial basis (including the nonprofits and universities). Environmental tourism is not about building exclusive hotels in the wilderness; it's about learning how to minimize and even counteract destructive habits.

Since ecotourism is difficult to define, John Shores, a grassroots environmental consultant and head of the U.S. Peace Corps division of ecotourism, proposes a system that would rate operations on a 0-to-5 scale that classifies the levels of ecotourism, much like the difficulty scale used to classify white-water rafting or technical climbing. Shores' proposed levels are:

Level 0: The ecotourism entry level. Requires that travelers be exposed to or made aware of the fragility of the ecosystems they have come to enjoy. This is the very lowest "awareness" threshold. Incidental nature travel would usually qualify at this level.

Level 1: Requires that a net positive flow of monetary support occur between the traveling ecotourist and the ecosystems visited. Financial earmarks, whether airport departure taxes or designations of a portion of land travel costs, would qualify at this level.

Level 2: Requires that the ecotourist engage in a personal way in supporting the environment. Some ecotourists have planted trees, others have participated in litter cleanups.

Level 3: Requires certifying that the specific tour system is benign to the environment. The system should include the international air travel as well as on-site transportation and accommodation. Level 3 requires demonstrating that the net effect of the traveler's presence is neutral or positive.

Level 4: Requires demonstrating that the net effect of the traveler is positive. Eco-friendly actions such as using appropriate technology, low energy consumption, recycling, organic agriculture, sustainable harvesting methods, and personal contributions to ecosystem restoration can balance less environmentally benign aspects of the larger tour system, such as air travel, stays in luxury hotels, and excessive energy consumption.

Level 5: This level should be the ultimate goal for ecotourism supporters, whether they are tour operators, travelers, or resource management agencies. A perfect "5" in ecotourism is a trip in which the entire system operates in an environmentally sound way. Advertising, transportation, accommodations, treatment of residual products—all are considered. No deluge of third-class mail solicitations, no advertising in non-recyclable magazines. Transportation is environmentally benign (limited use of petroleum products—in fact, maybe only solar and animal transport, and walking, biking, and swimming qualify). On-site accommodations and all visitor and staff activities are benign to the environment. Heating and air conditioning are solar and low-impact. Foods and souvenirs are produced in sustainable ways. All residual products are handled in a benign way. Sewage containment and treatment are carefully monitored. Used products are recycled, soaps and cleaning solutions are biodegradable, and non-degradation of the environment is the standard.

Shores' 0-to-5 scale offers a great deal to the dialogue and debate about ecotourism. It also suggests the need for a council that can offer accreditation. Perhaps by the time the next edition of this book appears, we will be able to offer a case-by-case evaluation of tourism destinations in Honduras. As it stands currently, most of the destinations would rank between Levels 0 and 3.

At this time, we choose not to rank the tours, hotels, and resorts of Honduras, but attempt to convey information about environmentally friendly or unfriendly activities. We invite your observations and comments.

RESPONSIBLE TOURISM

The purpose of *Adventures in Nature: Honduras* is to help travelers understand the nature of development/conservation compromises and, in so doing, to guide them toward the environmental destinations where their visit is a vote for conservation and local economic well-being. When travelers support tours and destinations that play an active role in environmental protection and local development, tour operators and resort owners come to see that there is a significant new niche in the tourism market comprised of travelers who are more interested in the local environment than in duplicating their home environment, complete with First World comforts.

Responsible tourism is mindful and meaningful travel. If you want to experience a new culture, learn a new language, or understand the challenges of conservation, unlimited options await you in Honduras. Both the tourism sector and environmental groups in Honduras are actively developing ideas and infrastructure to better present the nation's wilderness to foreign visitors and Honduran nationals alike.

As you pass through the wilderness, take only pictures and leave only footprints—but don't leave footprints on the coral. And don't buy souvenirs made from threatened resources such as black coral or any endangered species. Instead, support the work of local artisans whenever possible, and show that you appreciate their skill.

Although we are serious about ecotourism, we are not implying that responsible travel has to be hard work and no fun. Far from it! We believe that if you are interested in finding out the answers to the questions above, and if you

Garífuna Tours office in Tela

James D. Gollin

49

find yourself asking other questions as you travel through the country, your experience in Honduras will be greatly enhanced. The process is one of adding meaning and knowledge to your adventure.

By educating yourself about the complex interactions between natural systems and the human economy, you will magnify what you gain from your travel experience. Too often travelers build walls around themselves—but the purpose of travel is to break through the walls that separate us from the rest of the world.

Be as inquisitive and diligent as seems appropriate to your own level of interest. And don't be surprised if many of your questions can't be answered immediately. But by asking yourself as well as local residents the type of questions listed above, you'll arouse an interest in the issues, which will determine whether or not nature-based travel is indeed sustainable. Asking questions about the natural world places a tangible value on resources that have too often been neglected or exploited. Initial inquiries often result in further exploration by the locals. If they can't answer your question, or that of the next traveler, they'll probably find out the answer before the third person asks the same question. If native Hondurans don't like what they find out, they might well attempt to change things. And so your curiosity can help change things for the better.

One caveat should be mentioned. Many tourism agencies and officials do not place a high value on environmental protection. Their focus is on the utilization of resources for profit, not on conservation. Conservationists, on the other hand, often hold the attitude that environmental problems are caused by people, and so people, including tourists, should go away!

As a result, the two components of ecotourism—economic development and environmental conservation—are seemingly at odds. Those who respect both tourism and conservation are in fact few and far between. Our challenge is to find a bridge across this gap. This ought to be the shared goal of conservationists, tourism officials, and travelers alike. Who can argue against development that is sustainable, or against income that provides locals with a financial incentive to protect their resources?

Your visits will further the conservation of many of the protected areas. Honduras is a poor country, and the national strategy (which could be a world model, if things work out) is to entrust local groups in the administration of the parks.

And what an incredible difference you'll find among environmental groups in Honduras. Some of the groups are relatively wealthy. Others are long on intent and short on financial capital. Ironically, the richest groups charge the most for entry into the parks.

Only a few parks collect entrance fees. For example, Jeannette Kawas National Park charges 10 lempiras, and the fee is handled by the ecological group PROLANSATE. Cusuco National Park charges $10 for non-Hondurans and the fee is collected by the Fundación Fasquelle.

THE POLITICS OF ENVIRONMENTAL TOURISM

Honduras seems to be pursuing two strategies simultaneously— "top-down" and "bottom-up" ecotourism. Starting at the top, an often cited but unnamed World Bank consultant touted the development of a handful of luxurious five-star hotels near various recreational parks—Cusuco, Jeannette Kawas, La Tigra, Celaque, and Copán. The Tela Bay Project, in particular, has had a long history of development, and many Hondurans would like Tela to be the nation's Cancún—just a bit more environmentally and culturally sensitive. Developments in 1997 hinted that the mega-project will actually go forward, but this has been said before without success.

In 1992 Honduras convened a National Conference for Sustainable Ecotourism in Protected Areas that gathered environmentalists, businesspeople, and tourism officials. But despite the enthusiasm, not much developed from the conference. That same year the U.S. Aid for International Development (USAID) sponsored a National Ecotourism Council, which, like its sibling chapters in Guatemala and Costa Rica, died on the vine. These attempts to create "trickle-down ecotourism" have yet to work in Central America.

In devising tourism strategies, Honduras thinks big. In 1996 the government promoted nothing less than the Gran Proyecto de

Transformación Nacional (Great Project of National Transformation). "¡Marcha el Gran Proyecto!" screamed the daily *El Periódico*. The multimillion-dollar project relies on a series of loans from Inter-American Development Bank (IBD), Central American Bank for Economic Integration (BCIE), and other sources.

However, environmentalists from grassroots groups such as the Committee for the Defense and Development of the Flora and Fauna of the Gulf of Fonseca (CODDEFFAGOLF) insist that all projects must comply with environmental-impact studies.

Another approach promotes community-based efforts that, it is hoped, trickle up to benefit both the society and the environment as a whole. USAID has sponsored the creation of the Honduras Ecotourism Promoters Association (APROECOH), which has trained dozens of Hondurans. This type of grassroots community development deserves to be more successful.

Likewise, initiatives from the private sector have done a great deal for ecotourism. Honduras has excellent travel operators who have reached out to European, U.S., and Asian clients. In an initiative led by the private sector, businessmen from La Ceiba, including the late Tom Ellis, organized two national conferences on ecotourism, in 1995 and 1996. The 1996 conference attracted 150 people, including tourism industry leaders, environmentalists, and both local and international Honduras enthusiasts. The conference was flawed and disorganized—but due to Tom's persistence and vision, it successfully took place two years in a row. At conferences such as these, plans are laid that lead to further action.

What is the government doing? A plan to prioritize alternative tourism has been developed by Erasmo Sosa, a noted biologist working within the Honduran Institute of Tourism. Tourism could be used as a central axis for sustainable development. This plan highlights five different tours in Honduras: (1) The Atlantic coast from Tela to Trujillo, (2) the Northwest, including the Copán Ruins and Celaque National Park, (3) The Bay Islands, (4) Tegucigalpa and the nearby colonial cities, and (5) La Mosquitia. Efforts are underway to improve infrastructure in all of these areas.

Time will tell how Honduras develops its environmental tourism. Meanwhile, it's up to the individual tourist and travel company to propagate common-sense strategies.

NASCENT ENVIRONMENTALISM IN HONDURAS

Environmental consciousness is new to Honduras, but the country has made great strides since the initial steps taken in forming the system of "paper" parks and protected areas (areas protected at least on paper, if not in actuality). The first national environmental law was passed in 1993. Numerous environmental groups address issues from local, regional, and national perspectives and are entrusted with the administration of the nation's protected areas and parks.

The cause of environmental protection took a great step forward when President Callejas named Dr. Carlos Medina as Director of the Environmental Secretariat (SEDA), the Honduran equivalent of the U.S. Environmental Protection Agency. Though a gynecologist by training, Dr. Medina was a quick study who surrounded himself with such able advisors as American-born Dr. Becky Myton. Medina increased the efficiency of SEDA and instituted a system of Environmental Impact Studies (EIS) that needed to be completed before the initiation of any major new public or private projects.

When a giant Kuwaiti-backed oil refinery project threatened the coast near Trujillo in 1995, Medina announced that a project of that scale could not go forward without EIS based on serious scientific analysis of the risks. Shortly thereafter, the project died. Or seemed to. President Reina, it was rumored, had appointed Dr. Medina to his cabinet under pressure from the United States to keep a professional man in the post. But in early 1997 Reina merged SEDA into the new Secretariat of Natural Resources and Energy (Secretaria de Recursos Naturales Ambiente y Energía, or SERNA) and let Medina go, replacing him with Jeronimo

Seedlings for reforestation at Amaras

James D. Gollin

Sandoval Sorto, a veteran cabinet minister nicknamed "Super Chombo." As soon as he was in office, Sandoval declared that "environmentalists are all opportunists" who get money from gringos to raise trouble and obstruct progress, and the Trujillo refinery was suddenly back on. It is yet to be seen whether the environmentalists and those interested in tourism development in Trujillo will be able to summon the political clout to once again shut down the refinery.

A second Trujillo-area project pushed by Sandoval, sans EIS, involves a Japanese company called Intermar. On the surface, the project seems simple and beneficial. With Japanese government funding, the primarily Garífuna local fishing community is to be provided with larger boats and a fish processing and freezing plant. All of this will allow for greater catches that can be preserved and exported to Japan, creating hard currency earnings. But environmentalists point out that fish stocks in the area are already in a dangerously low state and that the introduction of such new technologies will surely wipe out the resource. According to *Honduras This Week,* Intermar was forced to shut down its plant in Alaska when overfishing sharply reduced fish populations there.

Though he later gutted SEDA and reorganized it as a subministry under Natural Resources, Reina can be credited with creating what, in retrospect, was a golden era of forest-use policy. Prior to the term of Reina's choice as Secretary, Rigoberto Sandoval (no relation to Super Chombo), the Honduran Forestry Development Corporation (COHDEFOR) was in charge of helping the private sector cut trees. COHDEFOR built roads and handed out permits freely, helping the cause of deforestation. Upon closer examination, it appears the permits were often handed out to political cronies of the administration in power and to whoever spread the right kind of money around to the COHDEFOR hierarchy.

Under President Reina, former head of COHDEFOR Mario Coello was jailed for two years on corruption charges relating to the granting of timber-cutting concessions without approved forestry management plans. Meanwhile, under Sandoval, COHDEFOR has reinvented itself as a forest protection agency. While it may seem illogical that the department responsible for cutting trees should now be in charge of protecting them, COHDEFOR does have knowledgeable biologists and a nationwide infrastructure with numerous field offices. Under the present scheme, COHDEFOR has been given primary responsibility for the oversight of the nation's parks and protected areas system. Sadly, under President Reina's successor, Carlos Flores Facusse, COHDEFOR has slipped back somewhat toward the bad old days of concentrating its energies on cutting timber.

In fact, though, COHDEFOR generally has very little to do with the day-to-day management of protected areas. That work is left to a decentralized network of nonprofit non-governmental organizations (NGOs) that have sprung up throughout the country. The Bay of Chismuyo in the South, for example, is watched over by the Committee for the Defense and Development of the Flora and Fauna of the Gulf of Fonseca. The West-End-Sandy Bay Marine Reserve is supervised by the Bay Island Conservation Association (BICA), while the Cuero y Salado Wildlife Refuge is managed by the Cuero y Salado Foundation (FUCSA). Generally, each NGO raises money on its own from ecotourism and park entry fees, wastes no funds on central Tegucigalpa offices, and works with local communities, building coalitions to protect the immediate environment of each region.

Honduran environmental groups were once far more centralized. In 1986 the then-largest national group, Asociación Hondureña de Ecología (Honduras Ecological Association, or AHE), released a watershed review of the country's natural areas. This compendium—the first of its kind—was used by the environmental community to bolster its demands that the country protect its remaining cloud forests. The national congress passed a law in 1987 establishing 37 new protected areas.

Unfortunately, as AHE evolved, it gained the attention of various international environmental groups, including the World Wildlife Fund (WWF). As one of AHE's founders, biologist Gustavo Cruz, would later say, "If you want to destroy an environmental group in Central America, all you have to do is give it money." Under the leadership of Rigoberto Romero Mesa, accusations were made that the AHE headquarters was changing dollar contributions for lempiras at the black market rate, declaring only the official rate, and was unable to explain where to the resulting difference had disappeared. Elena Fullerton took over and induced a similar flurry of financial scandals, but WWF kept sending the dollars, declaring that it did not want to get involved in internal Honduran affairs. A more likely explanation is that WWF officials in charge did not want to admit their mistake in funding a corrupt organization. Once the linchpin of the environmental movement, AHE faded into obscurity. Finally, WWF pulled its funding and the AHE disappeared altogether.

As AHE dissolved in the early 1990s, the collapse of this well-funded NGO led to a "boom" in environmental groups and domestic foundations—many of which are now struggling to be self-sustaining. Currently there are dozens of environmental groups in Honduras working for the protection of local areas and to incorporate the needs of the often poor inhabitants of the protected areas within a framework of environmental conservation. Some of these "nongovernmental" organizations receive direct funding from the government and employ past government officials. Others, such as the north coast NGOs PROLANSATE of Tela, FUCSA and FUPNAPIB of La Ceiba, and FUCAGUA of Trujillo, have recently received $100,000 each per year from a semigovernmental foundation, the USAID-funded Fundación Vida. CODDEFFAGOLF, on the other hand, is a network of local fishermen with a distinctly antigovernment political stance, funded by the tiny contributions of the local population and backed up by international groups such as Greenpeace.

Each of these environmental groups is unique. The groups closest to the larger cities, such as Amitigra in Tegucigalpa and the Fundación Pastor Fasquelle in San Pedro Sula, tend to be led by wealthier Hondurans. Groups in more rural areas (FUCAGUA in Trujillo, Ecological Group of Olancho [GEO] in Catacamas) are run mostly by schoolteachers. What they share in common is a determination to develop local strategies for environmental protection, including ecotourism, environmental education, and—in every case—pride in one's backyard.

International environmental agencies and groups have also turned a spotlight onto Honduras. The country receives an increasing number of globetrotting consultants who stay at the Hotel Maya Honduras in Tegucigalpa and do lengthy studies that will eventually store dust on a shelf at a multinational institution in Washington, New York, or Geneva. Honduras has also benefited from many hard-working visionaries who are helping promote the cause of sustainable development. A notable success is the stellar environmental program of the U.S. Peace Corps. Under Section Director Jorge Betancourt—

another early founder of the AHE—Peace Corps volunteers throughout Honduras integrate environmental education and sustainable development.

Again, AHE co-founder Gustavo Cruz: "Honduras needs training more than money. Giving money will never be enough. NGOs have nice offices, faxes, cars. In Honduras we then see each other as competitors for the international money. Likewise, the international groups compete with each other as well. They want to show 'total coverage' of the world to their members, but there's no continuity in the countries themselves." Jon Kohl of the RARE Center (originally Rare Animal Relief Effort, then the RARE Center for Tropical Bird Conservation, now the RARE Center for Tropical Conservation) is attempting to balance this need for training with a series of projects, including one designed to equip park guides with the skills they will need to take tourists around protected areas, including basic English and zoology.

PARKS AND PROTECTED AREAS

If all goes according to plan, Honduras will soon have one of the best-managed national park systems in the region. The government laid the groundwork over the past decade. Parks and reserves already protect all eight major life zones in the country, yet comprise only about half of the total 25,000 square kilometers (9,652 square miles) earmarked for eventual protection.

Of course, there are numerous obstacles, including the lack of legal authorization for the parks. One environmentalist who dismissed the parks as being mere "paper parks"—meaning that they exist only in government records—further complained: *"Hay parques en papel y lo peor es que algunos no tienen papel!"* ("There are parks on paper, but what's worse is that some don't even have the paper!")

Most Honduran parks and protected areas are divided into buffer zones, known as *zonas de amortiguamiento,* and nuclear zones. Establishing a major precedent, the "cloud forest law" established 37 areas as protected, defining them not only as natural areas but as human-use zones as well. By law, each protected area in Honduras must have a nuclear zone, or core area, but must also have an encircling buffer zone where people (mostly farmers) can live and work, and where human-versus-

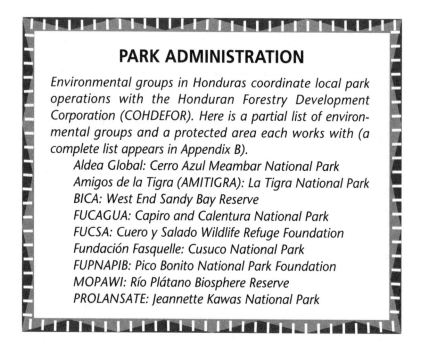

PARK ADMINISTRATION

Environmental groups in Honduras coordinate local park operations with the Honduran Forestry Development Corporation (COHDEFOR). Here is a partial list of environmental groups and a protected area each works with (a complete list appears in Appendix B).

Aldea Global: Cerro Azul Meambar National Park
Amigos de la Tigra (AMITIGRA): La Tigra National Park
BICA: West End Sandy Bay Reserve
FUCAGUA: Capiro and Calentura National Park
FUCSA: Cuero y Salado Wildlife Refuge Foundation
Fundación Fasquelle: Cusuco National Park
FUPNAPIB: Pico Bonito National Park Foundation
MOPAWI: Río Plátano Biosphere Reserve
PROLANSATE: Jeannette Kawas National Park

nature conflicts can be remedied. Limited organic farming, for example, would be an appropriate buffer zone activity. Ecotourism is another. But don't be surprised to see banana, coffee, or palm oil plantations in the buffer zones, and don't expect them to be organic.

Currently there are over 100 protected areas in Honduras. Most of these areas are rather inaccessible. Some are protected in name only and have been deforested (see sidebar for a complete list of protected areas).

A FINAL WORD ON EDUCATION

One of the most urgent needs in ecotourism is not the sale and promotion of natural destinations—or more likely, the hotels nearby—but the education of the traveler.

As Honduras promotes more of its parks and reserves as environmental tourism destinations, the country will need to earmark

PROTECTED AREAS IN HONDURAS

Biosphere Reserves
Río Plátano
Tawahka Asangni (proposed)

National Parks
Capiro and Calentura
Celaque
Cerro Azul
Cerro Azul Meambar
Cusuco
Jeannette Kawas (formerly
Punta y Sal)
La Muralla
La Tigra
Montaña de Comayagua
Montaña de Yoro
Montecristo-Trifinio
Pico Bonito
Pico Pijol
Santa Bárbara
Sierra de Agalta

Proposed National Parks
Bay Islands
Cayos Cochinos
Patuca
Punta Izopo
Sandy Bay/West End
Swan Islands
Turtle Harbour

Wildlife Refuges
Bahía de Chismuyo
Barbareta
Cuero y Salado

Erapuca
Laguna de Caratasca
Laguna Guaimoreto
Lagunas de Invierno
Puca
Texiguat

Biological Reserves
Carias
El Chile
El Pital
Guajiquiro
Guiysayote
Lancetilla
Montecillos
Río Kruta
Uyuca
Volcán Pacayita

Natural Monuments
Cerro el Cedral
Cerro los Cuscos
Cerro los Hoyos
Cerro los Tornillos
Cueva el Tigre
Cuevas de Talgua
Cuevas de Taulabé
Cuevas del Sitio
El Boqueron
El Sitio
Puente en San Antonio
Río Toco

more time and resources to convey the tenets of responsible environmental travel to the public.

Travelers will also be seeking more information than is provided by the traditional brochures selling five-star hotels on the Bay Islands. That said, the journey is often a difficult one.

There are few books on the environment in Honduras, let alone on environmental travel. Visit a bookstore and ask for books about *el medio ambiente*. You might find the translation of a book about general ecology, but that's about it. If you want a map of Honduras's national parks and reserves, request a copy from the Honduran Institute of Tourism (IHT). IHT's Miami office (800/410-9608) is extremely helpful and can even supply you with a copy of *Honduras Tips* magazine, if you pay postage.

Simply put, if you are heading south, read up on Honduras. We've compiled a bibliography (in Appendix B) of travel, historical, and environmental titles; Honduran periodicals; online resources; tourist information offices; map sources; and more. Updated information about additions to and future editions of this book will be available on the Eco Travels in Latin America website (http://www.planeta.com). Before you go, buy some maps and mark out prospective routes from the comfort of your own home. And finally, before you take a step out the door, begin a dialogue with fellow travelers. What have they experienced in Honduras? Do they have recommendations? Travelers love to share information.

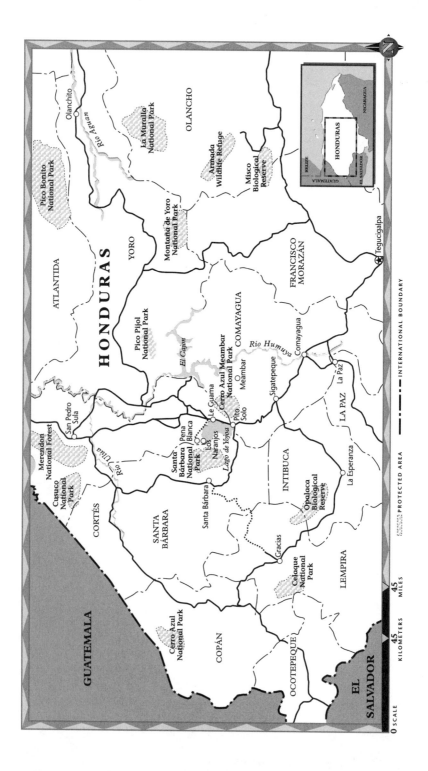

CHAPTER 3

Forests in the Sky: Central Honduras

While Honduras has four international airports and plenty of land crossings, nearly 85 percent of foreign visitors to Honduras enter through Ramón Villeda Morales International Airport, just outside San Pedro Sula, 60 kilometers (37 miles) south of the Caribbean Coast. Most of these immediately hop a small plane for the Bay Islands to the north, head east to the white sands of the Caribbean coast, or head west to the ancient ruins at Copán. That's understandable, of course. But a smaller number of wise travelers pause on their way into or out of the country to explore the great lakes, tall mountains, and thick cloud forests of central Honduras. In Honduras, wherever there are tall mountains there are also cloud forests, and those of the central region are as accessible as they are impressive. These zones of seemingly eternal mist and dampness are home to bromeliads, orchids, and ferns. Quetzals and other exotics flit from tree to tree, while tapirs and sloths move quietly through the foliage.

While it is true that industrial San Pedro Sula has few nature-based tourism attractions, there are things to see and do just outside of town. Mountains to the west and south, some visible from the city's Parque Central, boast lush cloud forests. To the south are the recently rediscovered archaeological sites at Los Naranjos, a majestic waterfall at Pulhapanzák, and beautiful Lake Yojoa, surrounded by almost impossibly steep, rain forest–cloaked mountains. Visitors can follow the hiking trails in Santa Bárbara National Park or trek through the newly developed hut system in Cerro Azul Meambar National Park. From there, it's only a short distance to the colonial capital of Comayagua, worth a stop if you are continuing down to Tegucigalpa.

VISITOR INFORMATION

San Pedro Sula, located 60 kilometers (37 miles) south of the Caribbean coast and 265 kilometers (165 miles) from Tegucigalpa, is one of the fastest-growing cities in Latin America. It is also the commercial capital of Honduras, home to traditional businesses such as banana export and newer ones such as the *maquila* factories that assemble clothing and other labor-intensive items for eventual export to the United States and elsewhere.

The Parque Central of San Pedro Sula, with the
El Merendon Mountains in the background

The city's Ramón Villeda Morales International Airport is the busiest in Honduras—you'll probably land there at some point during your trip. American and Continental airlines offer regular flights to and from major U.S. cities, including Miami, New Orleans, and Houston. Central American carriers such as LACSA, TACA, and COPA fly to the United States and throughout the region; Caribe flies to Cancun; and the main domestic carriers such as Isleña (now part of Salvador-based Grupo TACA) and Nicaragua-based Atlantic Air make regular flights to Tegucigalpa, La Ceiba, the Mosquitia, and the Bay Islands. The airport is modern, reasonably efficient, and a great place to rent a car, buy a cappuccino, or otherwise prepare to travel into the hinterland.

San Pedro Sula was founded in 1536 by the conquistador Don Pedro de Alvarado; he named it Villa de San Pedro de Puerto Caballos. The word *sula* means "valley of birds" in the local dialect. There are not too many birds left in the valley today, but there are quite a few banks, tour companies, and stores selling items harder to find in more rural areas, as well as immigration offices and other modern conveniences. San Pedro Sula makes an excellent base for gathering information about both regional trips and the entire country. San Pedro is also a good place to rent a car, at the airport, at larger hotels, or at one of the agencies in town. You'll have no problem finding your way around San Pedro, as the town is flat and laid out on a grid pattern, with numbered streets and avenues.

With a population of 600,000, San Pedro Sula is one of the most multicultural cities in Central America, with the dominant mestizo culture mixing relatively easily with black island culture and that of the "Turcos." The Turks, as they are called, are Middle Easterners, often Lebanese or Palestinians, who emigrated to Honduras during the Ottoman Empire period. Some are Christians, many are Moslems, and many are Jews, but they all seem to get along fairly well together and with the mestizo majority. In fact, many leading Honduran businessmen, from Jaime Rosenthal to Miguel Faucusse, are of Middle Eastern descent, as are politicians such as Carlos Flores Faucusse and environmentalists such as the late Jeannette Kawas. The economic and political power of the "Turcos," of course, engenders some envy. In San Pedro Sula, avenues *(avenidas)* run north–south, streets *(calles)* east–west. From the Parque Central, located at the exact center of

HERENCIA VERDE

Near San Pedro Sula the land is barren, as if set upon by a plague of locusts. The locusts, of course, are human beings with simple needs, people who, out of economic necessity, have migrated to the San Pedro metropolitan area. They have become urbanites, living in crowded conditions, but have been supplied none of the amenities that people from wealthier countries associate with cities. In many neighborhoods, especially in the unofficial "colonias" that ring the city, there is no running water, no sewage facility, no electricity. People still burn wood for cooking and light. Small wonder there are not many trees standing in the area.

Searching for a place to live, access to firewood, and some land on which to plant a crop, poor Sampedranos have gradually colonized the Merendon Mountains to the west of town. The municipal government, realizing that a healthy ecosystem in the Merendon is essential to preserve San Pedro's water supply, has begun to enforce conservation-oriented laws with increasing severity, evicting the campesinos and relocating them to poor land nearby.

Next to one of these municipally owned plots filled with the shacks of evicted Merendon-dwellers is an unlikely site: the environmental education center and model organic farm of a group known as Herencia Verde, or "Green Legacy." Herencia Verde, in a program funded by Fundación Vida, USAID, and the California-based sustainable development partnership group Katalysis, has developed an educational model that aims to improve the lives of tens of thousands of campesinos in the San Pedro area and, at the same time, put a brake on the relentless process of deforestation that is destroying Honduran and other tropical rain forests.

At Herencia Verde, farm families stay at the model farm in simple dormitories and learn about farming techniques such as mulching, green manure, and environmentally friendly forms of pest control. Instead of burning excess foliage each dry season, campesinos are taught to pile it up in simple containers, keep it moist, and let it decompose into rich mulch they can later spread on their fields. The mulch has more nutrients than ash, helps keep the ground moist, and discourages the growth of weeds. "Green manure," made from plants that fix nitrogen into the soil, can replace chemical fertilizers at a fraction of the cost. And "companion planting"—planting mutually beneficial and insect-repelling plants near each other—can protect crops without the use of insecticides. Marigolds, for example, will keep most insects away from tomatoes planted nearby. Herencia Verde practitioners are now growing organic seeds for the North American seed company Seeds of Change and selling their production directly to consumers at six farmers' markets in the San Pedro area.

Close to Herencia Verde is the famous Ocotillo refuge, a tropical dry forest where people go to view birds and mammals such as guatuzas and deer. To arrange a visit to Herencia Verde, contact the community-banking group ODEF (Organizacion de Desarrollo Empresarial Feminino). Their address is: 13 y 14 Ave., 3a. Calle, Salida Vieja a la Lima, Apartado Postal # 357, San Pedro Sula. Their phone number is 558-1280, and their email address is odef@sdnhon.org.hn.

town, radiate the two most important streets, Primera Calle y Tercera Avenida (First Street and Third Avenue), written as 1a Calle y 3a Avenida. After most San Pedro Sula addresses appear two capital letters, NE, NO, SE, or SO, standing for Northeast, Northwest, Southeast, or Southwest of the Parque. (Northwest is abbreviated NO because that direction is *norteoeste* in Spanish; southwest is *sudoeste.*)

A note of warning: Street crime in San Pedro is as bad as it is in the poorer neighborhoods of most U.S. cities. Especially if you are alone and especially at night, be careful where you walk. Don't leave anything of value in a parked car and, if you are leaving a car overnight, ask your hotel to recommend a safe parking space. Another note of caution: The active nightlife in San Pedro includes many adult establishments and both male and female prostitutes. AIDS levels here are high and you'd be well advised to steer clear of this underworld.

THINGS TO SEE AND DO IN SAN PEDRO SULA

Especially if you are planning a trip to Cusuco National Park, you might want to visit **Fundación Pastor Fasquelle,** (552-1014, e-mail: fundeco@netsys.hn) the NGO that oversees and protects the park, located at 1a Calle and 5a Avenida NO, northwest of the Parque and just above the Pizzeria Italiana. (While you're in the neighborhood, have a pizza. They're great!)

Visit the past at the colorful **Museum of Anthropology and History,** 3a Avenida and 4a Calle NO. The museum is open Tuesday to Sunday from 10 a.m. to 4 p.m. The entrance fee is 5 lempiras (abbreviated 5L).

At 4a Avenida and 3a Calle NO is the **Centro Cultural Sampedrano** (553-3911), "Sampedrano" meaning, of course, "of San Pedro." The center hosts a variety of cultural events and exhibitions and houses the local public library. Call the center at the number above or ask at your hotel if anything interesting is going on at the center while you are in town.

Backed by the tourist office, the **Mercado de Artesanías Populares,** at 6a Calle and 8a/9a Avenidas NO, sells sculptures, hammocks, and other handicrafts. (The "8a/9a" indicates that the mar-

BANANA LIFE TOURS

Anyone who has ever sliced a banana into her morning cereal should be interested in the offering of Banana Life Tours (if, in fact, the tours are still being offered). A clever entrepreneur, Claudette Rodriguez, arranged to rent out the use of the banana companies' railroad tracks, then fitted out a few old cars with comfortable seats suitable for tourists. The train meanders through the heart of banana country while guides explain more than you ever realized you could want to know about banana cultivation. Unfortunately, unscrupulous businessmen have attempted to profit from the business by raising track-rental rates high enough to shut down the entire operation. Negotiations are underway to reopen the tours. For information on the status of the operation, contact the office in Miami, Florida, at 305/371-9442, fax: 307/371-4006.

ket is to be found between 8th and 9th Avenues.) For souvenir shopping, your best bet is the Guamilito market, located between 8a and 9a Avenidas and 5a and 6a Calles NO. The market is roughly divided into halves, one selling vegetables and flowers and one selling handicrafts, T-shirts, and souvenirs.

Across the street, at 6a Calle, 8a y 9a Avenidas, is the **Casa de Sol shop** (557-9321), where Rosibel Janania sells very high quality artisan work from all over Honduras, including unusual felt Christmas ornaments (toucans and parrots) from the Mosquitia. Some profits from the sale of such items go to support MOPAWI, the Miskito Indian group. Rosibel opened the shop on a family dare after complaining about the quality of the handicrafts at Guamilito. She has been so successful that the family is now opening a branch across from the Hotel Copantl. Although the merchants at Guamilito reacted badly at first to the increased competition, they eventually realized that their best strategy was to improve the quality of their goods and offer better services to the traveler.

San Pedro Sula is also home to *Honduras Tips,* the magazine-format "Official Travel Guide of Honduras," published by expatriate John Dupuis with the help of the Honduran Tourism Institute, that lists hotel and restaurant prices and is filled with advertisements from outfitters, language schools, and other businesses interested in contacting tourists. Pick up a copy at your hotel, or check it on-line at www.hondurastips.com. Another local publication of interest is *Flora y Fauna,* a monthly newspaper that covers environmental issues. I found an outdated copy for sale at a newsstand at the

Trail in El Cusuco National Park

James D. Gollin

Hotel Copantl and when I asked about a more recent edition, the shopkeeper responded with a shrug and said, "It's environmental news. It doesn't really change that much." The monthly does, in fact, cover the changing environmental situation throughout the country. Publisher Juan de Dios Fajard, an award-winning photographer, deserves many kudos for raising ecological awareness throughout his country.

NATURE AND ADVENTURE SIGHTS IN NORTH CENTRAL HONDURAS

El Cusuco National Park

From an environmental point of view, the greatest attraction in the San Pedro metropolitan area is El Cusuco National Park. El Cusuco, which was granted National Park status in 1987, is home to pine trees that are said to be among the tallest in Central America. It also houses a variety of birds, including quetzals, trogons, motmots, jays, woodpeckers, flycatchers, and warblers.

Much of Cusuco was cut by an American timber company in the 1950s. The park has been protected since 1959, when enough virgin forest remained to provide a genetic bank. While some environmentalists warn that rain forest, once destroyed, will never regenerate, the tall trees of Cusuco, dripping with bromeliads and surrounded by bird and animal life, demonstrate the resilience of nature.

Cusuco is managed by the Fundación Ecologista Hector Rodrigo Pastor Fasquelle (HRPF). The foundation is named in honor of Hector Rodrigo Pastor Fasquelle, who was assassinated at his farm in El Jaral in 1990. The reasons for his murder remain unclear. An ardent environmentalist, he was committed to protecting Honduras's forests. The foundation is the recipient of 12.8 million lempiras from Fundación Vida for conservation efforts in El Merendon and also receives income from tourist visits to the park.

Cusuco is quite close to San Pedro Sula, located in the Merendon mountain range that is visible from the Parque, but the road up the mountain is long and steep enough to require a four-wheel-drive vehicle, especially during and after a rain. Most notably, the roads are poorly marked from the town of Cofradia to Buenos Aires. All tour agencies make regular trips up to Cusuco, and you should be able to book at your hotel.

If you are driving yourself, take the road out toward Copán and leave the highway at Cofradia, winding through the town and exiting on the smaller road toward Buenos Aires. As you climb, the habitat changes from secondary pine growth to thick tropical woods and back to pine. About two hours from San Pedro, the town of Buenos Aires appears atop a mountain ridge, with a soccer field on the right. Just beyond the soccer field is the house of Mario, where you can get drinks, meals, and even natural medicines.

Mario and his family host regular Buenos Aires visits by doctors and dentists, a program funded by Fundación Fasquelle. Another good program at work in the Buenos Aires area is run by FunBanCahfe, a coffee growing cooperative that emphasizes natural methods and sustainable yields.

Beyond Buenos Aires, the road climbs steeply, up to about 1,525 meters (5,000 feet) at the park entrance, where you will be charged the equivalent of $10. At the visitors center, there are maps (5L) and environmental education exhibits. You can arrange for a guide to

LAND OF THE RAINING FISH

Southeast of San Pedro Sula, Yoro beckons the adventurous tourists. According to national folklore, Yoro is the site of the famous "Lluvia de Pesces" (Rain of Fishes) phenomenon. It is said that small fish literally rain from the skies above Yoro, though no one can explain it. The sky reportedly becomes very dark before the torrent of fish. Of course, it's hard to believe this story, but everyone from Yoro seems to insist that it's true. If you're in town and the fish aren't falling, look up the local environmental group AMY (Asociación Ecologica Amigos de la Montaña de Yoro) on the Parque Central, check out the vegetarian food at Comedor Copáneca, go hiking in Yoro Mountain National Park. But don't forget your umbrella. You never know when it will fish. Er, rain.

take you on one of the five paths leading from the base camp of an old logging company, presently the park's visitors center, out through some spectacular cloud forest scenery.

Trails in Cusuco National Park are well marked and generally easy to follow. The Danto (Tapir) Trail takes 90 minutes to hike, including stops at the 21 markers to read the self-guided tour booklet (available at the visitors center). The Quetzal Trail can be hiked in two hours, climbing to an altitude of 1,700 meters (5,575 feet). Other trails include the Pizote, the Colorado, and Las Minas, but these are not as well marked. While you should be able to find your way around the well-developed trail system on your own, first-class guides such as Rene Alvarenga, Danillo Alvarenga, or Carlos Alvarenga will point out edible fruits, medicinal plants, and exotics that you would miss on your own. They will also warn you away from stinging nettles and poisonous insects. You can contact these guides through Fundación Fasquelle (see Details, p. 75, for contact info).

The forests are quite safe as long as you follow basic safety rules and make sure that accompanying children do the same. Do not brush your hands through the leaves at random. Look before you touch. If you are going to use tree limbs for support as you climb or descend steep paths, look carefully for giant "bullet" ants, spines, or other unpleasant surprises before you grab. The park is habitat for several poisonous snakes, so you do need to watch your step. But snakes and dangerous animals will generally hear you long before you approach and will keep out of your way. If you startle a sleeping snake, stand still or back up very slowly. The snake will leave you alone if you leave it alone.

For an alternative or addition to the main park trails, visit **Carlin's Ecotourism Camp,** Before you reach the visitors center, take a right at a large roadside sign erected by the Orion company. In a few hundred yards you'll arrive at a clearing that is home to Carlos, known as "Carlin," and his family. Carlin grew up on this site and, because it is in the buffer zone, he is allowed to stay on and run a small ecotourism camp. There is no charge to visit, but he charges 25L for a meal that includes coffee from the trees on the property and 20L to sleep on the bunk beds constructed by Cambio for just that purpose. Bring your own sleeping bags and pads. Take caution, warns Suyapa Dominguez, an environmental education specialist with the San Pedro Sula–based EDUECO: "*Chinche de Chagas* is a bug that bites at night when you are sleeping and then later 15 to 20 years can kill you by causing your heart to swell. They are abundant in houses made of mud. In Honduras many people die of these sicknesses, especially campesinos, so you have to take precautions if you sleep on the floor." There are also camping sites for those who bring tents, but be aware that ocelots hunt in the area at night.

One of the best hikes on Carlin's property is a one-hour round trip down to a waterfall and swimming hole. The path is steep, but ropes tied to trees make the difficult ascents and descents rather fun. (We wonder why more trails aren't equipped with such handy ropes.) Look carefully at the details of all that is around you. If possible, ask Carlin or another guide to accompany you so you won't get lost or miss too much. Those tiny mud bells hanging from a leaf? They are the homes of little wasps. Those giant shafts of the liquidambar tree? Each can be tapped like a maple tree, generating 5 liters (about 1 gallon) of fluid that fights skin infections and can be mixed with honey for use as a cough suppressant. The tall, straight tree's white wood is quite like that of a maple, and its leaves and flowers smell wonderful. At the end of the path, water pours out of a narrow rock canyon, looking, like Hollywood's idealized depiction of a rain-forest scene.

Details: *While it is actually quite close to San Pedro as the crow flies, it takes about two hours by four-wheel-drive to reach the park. The area of the nuclear zone is 1,000 hectares, and fees are 10L for Hondurans, $10 for foreigners. For more information, contact Fundación Ecologista Hector Rodrigo Pastor Fasquelle (HRPF), 552-1014 or 557-6598; fax: 557-6620, fundeco@netsys.hn.*

NATURE AND ADVENTURE SIGHTS IN SOUTH CENTRAL HONDURAS

Cerro Azul Meambar National Park

Parque Nacional Cerro Azul Meambar, known as PANACAM, is a 320-square-kilometer (123.5-square-mile) park with everything from dry tropical forests to humid tropical forests to cloud forests, starting at an elevation of only 415 meters (1,361 feet) and climbing to a height of 2,080 meters (6,824 feet). The nuclear zone is approximately 100 square kilometers (roughly 40 square miles). Nearly all the people who lived in the nuclear zone have moved to the buffer zone or elsewhere, but those who had recently planted coffee trees will be allowed to stay on for five years, by which time the production will decline naturally. In the buffer zone, no burning of the forest is allowed, though residents can easily receive permits to cut a limited amount of timber for home use.

The park is managed by the Tegucigalpa-based NGO Proyecto Aldea Global (PAG), which in 1997 opened a small in-park visitors center and a cluster of cabañas that can sleep three dozen. About 1,000 people visited this center in 1998, and about 400 spent the night, but this number will probably shoot up after the opening of the visitors center on the main road in early 2000. For reservations and information, contact PAG in Tegucigalpa at 232-8287 or 773-0539, fax: 232-6511. The organization will radio ahead to the park. If you don't speak Spanish, say, "Park reservation, please" when the phone is answered and you will be passed to an English speaker. The park entrance is located just 2.5 hours from Tegucigalpa and about an hour from San Pedro Sula, quite accessible to Honduras's largest population centers. The hope is that, as one of the most beautiful and accessible parks, PANACAM will serve as proof to Hondurans that their parks are valuable resources.

A 500-meter (1,640-foot) hike leads to a waterfall, and further on, 17 kilometers (about 10 miles) of trails have been constructed through the mountains. The cabañas are at 800 meters (2,624 feet) and reachable by dirt road. In 1997 the visitors center began offering tent and backpack equipment rental for those who want to head further into the park. By 1998 a network of six rustic B&Bs was established, one each in the hamlets of Planes, Palmital, Cerro Azul, and San Antonio de Yuri, and two in Las Delicias. Each consists of a simple room attached to a campesino's house, with its own clean toilet, potable water, and simple meals. The B&Bs are located at trailheads throughout the park and eventually 15 of them will be spaced so that trekkers can hike a circular path through the park, enjoying the view of Lake Yojoa one day, caves with Indian altars another, and waterfalls yet another.

PANACAM presently employs 19 guards, including seven in Siguatepeque, the highest number of any park system in Honduras. At present, throughout the park, there are 30 kilometers (about 18.5 miles) of trails, but another 50 kilometers (31 miles) will be opened up over the next two years in conjunction with the opening of the B&Bs; this will allow longer-range trekking. A variety of day hikes are possible from the visitors center, many of which end up at a crystal-clear waterfall. The park, after all, provides 70 percent of the water for Lake Yojoa, as well as 20 percent of the water for the giant El Cajón reservoir.

On the east side of the park are **El Palmital Caves,** with extensive petroglyphs and even holes in the ceiling to allow in light. Niches carved into the wall were probably used for religious purposes. There are still human remains in many of these caves. You will reap good karma if you visit and appreciate, but bad karma if you disturb artifacts and remains that have been lying peacefully for centuries. If you are interested in the caves, ask PANACAM guard Don Julio about "La Savana de las Cuevitas," the field of caves.

In the town of Meambar is an old bridge built with egg white mixed with lime, from the days before cement was available, as well as a nice 19th-century church. Ask for Sr. Adorcas Oseguera, who has gathered pottery shards and made a study of the local antiquities.

In the nuclear zone of the park there are tapirs, jaguars, monkeys, quetzals, and toucans. The nuclear zone is protected by the natural barrier of the mountain slopes' steep grade—at 70 degrees in many places, they are more like cliffs than slopes.

A terrible problem in the Cerro Azul Meambar area, and in other parts of Honduras, is the traditional practice of charcoal making. The carboneros dig pits in the earth, fill them with freshly cut wood, start a slow fire, and cover the pit with dirt to keep things from breaking into open flame. If everything turns out correctly, the oxygen-deprived fire turns the wood to charcoal. Because it is hard to control the strength of the fire, carboneros like to work where trees grow near rivers or streams so they can pour water into the pits and slow things down if necessary. As a result, charcoal-related deforestation is concentrated in the most fragile and environmentally important mini-watersheds in the cloud forests. To control this practice, every community in or near the park has joined one of 23 watershed protection committees.

Proyecto Aldea Global (PAG) may have a hand in opening an environmental education center slated to be located at the intersection of the main highway and the turnoff toward the lakeshore near Agua Azul motel. The center will include a restaurant, grocery, artisan shop, house-plant nursery, and a theater showing environmentally oriented films, including one profiling all the parks of Honduras.

In the PANACAM buffer zone, PAG has helped local farmers to plant 300,000 cacao, mango, achiote, avocado, and citrus trees. Besides its work in Cerro Azul Meambar, PAG has also developed integrated rural development projects in other parts of Honduras. In the region around Celaque, the group has developed and integrated health and literacy programs in conjunction with Lenca Indians. More than 1,000 families in the region have planted 300,000 trees, including apples and peaches that produce not only nutritious food but a great cash crop. The Yure River Basin project tackles soil and water conservation; the planting of citrus, achiote, and black pepper for cash crops; the construction of Habitat for Humanity housing;

and the development of potable water sources for all local families. The Humuya River Basin project, to the south, has planted 500,000 trees, mostly cacao, mango, citrus, and spice, and constructed nurseries for hardwoods.

In accordance with PAG philosophy, nothing is given to the local campesinos except advice. They must buy the rootstock they wish to plant, giving them an incentive to protect the trees from natural predators and fire. Once the trees begin to produce, providing food and income, the farm families will no longer migrate into the rain forest but will learn techniques to improve the agricultural land where they live.

Details: *The park encompasses most of the mountains due east of Lake Yojoa, with the main entrance 25 kilometers (15.5 miles) north of Siguatepeque. It's area is 25,600 hectares (63,200 acres).*

For more information, check in with the Visitor's Center or contact Proyecto Aldea Global (232-8287) or Enrique Campos at the Agua Azul motel (557-3982). To enter the park, leave the main road at La Gauma, heading slightly east through Santa Elena to San Isidro. After 2.5 kilometers (1.5 miles), take a right at the park sign, then drive through beautiful rolling hills on a good dirt road past pineapple and coffee plantations. The road gets steeper, suitable for two-wheel-drive vehicles only with aggressive drives, and finally ends at a small in-park visitors center.

Lake Yojoa

Lake Yojoa is a gorgeous natural lake set between towering mountains cloaked in cloud forest. Like a tropical Swiss valley, the blue lake is surrounded by intensely verdant mountains rising up to nearly 2,450 meters (8,000 feet). The area is rich in biodiversity, with 373 bird species confirmed.

Lago de Yojoa is constantly refreshed by the water coursing out of the surrounding cloud forests. The lake is 22 kilometers (13.6 miles) long and 10 kilometers (6.2 miles) wide. The maximum depth of the waters reaches around 18.5 meters (60 feet) in May, swelling to about 24.5 meters (80 feet) in the rainy season, so the shoreline varies significantly. The lakeshore itself is at an altitude of 670 meters (2,200 feet), making it noticeably cooler than the coast.

Another significant threat to the long-term health of the lake is the Rosario mine on the southwestern shore, near the town of El

Mochito. The mine, a tremendous producer of gold, platinum, lead, and silver, has poured unmeasured tons of contaminants into the lake over the decades, but scientific studies show that the heavy metals have sunk below the mud floor of the lake and rise into the food chain only when great storms rile the lake bottom. According to UNICEF water expert Tony Brand, there is no risk for a tourist who eats a few bass, but the impact on people who eat the fish every day of their lives has yet to be fully studied. A series of sedimentation ponds now keep heavy metals from leaching into the lake, and Ecolago (see below) occasionally takes samples for analysis.

James D. Gollin

Lake Yojoa

Giant pumps work constantly to keep the mine functioning, and locals say the electric bill for the pumps runs at $100,000 per month. The mine shut down temporarily, partly due to union conflicts, but was purchased by American Pacific as part of a debt swap with the Honduran government. Mine employment was reduced from 5,000 to around 1,200, and a system of sedimentation ponds was installed to keep the heavy metals from washing into the lake.

In years past, the lake's water level was ruled by complex seven- and 21-year cycles, but these have been interrupted somewhat by a canal built to supply water to a hydropower plant below the north shore of the lake. During low-water periods, it is possible to walk from the archaeological sites near El Jaral across to the Isla de las Ventanas. During the "green," or wet, season it's quite a swim.

The environmental group **Ecolago,** founded in 1990, seeks a balance between conservation and agriculture in the vicinity of the lake. Ecolago (337-5028 or 338-2507) sponsors an annual "adopt-a-tree" campaign in which nature lovers donate 15L to support the planting of native tree species in once-forested land around the lake. This assists a regional reforestation effort through which more than 20,000 trees have been planted. The organization also coordinates with PAG in Tegucigalpa (332-8287), which manages the nearby Cerro Azul Meambar and keeps an eye on the Santa Bárbara National Park.

Yojoa is a great base from which to visit the Los Naranjos eco-archaeological park on the north shore or hike up into the Santa Bárbara National Park to the west. Or spend some time relaxing by the lake itself. The town of **Peña Blanca** has banks and an office of Hondutel (the Honduran telephone monopoly; telephones are available for use at Hondutel offices). Most of the hotels are located on the eastern shore of the lake.

Just north of the southern end of the lake, 6 kilometers north of Pito Solo and 4 kilometers south of Le Guama, is a new **Visitors Center** built by PAG, just finishing construction as this book is being published. When fully operational, it will show videos and slide shows of the local parks and natural attraction, and also showcase Honduran nature with videos shot at parks and protected areas from around the country. Changing exhibits will highlight the Honduran environment, the culture of Honduras, the ancient Lencan and Mayan civilizations, etc. There will also be a small natural-foods supermarket and a restaurant serving organic produce. Just one hour from San Pedro Sula and two hours from Tegucigalpa, this center could receive enough traffic to make it an important center for environmental education.

Nearby, another environmental center, **Tropical Eco Center for the Study of the Environment and Biodiversity,** is planned but not yet built. This center aims to highlight the environment of the Lago de Yojoa region. Twenty manzanas (32 acres) of land were donated to the center by the Campo family, owners of Agua Azul (Enrique Campo is vice president of Ecolago), and construction and operating funds are expected from the University of Las Vegas. An additional 100 manzanas (160 acres) will be added to create a wildlife refuge.

The lake is a paradise not only for birders, but also for anyone interested in **bass fishing.** Black bass fishing, the insiders will tell you, is best five days before and five days after the full moon. The bass were introduced 40 years ago by United Fruit Company as a result of a strange accident. The live fish, originally destined to stock a lake in Colombia, were stuck on the tarmac at San Pedro Sula airport due to an airplane's mechanical problem. Rather than let the fish die, it was decided—with no environmental impact studies whatsoever—to dump them in Lake Yojoa. The bass prospered, displacing native species. Agua Azul was a fishing camp that boomed during the 1970s, attracting most of its clientele, including Texas oil millionaires, from the southern United States.

During the 1980s, the population around the lake exploded from around 2,000 to about 50,000, seriously stressing both the local economy and the ecosystem. The newcomers were able to feed themselves a high-protein diet by spearing or netting as many fish as they desired from the seemingly boundless supply in the lake. But soon all the larger fish were consumed. Next, a second disaster for the bass took place, this one stemming from the folly of poorly thought-out good intentions.

In 1982 the government constructed fish ponds in streams that flow into the lake and stocked them with an African fish species, black tilapia. According to the university studies, the tilapia would stay in the ponds, well set back from the lake. But with tropical weather being what it is, monsoon rains regularly flooded the experimental area, washing the tilapia into the lake. The relatively tasteless mud-dwelling fish rapidly displaced the bass from their spawning grounds. In 1986 the silver galaxia tilapia were introduced. While they still crowd out the bass, the grass-eating fish are at least good to eat. The Taiwanese government is now setting up a training center to teach fish farmers how to grow yet another species, this one a red tilapia.

During the early 1990s, the bass were fighting for survival. Whereas in the early 1980s a fisherman could regularly catch an 11- to 14-pounder, and even an occasional 18-pounder, a typical catch a decade later for an eight-hour period was only a 1- or 2-pound fish. Shortly after its founding, Ecolago commissioned a study that concluded that, for maximum fish population growth, the 1.5- to 4-pound fish should be left to breed, while the larger and smaller fish could be eaten.

Agreements were made with the fishermen to alter their nets so that they would catch only tilapia, allowing bass to escape. Tilapia grow from 1 to 6 pounds. Bass, which fetch 10L per pound, are now caught only by hand-lines, while the tilapia are caught with net and spear. In 1991, as the new policy was being instituted, a conflict arose in which a policeman shot and killed a fisherman, so the fishermen's association took over the responsibility to patrol the lake.

While poaching does oc-cur, the flexibility of the arrangement and the fact that it is their neighbors and not uniformed police who keep the fishermen in line has led to success. Have the reforms worked? A hand-line fisherman who caught only 1 or 2 pounds of fish a day in 1991 boosted his catch to 10 to 30 pounds per day by 1996, and fish stocks have remained strong since then.

Ecolago has been variously criticized as a club of wealthy city dwellers who keep country houses on the lakeshore and want to keep everything pretty, and as a cover for hotel owners to boost the sport-fishing industry. But the group's work in replenishing the bass population while allowing the subsistence fishermen to continue to fish is a good model. It's a strange situation: An undesirable exotic has crowded out a more desired one. No one talks seriously about reintroducing native fish species.

Swimming is a great way to cool off, and the lake water is clean and beautiful in unpopulated areas, but remember that there is no sewage treatment in the area—do not swim near populated areas.

Details: To get to Yojoa from San Pedro Sula, take one of the many buses to Tegucigalpa, Siguatepeque, or Comayagua, and get off at Le Guama, about 72 kilometers (45 miles) south of San Pedro Sula. By private car, the trip takes about an hour. From Tegucigalpa, take a bus heading toward San Pedro Sula and get off in Le Guama. For more information, Contact Ecolago at 337-5028 or 338-2507.

Los Naranjos Eco-Archaeological Park

Plans are underway for an "eco-archaeological" park to be built on the north shore of Lake Yojoa, near the community of Los Naranjos, which means "the orange trees." Due to the presence of Spanish aid money there should be at least a minimum of infrastructure by the time you visit. A pictograph representing the sun will be the symbol of the park. The park will be bounded by the Río Blanco to the west, El Eden to the northeast, La Jara to the east, and the lake to the south. There is a plan for a hanging bridge over the canal, to be built by ENEE, the electric utility. By the lakeshore there is a rocky beach and a few small islands. Originally excavated by a French group between 1933 and 1954, the site was all but forgotten until recently.

The project has been pushed by both Fund Copán and the Honduran Institute of Tourism and funded by Spain; Cooperación Español has an office in Peña Blanca.

Who were the original occupants of Los Naranjos, a group colloquially referred to as "the ancient Lencas"? Were they a southern branch of the Maya? No, the ancient Lencan civilization prospered, built 30-meter-high (100-foot) stone temples,

James D. Gollin

The Acropolis at Los Naranjos

and then disappeared while the Maya were still running around naked in the woods, chasing birds with arrows and living in grass huts. Researchers have identified 70 or so sites around the northwest end of the lake, near the towns of El Jaral and El Eden. The Lenca structures appear to date to around 900 b.c., long before the Maya invented their math or astronomy.

The main ruin area has three principal structures including a 17-meter (55.5-foot)-high acropolis and two others, inventively named structure #6 and structure #1, set around a central 200-square-meter (2,129-square-foot) triangular plaza.

The plan for the eco-archaeological park is to clear a bit of land immediately around the ruins, but to leave most of it in its natural state, hacking out only a few trails for visitors; hence the prefix "eco." The biodiversity of the area is tremendous, including three bio-zones nearby. These include the wetlands at the lakeshore, a niche for mollusks, crustaceans, and aquatic birds; the primary forest, filled with bromeliads and orchids in the deep shade of the gualiqueme trees; and a secondary forest that has a wide variety of fruit trees. Armadillos, gua-

PALMEROLA

Twelve kilometers south of Comayagua, at Kilometer 75, is the largest military outpost in Honduras. Once simply a Honduran military base and the site of the Honduran Air Force Academy, Palmerola was expanded by the U.S. military during the Central American civil wars of the 1980s. Over $150 million per year in official U.S. aid poured into Honduras during the Contra–Sandinista struggle (compared to $25 million in 1997), and much of that money was spent in or around Palmerola, building an air base capable of handling everything from B-52s to C-130s to fleets of helicopter gunships. While activity at the base has been scaled back in peacetime, it is still the primary fallback position for the U.S. Southern Command should it be forced to leave its bases in Panama at the turn of the century. Palmerola has also been discussed as a center for joint drug interdiction efforts in all of Central America. A few years back, Americans were asked to pay rent for their continued use of the base, but the United States refused. U.S. Ambassador James Creagan told the Hondurans, "The presence of U.S. military bases in the world responds to a

tusas (agoutis; strange creatures that seem to be a cross between a rabbit, a rat, and a deer), and jaguarundi abound, as does a critter known as the pericolgero (a type of two-toed sloth), in danger of extinction. The biodiversity of the archaeological zone has been protected while much of the rest of the region has been degraded by human encroachment, largely because ENEE fenced off and guarded the area to protect the water intake canal for its downstream power-plant system.

Details: *The main site is about 1 kilometer (.6 mile) from the lake. From Le Guama, regular buses run up the eastern shore of the lake toward* spirit of cooperation and it is based on relations of friendship and respect between nations." In other words, no money.

Some Hondurans have suggested that U.S. forces be made to leave Palmerola. The facility could then be transformed into a new Tegucigalpa international airport or a dual-use airport, with a civilian terminal at the far end of the runway, away from the military installation. The move would benefit Honduran agricultural interests as well—civilian shipping from Palmerola would allow mangoes to get to Belgium and avocados to Boston without first having to be trucked over the mountains. Nearby, about one hour southeast of Comayagua, just east of Palmerola, the mountain fortress of Tenempua is a good stop for history and archaeology buffs. Tenempua was the base of the Lencan leader Lempira, who kept the Spaniards at bay in the 16th century. After attempts to take Tenempua were repulsed, the conquistadors lured Lempira into negotiations and, under a flag of truce, murdered him. Not much remains visible to the untrained eye, but the steep mountainsides around Tenempua were once extended with high stone walls and other defenses. Archaeologists have found evidence of a ball court and other artifacts in this fortress town.

Peña Blanca. If you are heading to Peña Blanca itself or to Los Naranjos, take a bus from San Pedro Sula to El Mochito and get off in Peña Blanca. To get to Los Naranjos from Peña Blanca, take the La Mochito Road for 1.5 kilometers (.9 mile).

Pulhapanzák Falls

Can you say the name of this waterfall three times in a row without cracking a smile? You may have to in order to find your way here, but the effort is well worth it.

Pulhapanzák Falls

The first spot you come to seems like a nice calm place to swim with some cascading rapids above you, but beware. Pulhapanzák Falls is not above but below the spot in which you are lolling. The Río Lindo snakes through reeds and grasses then bursts out over a 100-meter (328-foot)-high cliff to pound spectacularly down through the jungle into the deep canyon below. Take a path around to the right to get the best view of the falls, and bring plenty of film. You can work your way down to the swimming area at the base of the falls, but be careful: The area is covered in mist and is quite slippery.

Above the falls are lovely grounds, bridges over streams that flow into the Lindo, and picnic tables. Pulhapanzák is a popular picnic site ʼn weekends, so if you would like to dally tranquilly in the pools, head ʼre midweek. If you are heading down to Lake Yojoa, it's another kilometers (about 11 miles) to Peña Blanca on the north shore.

There is a 5L fee to enter the *balneario* (bathing resort), where ʼan park, picnic, or eat at the local small restaurant, and even e night in a private house.

Details: *The falls are 19 kilometers (12 miles) north of Lake Yojoa, a great spot for picnicking and swimming. For more information, contact Ecolago at 337-5028. To get there from San Pedro Sula, head south on the main highway toward Lake Yojoa, but exit to the right, near Río Lindo, in the direction of El Mochito. About 12 kilometers (7.5 miles) south of Río Lindo, turn west at the town of San Buena Ventura. From there it's about 1 kilometer (.6 mile) to the falls. Follow signs or ask for the* "balneario."

Parque Nacional Montaña de Comayagua

Much of the area around the colonial town of Comayagua has been deforested, but the Parque Nacional Montaña de Comayagua has a core zone of 6,000 hectares, two-thirds of which is still covered with primary tropical cloud forest, at altitudes of 1,800 meters (5,905 feet) and up, with the highest point in the park at 2,407 meters (nearly 7,900 feet). Including the buffer zone, the park comprises 24,000 hectares (59,280 acres) and 62 communities. The park, especially the nuclear zone, is a refuge for many species of wildlife including quetzals, toucans, white-faced monkeys, sloths, and others. As with most such parks in Honduras, a scientific inventory of the flora and fauna has never been undertaken here, so no one really knows the true extent of the park's biodiversity.

Infrastructure in the park is minimal, but a local NGO, ECOSIMCO, is attempting to control deforestation and has set up a system of environmental education projects involving schoolchildren in the Comayagua area. With the help of Peace Corps volunteer Karl Riber, ECOSIMCO has done wonders raising the awareness of the people of Comayagua about the precious resource so near their city. ECOSIMCO also works with the farmers in the buffer zone, most of whom grow coffee. Soil conservation and improvement methods have been introduced and chemical use has been reduced.

ECOSIMCO has promoted the idea of using ecotourism in a few areas of the park. One prime ecotourism site is the Río Negro, about 90 minutes by car from Comayagua, or one hour from the town of San Jeronimo. From the Río Negro, hike an easy path for 30 minutes to a waterfall called El Ensueño. The fit and adventurous can head on for about 45 minutes more on poor trails to another waterfall that tumbles down approximately 100 meters (328 feet). Ask for

SOLVING THE EL CAJÓN PROBLEM

The Honduran government and the IDB have recently spent more than $20 million to reforest and protect the El Cajón watershed, but these funds are too little too late. According to officials at SANAA, the government agency in charge of water resources, only 10 percent of the El Cajón watershed is still pure forest. Even if 10 million trees were planted per year and none were cut down, they say, it would take 20 years to restore the ecosystem.

The fact is that there are people living in the El Cajón watershed, people who have nowhere else to go. The only long-term solution is to develop land-use systems that allow people to produce value from the land without destroying it. A promising example is the work being done by NGOs such as PAG, the group active in Cerro Azul Meambar National Park. They have intensified efforts to help the farmers in the El Cajón region, teaching them regenerative agricultural techniques that improve the soil while encouraging them to plant cacao, orange, mango, and avocado trees. To avoid erosion, PAG-trained farmers plant regular rows of pineapples across their fields. To avoid the need for chemical fertilizer, they plant high-protein velvet beans among their corn stalks, plants that return nitrogen to the soil. Funding for such highly successful projects, however, is a pittance compared to the industrial reforestation projects preferred by the IDB.

guides Abilio Velasquez or his father, Don Maximo. They can take you to the waterfall or to other areas in the park. After a 90-minute hike from the Río Negro, you will be in the heart of the primary cloud forest.

Another good prospect is the area around **El Horno,** a three-hour hike from Comayagua. At El Horno, there are caves with ancient petroglyphs—ask ECOSIMCO or someone in El Horno for a guide.

"It's insane," says PAG's Chet Thomas. "They spent the better part of a billion dollars on the dam, but not $5,000 on protecting the watershed."

Since the El Cajón crisis, many Honduran officials have come to realize that, just as the outflow of water through the dam's turbines cannot exceed inflow to the reservoir, a society that cuts wood faster than trees grow cannot prosper for long. In wealthy countries such as the United States, debate over the environment is often discussed in terms of spotted owls versus loggers. But in a small country such as Honduras, the essential fallacy underlying the "jobs versus the environment" debate is exposed.

Without a healthy, sustainable environment, the economy of any nation will soon either collapse or, by importing precious resources, simply delay a more general environmental and economic collapse. Due to the mismanagement of the three-quarters-of-a-billion-dollar investment at El Cajón and at other sites throughout the world, institutions such as the IDB and the World Bank have begun to see the light. Washington conferences now concentrate on sustainable development and micro-credit. "Our aim has always been to abolish poverty," says Kenneth Newcombe, chief of Global Environment Coordination at the World Bank. "Now we understand that solving poverty and protecting the environment go hand in hand." The rhetoric, at least, has shifted.

The best time to visit the park is during the dry season, from February to late August. In the wet season, the hiking is more difficult, the weather is chillier, and it is harder to see the breathtaking sights. You can take a bus from Comayagua to San Jeronimo and hitch a ride from there if you don't have your own transportation. Most of the trails into the park depart from Río Negro on the north side of the park.

James D. Gollin

The controversial El Cajón Dam

Details: *Montaña de Comayagua National Park is located 12 kilometers (about 7.5 miles) east of Comayagua and has an area of 24,000 hectares (59,280 acres). For more information, contact ECOSIMCO 772-1575.*

Parque Nacional Santa Bárbara

Parque Nacional Santa Bárbara, just outside of the town of Santa Bárbara, consists of a mountain range separating the town of Santa Bárbara from Lake Yojoa, to the east. It's a beautiful area, though it has no infrastructure. Regrettably, the National Agrarian Institute (INA) has been giving landless campesinos land on the Yojoa side of Santa Bárbara, leading to the clearing of these beautiful forests. Creeping deforestation is claiming many of the habitats. Further, Canadian-owned zinc and lead mines at the base of the mountain logged much of the forest cover in the 1950s.

There is no clear trail to the summit, but a number of cool, shaded paths meander through the lower slopes. It is possible to hike up from Santa Bárbara, over the top and down to Lake Yojoa, but this should not be tried without an experienced guide or in the wet season. The crossing will take approximately two days. Intrepid mountaineers might want to hack their way through dense vegetation up through the virgin forest to the summit, Mt. Marancho. At 2,744 meters (9,000 feet), it is the second-highest peak in Honduras. Fauna regularly sighted in the park include peccaries, quetzals, trogons, and iguanas.

The town of **Santa Bárbara** is a great place for hiking and is relatively prosperous, its economy heavily dependent on the coffee crop. The department of Santa Bárbara produces one-third of Honduras's coffee. During the harvest season, December and January, many townspeople head off to their *fincas* (country houses) in the mountains around town. During that period, dying beans can be found spread on sidewalks, side streets, even the Parque Central. Santa Bárbara is also famous for woven mats made out of a type of straw known as junco. The junco hats of Santa Bárbara can be purchased throughout Honduras, but the best choice and prices are to be found, of course, in the Santa Bárbara region. Another nice souvenir is angels made from corn husks.

The nearby town of **El Nispero** is home to a hydroelectric dam that had overflowed during one of our visits to the area. A 300-meter (about 985-foot) stretch of road was completely inundated and it was impossible to tell how deep the water was. Having spent hours crossing rough mountain roads from Gracias, we were loath to turn back. We asked a campesino on horseback whether we could get through in our rented Toyota jeep. He looked at us and responded, "Just keep heading forward." As we rolled forward, the water rose to the hubcaps, then to the tops of the wheels, then crested over the hood of the car. We didn't want to stop and turn around, so we just kept heading forward, even as the water climbed over the bottom of the windshield and side windows. With thoughts of a long swim with wet bags and difficult excuses to Toyota Rent A Car, we just kept heading forward. Eventually the water level receded, and we passed through El Nispero and at last made it down to Santa Bárbara.

El Nispero is also where Hondurans weave *petates,* the mats campesinos throughout the nation use to sleep on. Just south of town is the waterfall known as La Chorrera; to reach it from the town of Santa Bárbara, follow the road up from the Colonial Hotel toward the mountain and keep going straight up until the road stops.

Details: *The town of Santa Barbara is 25 kilometers (15.5 miles) west of Lake Yojoa. The park itself is 125 kilometers (77.5 miles) north of*

Tegucigalpa and 75 kilometers (46.5 miles) southeast of San Pedro Sula, and has an area of 5,000 hectares (12,350 acres). To get there, take the branch road off the main San Pedro Sula–Teguz highway just south of Lake Yojoa and drive around the mountains of Santa Bárbara National Park. It is less than an hour from Pito Soto at the south shore of the lake to Santa Bárbara. If you are heading back to San Pedro Sula from Santa Bárbara, it will take about two hours. For more information, contact Ecolago, 337-5028 or 338-2507.

GUIDES AND OUTFITTERS

Two groups that emphasize environmental concerns are **EDUECO** (Edificio Diek, local 20-C, 3 Avenida y 4-5 Calle NO, 551-3956 in Barrio Gaumilito; e-mail: edueco@intertel.hn2.com) and **Maya Eco Tours** (239D Calle 9a SO and 23a y 24a Avenidas, Río Piedras, 557-4056; e-mail: mayaeco@globalnet.hn). Customized trips are designed by Javier Pinel, who is very knowledgeable about this part of Honduras.

Explore Honduras Tours is in Edificio Paseo del Sol, 2a Avenida y 1a Calle NO (552-6242 or 552-6093, fax: 526-239; e-mail: info@explorehonduras.com). Check out their full range of eco and other offerings, and even book your tours, on the web at http://www.explorehonduras.com/. Explore Honduras has been around for over a decade and boasts "the country's largest deluxe air-conditioned coach fleet dedicated exclusively to tourism." Their focus is on large tourism groups of up to 200 people, but they'll accommodate groups as small as one.

Mayan Caribbean Tours claims it's the largest tour company in Honduras, and they certainly have a major presence. They can be reached at 557-7339 or 557-6072, e-mail: info@mayancaribbean.hn. Don't confuse Mayan Caribbean with MC Tours, whose main office is at 10 Calle / 18 Avenida SO Casa #235 Colonia Trejo, near the Chamber of Commerce (CCIC); phone 552 4455 and 552 4549, fax: 557-3076. MC Tours also has an office in Ruinas de Copán in the lobby of the Hotel Marina Copán. Their e-mail is mctours@netsys.hn and you can check out all their services at http://www.netsys.hn/~mctours/.

Maya Tropic Tours, on the Parque Central inside the Gran Hotel Sula (552-2405) is an all-purpose agency that can help you rent a car, make plane reservations, call home, or book a tour. Jorge Molamphy and his staff are very helpful.

Any hotel in the Lake Yojoa area should be able to set you up with fishing gear, a boat, and a guide. If you don't like to fish, how about a sail? Sailing on the lake is available from **Honduyate** (339-2684 or 557-0774). Briton Richard Joint rents out sailboats and arranges for sailing expeditions that cost 1,200L for up to ten people, including lunch. Motorboats with a guide and a 25-horsepower engine go for 150L per hour, paddleboats are 30L per hour, and canoes are 50L for three hours.

LODGING

Simply put, there are two categories of hotels in San Pedro: business and tourist. Another way to put it would be expensive and nice or cheap and so-so. If you have a big budget or want to splurge (think U.S. big-city prices) on the way in or out of the country, there are "international" hotels such as the Camino Real Inter-Continental ($270), the Copántl ($155), and Los Proceres ($180), where a traveling business executive could feel at home, for a price. Of these, try the Honduran-owned **Hotel Copántl** (on the southern edge of town, 556-8900; e-mail: copantl3@simon.intertel.hn). It's a first-class hotel with all the amenities. One step down in quality and about half the cost is the original high-end hotel in San Pedro, the **Gran Hotel Sula** (1a Calle, 3/4 Avenidas NO, right on the Parque Central, 55-2999, $100). This is a good place to stay if you are on your way in or out of the country and don't mind spending a little extra. The coffee shop and poolside scene are a throwback to the 1950s, and everything is well maintained. The rooms and beds, however, are surprisingly small and resemble upgraded college dorm rooms. If you are on more of a budget, there are dozens of hotels in a more affordable range ($10–$30), most without a great deal of character. Again, for its proximity to the Parque Central, you might try the **Hotel Bolívar** (2a Calle and 2a Avenida, 553-3224; $20). For something a little homier, try **Maya Eco Tours Bed and Breakfast** (239D Calle 9a SO, 23a y 24a Avenidas, Río Piedras, 557-4056; e-mail: mayaeco@globalnet.hn).

When visiting Lake Yojoa, most visitors stay on the eastern shore of the lake at one of the hotels lining the road between Le Guama and Peña Blanca. **Agua Azul** (2 miles north of the shore road junction, 991-7244, $24) is the original fishing hotel on Lake Yojoa. Enrique Campo's "motel," consists of cabañas with no air conditioning but good ceiling fans and hot water. It's located lakeside near a central complex with a pleasant restaurant overlooking the lake, and a swimming pool for those who don't want to risk the lake water. Awaken to birdsong with the dawn light illuminating the Cerro Azul Meambar Mountains, wander among the wildflowers growing in the meadow along the lakeshore, then breakfast on the bamboo-roofed outside dining area, built on stilts to improve the view. Nearby, 4 miles farther up the shore road, is the original "upscale" lake hotel, the **Hotel Brisas del Lago** (553-4884, $53). Set back a bit from the lake, this hotel has a 1960s conference-center feel. It's a resort that has seen better days, but is a good place to book a tour. The newest addition to lakeside hotels is **Oasis Italiani** (991-1195, $28), with eight rooms and a well-deserved reputation for the best Italian food in all of Honduras.

A bit to the north, just south of Peña Blanca on the shore road, **Hotel Finca Las Glorias** (566-0462, 566-0461) has 31 rooms at roughly $40 per night, free for children under 12 years of age with their families. Comfortable rooms have double beds, air conditioning, and cable television. Motorized boats and aquatic bicycles can be rented by the hour. As the hotel is also a working farm, much of the fruit served in the restaurant is homegrown. The hotel has a separate pool and playground for children. To the south, where the San Pedro Sula–Teguz highway touches the south shore of the lake, **Hotel Los Remos** (557-8054) offers simple but clean cottages for around $20.

In addition to the hotels listed above, there are also many spots to camp near the lakeshore, and plenty of simple lakeside stands selling fish.

The **Cerro Azul Meambar National Park Visitors Center** boasts three newly built cabañas, each with two rooms. There is a total capacity of 36 beds, but as many as 40 people have stayed overnight on school trips. There is a kitchen available, but no food at present. The cabins cost $3 per night per person, with meals available for $1.50. Alternatively, stay at one of the rustic B&Bs scattered at trailheads throughout the park.

FOOD

In San Pedro Sula, you can get whatever type of food you want, from Mexican to Italian, Burger King to Pizza Hut. Restaurants specializing in Honduran food include **Las Carnitas, Toreros,** and **Chef Marianos,** all in the *"zona viva"* neighborhood. The latter serves Garífuna specialties. Not too far away, **La Tejana, Las Tejas,** and **Arte Marino** specialize in seafood. If you want to see where the extremely wealthy Hondurans eat, put on your best clothes and head to **Mediterraneo** at the Arab Club (founded by Hondurans of Middle Eastern descent. Nonmembers are allowed into the restaurant only.

In the Yojoa region, drop in to **Only Bass,** right on the lake just south of Agua Azul. The name isn't quite right, as they do serve other things, but you'd be a fool to not eat the bass. Nearby, **Oasis Italiani** serves excellent Italian food. If it's open, definitely try the natural-foods restaurant planned at the **PANACAM Visitors Center.** It plans to emulate the success of **La Granja D'Elia,** an Italian buffet, café, bar, and grocery on the main highway near Siguatepeque, also worth a stop.

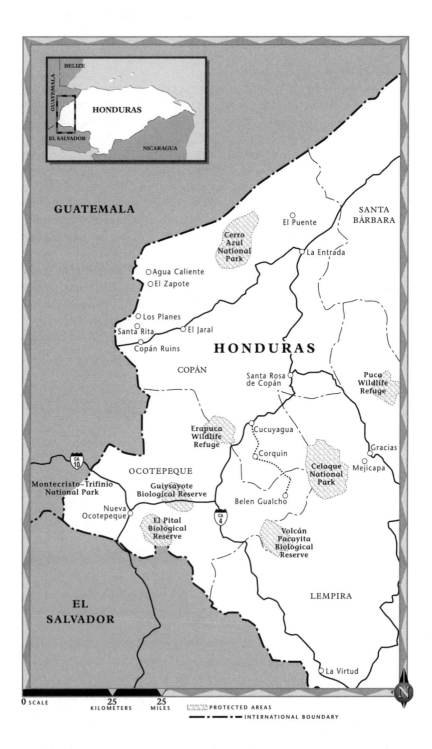

CHAPTER 4

The Lenca Trail:
Western Honduras

Western Honduras, a triangular wedge of mountains and forests bordering Guatemala to the northwest and El Salvador to the southwest, is best known for the site of spectacular Mayan Indian ruins at Copán. Travelers seeking the ruins of a grand civilization are often surprised to find the descendants of the Maya still living around Copán. Although the city of Copán collapsed around the year a.d. 900, the culture and traditions live on, accompanied by the plants and animals that played and continue to play a role in religious ceremonies. South of Copán, the population is heavily Lenca, descendants of a proud people who, under chief Lempira, fought off the conquistadors for two years before their chief succumbed to treachery in 1536.

While Copán is one of the most visited tourist sites in Honduras, with 100,000 visitors per year, its grace and beauty still emanate a powerful sense of history that overshadows any tour-bus crowds you might encounter. Nearby, smaller archaeological sites are all but ignored by conventional tourism, as are sites of natural beauty, including bird-rich forests, rivers with natural hot springs, and traditional villages tucked away behind tall mountains. A bit further afield, nascent tourism in towns such as Santa Rosa de Copán and Gracias, and in the parks of Celaque and Guiysayote, is supported by some basic facilities that allow you to explore the heart of western Honduras. Note that the IHT refers to much of this area as "the Quetzal Trail."

From San Pedro Sula heading southwest to the town of Ruinas de Copán (Copán Ruins), near the Guatemalan border, the highway is well paved. Following the path of the Río Chamelecón, the scenery changes from urban sprawl and banana plantations to small plots of corn and tobacco planted on steep hillsides.

VISITOR INFORMATION

The town of Ruinas de Copán is pleasant, cobblestoned, and white-washed, and well supplied with hotels, restaurants, and bars to suit every taste. Copán has banks, laundries, and even an immigration office, and is surrounded by opportunities for bird-watching, hiking, rafting, and of course visits to surrounding archaeological sights. The town, which is called "Ruinas" is actually about a half-mile from the main set of ruins themselves. Because it's about 170 kilometers (105.5 miles) from San Pedro Sula, or around 2.5 hours by car, many people make the mistake of day tripping in and out without pausing to let the atmosphere soak in. For some strange reason, many people day trip in from Guatemala, see the sights, and return all the way to Antigua in a grueling day of driving across terrible and often bandit-infested Guatemalan roads. What's the rush? If you've got the time, spend a week and study Spanish while getting to know the ruins intimately.

Southeast of Ruinas, Santa Rosa de Copán and Gracias are traditional rivals, each claiming to have the most charming colonial architecture or important history. If you have time, visit both. In terms of charm, Gracias, with its still-vibrant Lencan culture, probably has the edge on Santa Rosa, but Santa Rosa, a pleasant colonial city set at 1,066 meters (3,500 feet) elevation, has a secret weapon to lure a certain subculture among tourists: cigars. Both towns are excellent bases for exploration.

Chosen as the capital of Central America for a brief period—from 1544 to 1548—Gracias was superseded by Antigua, Guatemala, and the locals have never quite gotten over their loss.

The town was prosperous for another century, but then its potential for glory was eclipsed, they claim, by the curse of the Buleros. According to the story, monks from Comayagua, known as "Buleros," regularly came to Gracias to sell pardons for eating meat on Fridays and other such sins. One monk was caught cheating at cards and when publicly accused he slapped the mayor's wife. An infuriated crowd chased him into the church where he hid behind a statue of the Virgin of Mercedes. The statue was damaged by a rock and the monk was killed. Shortly afterward and throughout the early 1700s, the town was repeatedly destroyed by a series of earthquakes.

You can drive yourself to Copán quite easily, or book a tour with any San Pedro Sula travel agent. Many tour groups drive out early in the morning, cram in a visit to the ruins and the museum, then head back to San Pedro in the evening. Unless your schedule is horribly cramped, this is a foolish way to save time. Another option is to take one of the "luxury" buses such as Casa Sola Express, which departs every day at 7 am from the front of the Hotel Palmira (6a Avenida y 6a Calle) and returns at 2 p.m. from the Hotel Posada. Call 651-4078 to reserve or confirm. It's a comfortable under-three-hour trip by bus.

Copán is 170 kilometers (105.5 miles) southwest of San Pedro Sula and 12 kilometers (7.5 miles) from the Guatemalan border. Travel by public bus always takes longer than by "luxury" bus or passenger car. The last stretch of the road is freshly paved, but patches have already deteriorated to dirt, creating a few hairy spots on curves rounding cliffs over the river. Drive with caution, preferably during daylight. You can also travel overland from Guatemala, using the bus service from Chiquimula and Florida. This border is open from 7 a.m. to 6 p.m. daily.

To get to Gracias from San Pedro Sula, head toward Santa Rosa via La Entrada. A few kilometers before Santa Rosa, turn off at the sign for Gracias. It's another 46 kilometers (28.5 miles) to town—a total of 150 kilometers (93 miles) from San Pedro Sula.

From La Entrada, you can head to any of three destinations: Copán, San Pedro Sula, or Santa Rosa de Copán. If you have time, visit Santa Rosa and the land of the Lencas, a worthwhile 44-kilometer (27-mile) trip by highway.

THINGS TO SEE AND DO IN COPÁN

Downtown Copán itself boasts one of the most tranquil plazas in all of Honduras. A small community museum stands on the main square. The **Copán Museum** is not as elaborate as the new Copán Sculpture Museum, but it continues to house artifacts from the site. It's open Monday through Saturday from 8 a.m. to noon and from 1 to 4 p.m. The entrance fee is $2.

Want to learn Spanish? Copán is a great place to improve your language skills. **The Ixbalanque Language School,** run by ex–Peace Corps volunteer Darla Brown, offers one-on-one instruction. Think about dallying in Copán while learning Spanish and getting to know the ruins like you'd get to know a friend. Tuition and room and board with a local family are only around $125 for a week. Call 651-4432 or e-mail ixbalan@hn2.com for details

Watch out for the kids of Copán, who follow tourists, waving souvenirs and crying, "You buy only from Angie! I give you good price!" or "You want to rent horse? Maybe tomorrow?" Such urchin action is normal across the border in Guatemala, but rare in Honduras. If you're in the mood, befriend one of the little vendors, teach him or her some English, maybe purchase a necklace made of dried local seeds and beans. (Don't just give them money—it encourages begging and upsets an already unbalanced tourism-driven local economy.)

If you are interested in bird-watching, you'll want to look up Jorge Barraza. Jorge, known around town as El Viejo even though he is only in his middle 30s, runs **Xukpi Tours** (651-4435, 651-4503). "Xukpi" (pronounced "shook-pee") means "motmot" in Mayan. Give him a chance and he'll loan you a pair of binoculars, put you in the back of his blue Samurai, and lead you up muddy mountain paths, drag you up waterfalls (he always carries rope), and show you as many as possible of the 300 or so bird species that make their homes in the area around Copán.

Like vacationing North Americans, migratory birds from Baltimore orioles to ruby-throated hummingbirds spend their winters in the tropics, arriving in September and heading back north in April. Many of these familiar birds, however, take on completely different plumage while in Honduras, so you probably would not recognize them without Jorge's aid. Tropical birds such as the motmot with its pendulous tail feathers, the quetzal, the trogon, and the toucan, however, can be recognized even by the novice birdwatcher.

Jorge usually goes out birding two or three days a week, depending on demand. Out-of-shape naturalists can see 5,000 cattle egrets, great egrets, blue herons, and other birds just a 1-kilometer (.6-mile) walk from the **Hacienda El Jaral.** The birds depart en masse in the early morning and return each dusk during the dry season. Birders ready for a bit of a walk should head 12 kilometers (about 7.5 miles) from Copán to the Montaña de Zapote, 11 kilometers (about 6.5 miles) short of the Guatemalan border. The mountain is protected by the municipality as its source for water, and a rough but maintained trail leads up to a simple dam high in the cloud forest that supplies water for much of the surrounding area. Jorge will probably stop once or twice on the 45-minute trip out to the town, perhaps to sip homegrown, home-brewed coffee at a friend's house, and again at a hot spring on the way home.

A typical birding expedition starts at 5:30 a.m. and ends around 1 p.m. It typically costs around $75 with a ten-person maximum, but everything can be customized. Bring some extra lempiras with you to treat yourself and Jorge to *refrescos* (sodas). This helps put money into the rural economy—one of the objectives of ecotourism.

"Everything that exists has a reason for being," Jorge told us as we made our way up through a thickly planted coffee plantation. He explained how the local grower used to throw coffee husks into the river and burn firewood, but now he burns the husks to dry the coffee. Jorge might remind you of your favorite high-school teacher and, indeed, he teaches rural schoolteachers how to teach environmental education. He travels from town to town with a car battery–powered slide projector, organizing children to capture caterpillars and hatch butterflies, and, since 1992, training kids in the Copán school system to become tourism guides. So far, 100 percent of his graduates have found jobs.

Those interested in participating in contemporary Mayan religious rituals will probably do best by prearranging with outfitters such as Xukpi Tours. The traditional shamans make altars of flowers and leaves, burn copal incense, chant, and offer protections, divinations, and cures. The trips, usually in the evening, involve a four-wheel-drive trip to a local village, a 1-kilometer (.6-mile) or so walk, and costs around $50. Be careful to respect local customs regarding photography and the like on such trips. Hallucinogens are *not* part of the local shamanic tradition.

Horseback riding can be arranged at any of the major hotels, especially the Hacienda El Jaral, and by tour agencies such as Maya Atlantic. If you stand still around the Parque, chances are that a kid will come up to you and try to persuade you to rent a horse. If you're in the mood, it's a nice way to see some of the outlying sights such as Las Sepulturas or Los Sapos.

For those interested in rafting, there are some pleasant whitewater rapids, mostly Class III, between Santa Rita and the ruins, flowing through the archaeological park. While you can't actually see the pyramids from your kayak or raft, you can pull up on shore and visit. Ríos Honduras offers multiday tours including the Copán stretch. Tubing is also a fun way to cool off and can be arranged by local agencies.

James D. Gollin

Artifact at the Copán Museum

THINGS TO SEE AND DO IN GRACIAS

The best center of operations for the traveler in Gracias is **Guancascos Tourist Center** (898-4516), where staff members speak Spanish, Dutch, and English. But **Guancascos,** the restaurant across the street from the Parque Central and catty-corner to San Marco Church, is not just a café but also a major information hub for western Honduras. Guancascos (the café) is run by Froni Miedema, a Dutchwoman who fell in love with the quiet charm of Gracias and decided to stay, and she is part of the informal association called Friends of Celaque. Among many other things, she can provide visitors with maps and information about Celaque; rent tents, backpacks, and other equipment; and help arrange transportation into the national park ($10 per trip in their Land Cruiser—so the more people the cheaper it is per person).

At the entrance to the restaurant is a natural apothecary, the **Tienda Naturista,** selling herbal medicine to locals and tourists alike, and the fresh foods and juices within aren't bad for you either. Attached to the restaurant is **Los Lencas Popular Cultural Center,** which consists of a store that sells Lencan handicrafts and other souvenirs and a central place where cultural and environmental groups can get together to discuss strategy for the future.

The restaurant is named after a local dance, the Guancasco, in which neighboring tribes brought their idols and corn to rival villages and performed dances for each other instead of fighting. Such Lencan customs are still kept alive in modern times despite the church censorship known as *compustura.* The idols, of course, have been replaced by figures resembling saints. The dancers, on the other hand, wear long-whiskered animal-fur masks, tall conical hats with mirrors, and dangling strings of seashells. The dance takes place every December 13 in the nearby village of Mejicapa, on January 20 and February 24 in San Sebastian, and on January 6 in Calquin. Inquire at Guancascos for other locations and times.

Contemporary art and culture are alive and well in Gracias. Traditional handicrafts such as ceramics and basket-weaving have been preserved, while painters such as **Mito Galeano** fuse modern techniques with traditional themes. Ask if Mito is around and see if he'll show you his atelier, where dozens of canvases are half-filled with Guancasco dancers.

El Castillo de San Cristobal is a 120-year-old colonial fort that was designed to protect the city from the exiled Los Coquimbos, followers of Francisco Morazán (1789–1842), the Liberal leader who led the struggle against Conservative forces in the aftermath of Central America's independence from Mexico. The fort commands a terrific view of the park and is open daily from 8 a.m. to 5 p.m.

Other nearby sights besides Celaque include natural hot springs, just 6.5 kilometers (4 miles) south of town, accessible via a 20-minute drive or a 90-minute hike. The baths are quite pleasant, especially after a hike in the mountains. There's even a *pulpería* (general store) where you can buy *refrescos* and *cerveza*. The entrance fee is 10L per person.

Further south, about 13 kilometers (8 miles) from Gracias, is the beautiful colonial town of **La Campa,** noted for its traditional ceramics. A bit further along, on a rough road, is San Manuel de Colohete, a friendly, timeless town with a lovely colonial church. From there, you can hike to Belen Gualcho in five to eight hours.

THINGS TO SEE AND DO IN SANTA ROSA

The one must-see spot in Santa Rosa is **La Real Factoría de Tobacco,** the Flor de Copán cigar factory, located just off the Parque. Follow your nose to the pale yellow building where locally grown tobacco, after four to nine years of careful aging and partial fermentation, is blended by masters, many of them old Cubans who escaped Castro's regime with tobacco seeds in their pockets. You can just show up, or ask Max Elvir of Lenca Land Tours (662-0103) for a tour that can include a trip to tobacco farms and drying and aging facilities. In fact, you'd be foolish to do just about anything in the town of Santa Rosa de Copán without first checking to see if Max is available for hire to do it with you.

The cigar factory, founded by the Spanish in 1760, operates much as it did in past centuries. Inside, skilled employees roll, twist, press, and cut around 500 cigars per day, earning about 100L, more than double the typical local wage. A natural resin glue is used to affix the cover leaf, grown in Danlí, near Tegucigalpa. Then the cigars are inspected, affixed with brand names from Zino to Don Melo to Petrus, boxed in nonsustainably harvested cedar, then shipped off to Europe and the United States. This one factory makes cigars for many of the world's most prestigious cigar companies, producing around 10 million cigars per year.

La Real Factoría also has a small line of personal brands made solely for wealthy aficionados. Look closely and you might spot an Arnold Schwarzenegger Corona or a Sylvester Stallone Churchill. While to the novice the cigars all look pretty much alike, each has its own distinctive flavor and aroma. Each morning, half a dozen heavy smokers sit around the tasting room, drinking strong coffee and smoking up a storm to make sure that standards are being met. You can arrange for a taste test or just visit the cedar-walled sales room. Ask if there are any factory seconds available. But for their minor imperfections, these near-perfect cigars would cost $10 to $30 each in the United States. They are available here for a fraction of that

James D. Collin

One of the many colonial-era churches in Gracias

cost. If you aren't a big smoker, you might buy a box of smaller cigars, smoke a few, and give the rest away as tips.

Tobacco is not a new arrival to this region. Indeed, archaeologists found cigars buried in a 3,000-year-old Mayan tomb. A retired colonel, Juan Garcia de la Candelaria, settled the area in 1705 and began to plant tobacco. By 1760 a booming tobacco business led strong economic growth, eclipsing that of the neighboring town of Gracias. By 1805, wealthy tobacco growers donated funds to build a grand church, and tobacco has been the backbone of the local economy ever since. But the recent boom in North American consumption has driven prices up and upset the natural balance, encouraging the use of wood-burning drying facilities instead of the traditional sun-drying techniques, as well as increased use of agrochemicals.

NATURE AND ADVENTURE SIGHTS IN COPÁN

Ruinas de Copán

The ruins, like most great archaeological sites, are best visited twice. Go once with a guide or a tour book, paying attention to names and dates and archaeological history. Then return with nothing but your imagination to enjoy the timeless mood of the place. You'll probably learn more on your second visit.

The fertile river valley around Copán was settled about 4,000 years ago. As in the rest of the Mayan world, a complex calendar filled with rituals that developed along with a deep understanding of natural weather patterns, allowing for abundant surpluses of corn production. This surplus allowed the flourishing of art, evident in pottery, carvings, and, of course, architecture. A great deal of Copán's history is actually known, thanks to the ancient custom of inscribing stone with the names and great deeds of a succession of rulers, some with terrific names like "18 Rabbit" and "Smoke Jaguar."

Each ruler tended to build his temples and tombs directly on top of those of his predecessors, and patient work by archaeologists has untangled much of the web. Climbing in through a side entrance of Temple 16, you can squeeze through a recently opened tunnel to view its predecessor, the Rosalila temple, buried by the construction of Temple 16. As you gaze at the polychrome bas-relief carvings of quetzals and macaws, know that scientists are patiently chipping away at stone deep below you, unlocking a still older temple known as the Margarita, discovered by high-tech sonic measuring devices.

Copán's golden era spanned nearly four centuries, from a.d. 465 to 800. Toward the end, the city's growth surpassed its ability to feed its 20,000 residents. Scientists suppose that overfarming led to salinization of soil; overharvesting of the forests led to wood shortages and erosion; and overcrowding led to disease and, some scholars suspect, to mass rebellion.

In any case, the rain forest reclaimed the ruins until American diplomat and adventurer John Lloyd Stephens visited Copán in 1839. As he recounts in his *Incidents of Travel in Central America, Chiapas and the Yucatán* (New York: Harper and Brothers, 1841), he bought the site for $50 from a landowner who considered the area worthless as farmland (too many stelae in the way for good plowing). "There was never any difficulty about the price," Stephens wrote. "I offered that sum, for which Don José Maria thought me only a fool; if I had offered more, he would probably have considered me something worse."

Archaeologist Sylvannus Morley called Copán the "Athens of the New World." The massive structures of Tikal, Palenque, and Chichén-Itzá, each wonderful and each unique, do not match the refined artistry of Copán. Carved faces not only show individual characteristics, they also telegraph complex emotions. Courtyards, carvings, and stelae seem designed not to impress and overpower but to enchant. The Carnegie Institute oversaw early excavations at Copán and rebuilt the Great Stairway. Since the 1950s the Honduran Instituto Nacional de Antropología e Historia (INAH) has maintained the site. INAH is now responsible for the major excavations and the newly opened Copán Sculpture Museum.

The ruins, located a half-mile from the eastern edge of town, are best savored early in the morning, when mists rise above the pyramids. Hiring a guide for around $10 is usually a good investment. Before hiring one, chat with them a bit to get a sense of their language skills and knowledge base. A good guide can show you things you'd otherwise miss, while a mediocre guide can be irritating. Ask for Hector Cardona, known as "Muco." He grew up around archaeologists in the ruins and speaks perfect English (and Italian). He's a good person to know if you're considering heading out for some white-water rafting or mountain exploration later on in your Honduras trip. If it sounds like fun, he might even come along.

While there is no need to go into extreme detail about the ruins in a guidebook dedicated to natural destinations, here's a quick tour of the park:

North of the Acropolis is the ball court, rebuilt at least six times during the lifetime of the city. According to the inscription on a nearby stelae, the final dedication was made in a.d. 738. Representations of the macaw are found. The grounds of the ball court are off-limits due to their fragility.

The most visionary of the Copán leaders, 18 Rabbit erected stelae after stelae on the Great Plaza, generally portraying himself in the ritual costumes of different gods, and, in many cases, the personification of the World Tree itself. In Mayan thought, the World Tree is a multidimensional portal from ground to sky, or from the Otherworld to this earth. In the highly recommended book *Maya Cosmos*, author Linda Schele calls the series of stelae a "big-stone forest" that marked out the movements of the planet Venus as well as of a longer cosmic period known as the *k'atuns* (a period of 20 360-day years).

More than 1,000 glyphs record the history of Copán's rulers up to 755. The Hieroglyphic Stairway is considered the longest Mayan inscription. The stairway is covered for protection, but you can get a good view of the glyphs from the base of the pyramid. Excavations of a noble tomb took place in 1989. There were originally five statues in the middle of the stairway—one of which is now in Harvard's Peabody Museum. Some Hondurans are urging the university to return the relic.

On the southern side of the complex is a series of temples, a human-made mountain range called the Acropolis. Temple 22, for example, boasts one of the most famous doorways—the jaws of a serpent. In Mayan belief, portals are passageways to the otherworld, and this is echoed in the architecture. At the corners of doorways are figures of Chac, the rain god.

It is in this section that you will find Structure 16, beneath which Honduran archaeologist Ricardo Agurcia uncovered a much older temple dubbed Rosalila (because of its reddish coloring). The temple was another built to honor the deified mountains. Celestial dragons frame the top of the temple, and the sun's daily journey, together with the life cycle of maize, are depicted on the lower parts of the temple. The birds on the lower part of the building are representations of the first ruler and founder of the Copán dynasty, K'inich Yax K'uk' Mo' (meaning "sun-faced blue-green quetzal macaw"). When the building was covered over in a.d. 650, a ritual bundle of flints, knives, stingray spines, and marine animals was deposited on the first floor. The temple was then painted over in white and the Maya built their new temple over it. Only very recently have the tunnels used to excavate these sub-temples been opened to tourists—five people at a time. Make sure to ask and see the Rosalila and Los Jaguares tunnels. Carrying a flashlight isn't a bad idea.

If it is open, spend the middle part of the day in the impressive new Copán Sculpture Museum, the best museum of its kind in Central America. "If" is the operative word; the museum was closed due to structural problems in 1999 and the reopening date is uncertain. The museum's design, by Honduran architect Angela Stassano, was excellent, with a two-story central hall surrounded by galleries and an entrance modeled on traditional entrances to Mayan tombs. Exactly what went wrong is not clear but it seems that the contractor altered the plans somehow, and the building has been declared unsound. Given the amount of money involved, a retrofit or a rebuild will take some time.

In any case, the museum is located next to the ruins. Admission is no longer included in your $10 day pass, but it is well worth an extra fee. The museum houses 3,000 pieces of sculpture, and this is theoretically only the first of seven modules that will eventually contain some 25,000 artifacts. Native trees are planted around the base, and openings in the roof allow for a great deal of natural light. The building is aligned with the compass points, just like the Mayan buildings themselves.

Visitors enter through a long tunnel that resembles a passageway into a Mayan pyramid. At the end of the tunnel, in the center of the museum, is an exact replica of the Rosalila Temple. The rose-colored building is recreated in stunning detail. Imagine trying to keep the building plastered and painted in the steamy, tropical heat. Maya fans who have been long accustomed to seeing the weathered limestone

OTHER NATURE SIGHTS NEAR COPÁN

Nature trips around Copán can often be customized to your taste, but to see more birds and wildlife it's generally a good idea to head out early in the morning. For more information about visiting one of these sights, contact one of the guides listed toward the end of this chapter.

Agua Caliente—28 kilometers (about 17.5 miles) from Copán on a good dirt road, has outrageously hot water pouring into an icy stream. The water is pumped into concrete man-made pools that lack charm, but evening trips involving star-gazing and barbecues are quite pleasant.

Pena Quemada—Pena Quemada is a private reserve 20 kilometers (about 12.5 miles) from Copán. It has well-laid-out trails, lush vegetation, and a few rivers to cool off in after a hike.

La Calichosa—At La Calichosa, on the Río Blanco, 5 kilometers (about 3 miles) past El Jaral, a river resurfaces in a cave after running underground for a few kilometers. Inside the cave, reached by a 30-minute steep hike that begins near the detour to Río Amarillo, are stalactites, stalagmites, and a resident population of screeching bats.

ruins are in for a Technicolor shock. Even better, the color is not a Ted Turner innovation, but the original score.

The Maya had to produce a tremendous amount of lye to keep the temples in pristine condition. Ironically, it was the very opulence of Copán that led, in part, to its downfall. To honor the gods, the Maya expanded their temples. To consecrate the temples they plastered them using lye, which was created in very hot wood-burning fires. Forests were denuded and agricultural productivity suffered. To appease the gods for agricultural misfortune, the Maya again expanded their temples, repeating the cycle until the city was simply abandoned.

A well-designed nature trail winds between the new museum and the ruins. The deeply forested walk provides a feel for what the whole valley used to look like, even though it is now mostly secondary growth. The trail eventually leads to some smaller museums.

Take along a trail guide and read up on the medicinal and other traditional uses made of the various plants by both ancient and contemporary Mayas. Don't walk the path alone, especially at the end of the day, as at least one assault has been reported. The culprit, it seems, was a former street urchin who used his charm to live off of tourists and when charm failed, turned to crime.

Hold onto your Copán ticket if you are planning to visit Las Sepulturas or other outlying sites on the same day. Or rent a horse and trot out to Los Sapos, a place where women traditionally went to give birth, and Stele 12, built by the 12th ruler of Copán, Smoke Jaguar, in a.d. 652. The countryside around Copán is filled with clear-flowing rivers, dense forests inhabited by wild birds, and traditional Mayan villages off paved roads and off the electric grid, still living a lifestyle dominated by ancient culture and the rhythms of nature.

Details: The ruins are open from 8 a.m. to 4 p.m. Visitors who are not residents of Honduras must purchase a $10 pass, which includes admission to both nearby ruins and the museum, for each day of their visit. There is an extra charge of $5 for the sculpture museum, and there is sometimes an extra charge of up to $10 to visit the Rosa Lila and Los Jaguares tunnels. Ask for details at the main entrance.

Cerro Azul National Park

The closest high cloud forest to the civilization at Copán is located in what is now Cerro Azul National Park (not to be confused with Cerro Azul Meambar National Park, near Lake Yojoa). The buffer zone has been badly overgrazed and overharvested for firewood, but the nuclear zone, almost inaccessible, remains pristine. Atop what a local environmentalist calls "a perfect mountain cloaked in a perfect forest" is Laguna de los Pinares, home to many species of wildlife. While no archaeological sights have been excavated in the park, local caves are said to be filled with artifacts. It is likely that ancient Maya hunted in this area for the jaguars and quetzals that played such an important role in their religious life. The main entrance is about 10 kilometers (6 miles) northeast of the town of Florida and the total park size is 150 square kilometers (nearly 60 square miles).

Details: *If you'd like to explore the park, leave the main road toward Copán at Florida and take a dirt road toward El Paraíso, about 1.25 hours distant. At El Paraíso, inquire at the local COHDEFOR office. There are officially two park entrances, but in fact there is no infrastructure to speak of yet. From Copán, take the good dirt road 90 minutes to El Paraíso, looking across the border to a neighboring valley in Guatemala. On the way, you'll pass unmarked caves still filled with Mayan artifacts and the natural hot springs at Agua Calientes.*

El Rubi Waterfall

Jorge Barraza, Rene Hernandez, and other local guides take nature-oriented tourists to a variety of local sites, including the El Rubi waterfall, a 9-meter (30-foot) cataract pouring out of a rock wall into a natural swimming pool near the town of Santa Rita, 8 kilometers (about 5 miles) from Copán. You'll have to hike and swim upstream and maneuver past slippery boulders, but it's worth the effort.

A good half-day expedition includes a hike up the Quebrada Santa Rita to El Rubi for a swim, followed by a further hike to the tile-making village of Los Planes, circling back to Santa Rita in time for lunch or by dusk. Make sure to look for the leaf-nosed vampire bats that live under a giant boulder just before the descent to the stream. Local Indians believed that this was the spot where their Spanish overlords made human sacrifices.

Details: *If you're going on your own, make sure to bring a rope and good water shoes, leave plenty of time, and be careful. Park at the Esso station in Santa Rita, take the rough dirt road up from the east side of the bridge, cross the pasture, and follow the river up to a waterfall. Above the waterfall, reached by a path around to the right, water fills a tightly winding canyon 3 to 6 meters (10 to 20 feet) wide and 18 meters (60 feet) deep. A tourist information office is scheduled to open in Santa Rita soon, but for now the pretty little town captures little of the Copán tourist trade.*

Hacienda San Lucas

A great recent addition to nature-oriented tourism in the Copán Ruinas area is the Hacienda San Lucas, a working farm, or "finca," located near the Los Sapos archaeological site. Run by a local woman who went to the U.S. and raised a family before taking up the eco-tourism challenge, the Hacienda is a great place to stop in for a hike and a drink, a meal, or an overnight stay. You can help the Mayan chef slap tortillas over a wood fire, or just relax in well-situated hammocks. With great views of the town of Copán Ruinas, the ruins themselves, and the surrounding countryside, and with miles of well-marked trails through cedar and oak forests, a visit to San Lucas is well worth the 20L admission charge, which includes the fee to visit the nearby archaeological sites.

Details: To reach the Hacienda by foot (a half-hour hike), head south from the Parque Central past the Banco de Occidente and the Hotel Plaza Copan. Take the right fork just out of town, cross the bridge over the Rio Copan, take a left, and follow the road along the river past fields of cacao, coffee, tobacco, and bananas. After the road climbs steeply, take another right. Alternatively, you can make the trip on horseback, or hail a cab. For more details, call 651-4106.

La Entrada/ El Puente (town/ruin)

The town of La Entrada, which lies between Copán and San Pedro Sula, is modern and rather ugly, but is a good spot to get gas or other supplies. If you're in the mood for more ruins and don't mind some travel on dirt road, follow signs for the El Puente ruins and head north for about 15 minutes. If you don't have a good vehicle, pickup-truck taxis make the trip every 15 minutes or so laden with campesinos from the neighboring villages. I once spent a few hours watching these pickups roll slowly by after a rented Toyota jeep skidded through a deep puddle and rolled off an embankment halfway to the ruins. No one was hurt, a truck laden with cinder blocks pulled the car out with a giant rope, and damage was minimal, but please let the incident remind you to drive slowly and carefully around these parts. You never know when a child will jump out into the road or the shoulder of the road will suddenly disappear.

The ruins at **El Puente**, a series of pyramids and courtyards surrounded by grazing land and tree farms, have been excavated with the financial support of the Japanese government. This explains why the high-budget visitors center has charts on the wall comparing the population, economy, and history of Honduras to those of Japan, and why the trees are so neatly labeled. The ruins have been open to the public only since 1994.

After a tour of the solar-powered archaeological museum, walk down a tree-lined path to the ruins. There are three temples here, each with access and lighting inside the chambers. The path winds through rich farmland and pastures. It becomes obvious why the founders of El Puente built their city in this fertile valley, surrounded by beautiful mountains.

About 45 minutes away, in the village of El Espíritu, is one of the most successful organic farming ventures in Honduras, PRODAI. Further still, near Techin, the Laguna de Villahermosa is a great spot for migratory birds.

Details: The 135-kilometer (84-mile) trip to La Entrada, where budget travelers may have to change buses, takes about two hours from San Pedro Sula. From there, it's another 48 kilometers (30 miles) to the ruins at Copán, an hour or so further. For more information, contact Armando Ortiz (898-5419), administrator of the ruins at El Puente Archaeological Park.

NATURE AND ADVENTURE SIGHTS IN GRACIAS AND SANTA ROSA

Belen Gualcho

In Belen Gualcho, the terrain rolls gently but the streets can be very steep. The prime attraction in town is the Sunday market, when Lencas and others come in from the roadless expanse surrounding the town to trade goods and entertain themselves. There's a waterfall just outside town and a network of paths great for hiking.

If the recommended Hotel Belen (run by the mayor) is full, try the **Hospedaje de Doña Carolina.** Note that the town does not have electricity, but hospitality is not lacking. Trained guides can be found at the mayor's office downtown.

For those who want to see Celaque National Park in an unconventional way, there's a path from Belen Gualcho to Los Naranjos, on the Gracias side of Celaque. While the hike can be done in two days, Max Elvir of Lenca Land Tours takes mules to carry the packs (and exhausted hikers) and does it in five days, stopping regularly to enjoy the flora and fauna of the forest and the spectacular vistas of the mountains. The trips cost around $35 per person per day, and can be arranged for six people.

CENCA, the Centro de Capacitación Ambiental (Center for Environmental Education), has its offices in the town of San Pedro, near Corquin, on the road to Belen Gualcho. Reacting to the threat of the "agricultural frontier" that is rapidly advancing toward the protected areas of Celaque, Guiysayote, and the nearby Erapacu Wildlife Reserve, CENCA aims to organize a cadre of community forest guards, demarcate the boundaries of the protected areas, develop a management plan, promote ecotourism, and train local schoolteachers in environmental education. On their 1-acre plot, a former forestry camp donated to them by COHDEFOR, CENCA has set up a teaching facility with the capacity to sleep 30 people. CENCA has received some support from CARE International, but is in need of further resources to carry out its ambitious mission. Contact Marco Aurelio Garcia, Executive Director, c/o the Santa Rosa de Copán offices of COHDEFOR, or 662-0212.

Details: Located about two hours southwest of Santa Rosa de Copán, via Corquin, the best time to visit Belen Gualcho is early on Sunday morning, for the Sunday Market.

Celaque National Park

Celaque means "box of water" in the Lencan tongue—and for good reason. Nine rivers and many streams are born in the mountain. This valuable watershed provides water for people throughout the department. The entrance to the 17,000-square-kilometer (6,563-square-mile) park is just 5 kilometers (about 3 miles) from town. About 2.5 kilometers (about 1.5 miles) farther is the visitors center, located at the site of an old hydropower plant that ceased operation in 1981.

In addition to Guancascos, the COHDEFOR office (on the road into town from Santa Rosa) is a good source of information on Celaque. If possible, contact Miguel Ayala Fuentes, who also serves as the park watchman and will happily take people to the summit or on day trips. He also maintains the Gracias visitors center, where travelers can pay $10 per night for a bed in the dormitory.

Just outside the park is Villaverde, where both Guancascos and Max Elvir keep cabañas set up with simple bedding and kitchens. Potable water is available in the kitchen, and rough beds sleep 16 people.

Just inside the park is a simple visitors center offering overnight accommodation and kitchen facilities. Take the opportunity to have a home-cooked meal prepared by Doña Alejandrina, who lives nearby: freshly ground blue-corn tortillas, rice, beans a scrambled just-laid egg, and some homegrown, home-roasted coffee costs around $2. After a long hike, nothing can taste better.

If you are fit and have located some camping gear, you might want to consider a trip to the highest spot in Celaque. U.S. Peace Corps volunteer Bill Jackson helped define trails to the summit at Las Minas, tying flags to trees at key points—an invaluable tool for visitors who don't want to spend a few weeks exploring the fern-filled wonderland of the cloud forest. The trip up and down requires an overnight stay for all but the super-fit.

Starting from the visitors center at 1,400 meters (nearly 4,600 feet), climb a steep path for 400 meters (1,312 feet), then another 250 meters (820 feet) of more gradual climbing to the Campamiento Don Tomas at 2,050 meters (6,725 feet). Drinking water is available, as well as rudimentary camping facilities that include a tin shack and sites for two tents. This early part of the hike passes through pine and oak forests that, while beautiful, are not terribly exotic for North Americans. From Don Tomas, it's another 500 meters (1,640 feet) of steep going through cooler, wetter, and more biologically diverse forest to the campamiento El Naranjo, about seven hours' slow hiking from the visitors center, 3.5 hours for fit mountaineers in a hurry. From there, it's another three-hour, relatively easy walk through a 12-square-kilometer (4.6-square-mile) plateau, known to travelers as the Ewok Forest, to the peak of Las Minas at 2,849 meters (9,347 feet), the highest point in Honduras.

In the words of Alex Aguilar of Friends of Celaque: "This plateau is where you find the most beautiful example of the cloud forest. The air is cool, the ground and foliage very moist. Trees and rocks are covered with moss, orchids, bromeliads, and vines. The sound of tropical birds fills the air. The whole hike is under a closed canopy. Most trees are thin and tall as they compete for sunlight. The diversity of vegetation is nothing short of amazing." The trip from the summit back down takes approximately six hours, which means that you have to start heading back no later than noon if you don't want to hike in the dark.

Those attempting the climb should be in good shape and either hire a guide or inform themselves extremely well about current conditions. Remember, cloud forests are wet places. Celaque gets up to 4 meters (157 inches) of rainfall per year. Your footwear will soon be drenched, and probably your clothes, too. That's fine down below, but up at the top at night it's rather cool. Pack extra shoes and clothes in a waterproof bag in your pack. For the less ambitious, there are several day hikes that give a good taste of cloud forest ecology yet allow for a warm meal and a bed at the end of the day.

WESTERN PARKS

Guiysayote Biological Reserve
Guiysayote is known as the drive-through cloud forest, since it is neatly bisected by the highway heading from Santa Rosa de Copán to Nueva Ocotopeque and El Salvador. Of the 42 cloud forests in Honduras, this is the most easily accessible. Waterfalls, screaming monkeys, and the flashing colors of wild birds line the road. A Peace Corps volunteer lives at the top of the road in the town of El Portillo, but there is very little in the way of developed infrastructure. In the nearby town of San Marcos, ask for Francisco Espinoza, a man who increasingly dedicates himself to the protection of Guiysayote. He sells a video about the park and provides information for travelers.

Guiysayote is about an hour's drive from Santa Rosa. Beyond Guiysayote is the modern town of Nueva or New Ocotopeque. What happened to Old Ocotopeque? It wasn't an earthquake. In 1969, Salvadoran troops crossed the border and demolished the town in what historians now refer to as the "Soccer War." The 100-hour war, triggered by a riot during a World Cup qualifying match, was the result of the migration of hundreds of thousands of Salvadoran campesinos into relatively underpopulated Honduras. More refugees came during the Salvadoran civil war of the 1980s, and some thorny border issues were not solved until 1996.

Details: *Guisayote is located about one hour west of Santa Rosa de Copán.*

Montecristo-Trifinio National Park
Currently, relations between Honduras and El Salvador are fairly smooth, a relationship which allows for a visit to **Montecristo-**

117

To see the animals in Celaque, you must be silent.

James D. Gollin

Trifinio National Park. Montecristo-Trifinio, located along the El Salvador border, is an trinational park and nature reserve shared with both Guatemala and El Salvador. Currently, only the Salvadoran section has a visitors center and trails. The best access on the Honduran side is from Nueva Ocotepeque. In Ocotepeque, simple lodging is available at the Hotel Maya Chortis (653-3377) and the Sandoval (653-3377).

Details: Guisayote is located about one hour west of Santa Rosa de Copán. Ocotepeque is just another 15 minutes down the road. From there, you can take a right fork for Guatemala or a left fork for El Salvador, or return to Santa Rosa.

GUIDES AND OUTFITTERS

In Copán, try **Go Native Adventure Tours,** near the Parque Central (651-4432; e-mail: ixbalan@hn2.com). Experienced guide Rene Hernandez, who has been leading tours for more than 20 years, runs this operation. Go Native organizes tours as far away as La Mosquitia and as near as the local hot springs. Rene also owns El Tunkal Bar and is the husband of Darla Brown, owner of the Ixbalanque Language School. Small world!

MC Tours (651-4453, fax: 651-4477; e-mail: mctours@netsys.hn) is in the Hotel Marina Copán and has an office in San Pedro Sula. It has a good reputation for its package tours, especially among visitors less interested in roughing it.

Jorge Barraza's **Xukpi Tours** (651-4435, 651-4503) is the place to call for bird-watching and other local adventures.

CONSERVATION EFFORTS

The people of Gracias are gradually realizing that their future is linked to the great mountains immediately to the west in Celaque National Park. The fight for Celaque's conservation began in the 1960s when local politician Pedro Iglesias, the mayor of Gracias, began to fine people who came down the mountain with loads of wood. He is buried in the colonial fort, El Castillo de San Cristobal.

*The local environmental group **Fundación Celaque**, or FUCELA, was (according to rumor) taken over by people more interested in the aid money that was expected to (but never did) pour in from U.S. and European environmental groups than in preserving the local environment. Javier Pinel wrote to tell us that the current president of FUCELA is Armando Mondragon, who is a fit walker and will take visitors in his four-wheel-drive from his Texaco gas station at the town entrance to the COHDEFOR house.*

*Established in 1996, **Friends of Celaque** does not have formal NGO status but is making progress in protecting the area. For information, contact Suyapa Diaz at the Guancascos Tourist Center in Gracias or contact Friends of Celaque, Attn: Alexis Aguilar, 759 Maydee St., Duarte, CA 91010; e-mail:alexagui@ucla.edu; http://www.generation. net/~derekp/celaque.html.*

In the Santa Rosa de Copán/Gracias/Belen Gualcho area, your best bet is Max Elvir's **Lenca Land Trails** (662-1375, 662-0805, fax: 662-1375; e-mail: lenca@hondutel.hn). Max, educated in the U.S. and experienced as a guide throughout Honduras, is happy to pick you up at San Pedro Sula Airport and shepherd you all around the region and beyond. He offers tours throughout the region, knows all the ins and outs, and is a great person to spend time with.

LODGING

In Copán Ruins, **Casa de Café** (3 blocks west of the Llama de Bosque and Tunkul restaurants, 651-4620; e-mail casadecafe@mayanet.hn) is owned by expat Howard Rosenzweig, a regular contributor to the *Honduras This Week* newspaper, and one of those gringos in Honduras whose enthusiasm for the country is highly infectious. At this cozy Bed and Breakfast, recently expanded and remodeled, rates are around $38.

Unless you really like Best Westerns, avoid the **Posada Real de Copán,** a colossal modern hotel overlooking a roadside shantytown at Kilometer 164 on the highway to San Pedro. A better choice for upscale rooms is **Hotel Marina Copán** (right of the Parque, 651-4070/1; e-mail: hmarinac@netsys.hn); rates are $65-85. There are also many cheaper hotels in town catering to travelers, including **Paty** and **Popol Nah.**

Hacienda El Jaral (about 11 kilometers [7 miles] back on the highway toward San Pedro, 552-4457) is a great $45 place for kids or for people who want a bit of nature surrounding them. Cabañas, from $20 to $60, are located on a working farm, and a nearby lake supports a rich variety of wildlife, including cattle egrets who flock to the lagoon every afternoon between October and May. Even if you don't stay at the Hacienda, plan on coming for a visit—and perhaps a drink at the restaurant—to see this natural phenomenon.

If you're one of those people who crave still more nature, head to the Hacienda San Lucas (651-4106) which has rooms on a working *finca* for around $40.

The best place to stay in Santa Rosa de Copán is **Hotel Elvir** (Calle Real Centenario SO y 3a Avenida SO, 662-0103, 662-0805). Newly remodeled, the hotel has great views from the roof-top, and rooms ranging from $25 to $40. It's also the best place to meet up with Max Elvir of Lenca Land Tours, whose family owns the hotel. If Elvir is full, try **Mayaland** (on the highway across from the bus station, 662-0233; $20) or the **Continental** (2a Calle NO y 2/3 Avenidas, 662-0801; $15). **Hospedaje Calle Real,** east of Pizza Pizza, $5, is a backpackers' favorite.

In Gracias, **Posada del Rosario** (656-1219) is a quiet place with a garden patio near the San Cristobal fort, and is owned by Froni, who also owns Guancascos restaurant. Rooms are around $16. Hotel Erik (1 block north of the Parque Central, 656-1066) offers cheap ($10), clean rooms; as does **Hotel Iris** ($7), 4 blocks south of the San Sebastian church. If you'd like cable TV and air conditioning and can pay around $18, try **Posada de Don Juan** (656-1020).

FOOD

In Copán Ruins, **Tunkul**, 1 block west of the Parque Central, is a great traveler's hangout in Copán, open from 7 a.m. to 10 p.m. They offer nightly happy hours, when first beer and then cocktails are two-for-one. At that point, you might as well stay and order a burrito or a burger. Across the street, **Llama del Bosque,** offers excellent, traditional meals at a reasonable price. A few blocks off the plaza, with great views, newcomer **Carnitas Nia Lola** now vies with Tunkul as the best place in town to eat, drink, and exchange stories with travelers, and make plans for further adventures. **Via Via Café** is a great spot for travelers, especially popular with Europeans. For an upscale meal, coffee, or cigar, drop in on the **Hotel Marina Copán**. **Macanudo Bar** is a place to go for rock music and late-night drinks.

In Santa Rosa de Copán, the **Hotel Elvir Restaurant** at the Hotel Elvir, with 24 hours' notice, can prepare local Lencan delicacies such as *gallo en chicha*, rooster meat marinated overnight in spiced molasses. Vendors at the local market serve specialties such as *atol chuco*, a hot, red, fermented corn drink served in a calabash; ground squash seeds; and *totopostes*, cornbread with molasses dunked in coffee. **Flamingos,**

James D. Gollin

Tortilla making

121

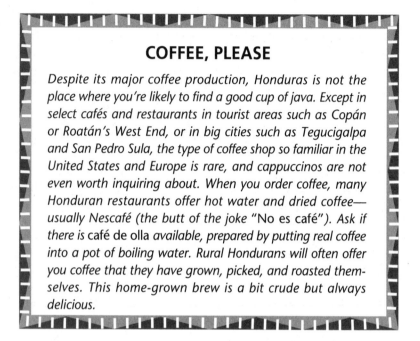

COFFEE, PLEASE

Despite its major coffee production, Honduras is not the place where you're likely to find a good cup of java. Except in select cafés and restaurants in tourist areas such as Copán or Roatán's West End, or in big cities such as Tegucigalpa and San Pedro Sula, the type of coffee shop so familiar in the United States and Europe is rare, and cappuccinos are not even worth inquiring about. When you order coffee, many Honduran restaurants offer hot water and dried coffee— usually Nescafé (the butt of the joke "No es café"). Ask if there is café de olla available, prepared by putting real coffee into a pot of boiling water. Rural Hondurans will often offer you coffee that they have grown, picked, and roasted themselves. This home-grown brew is a bit crude but always delicious.

half a block south of the Parque Central, is a good place for an "international" menu.

Pizza Pizza (on Centenario 530, 4 blocks east of the Parque Central, 662-21104; e-mail: wpost@hondutel.hn) is a must if you're in the mood for pizza. Even if you aren't, stop by to meet Warren Post; he came to work at the U.S. Embassy in 1986, married a woman from La Mosquitia, and decided to move to Santa Rosa de Copán because, he claims, his kids liked to play in the local park. The restaurant and its owners are a great source of information for travelers, and the place doubles as an internet café.

In Gracias, **Guancascos,** right on the Parque Central, is a must for visitors to Gracias. The vegetarian dishes and fruit juices are excellent but mostly the restaurant is the best source of information on Celaque and other local sites. **La Fonda,** within site of the Parque Central, is another good choice. Proprietor Jesus Navarro also owns the nearby **Alameda,** specializing in roasts. **Rancho Lily,** an informal bar not far from the Parque Central, serves sandwiches and a good *plato tipico.*

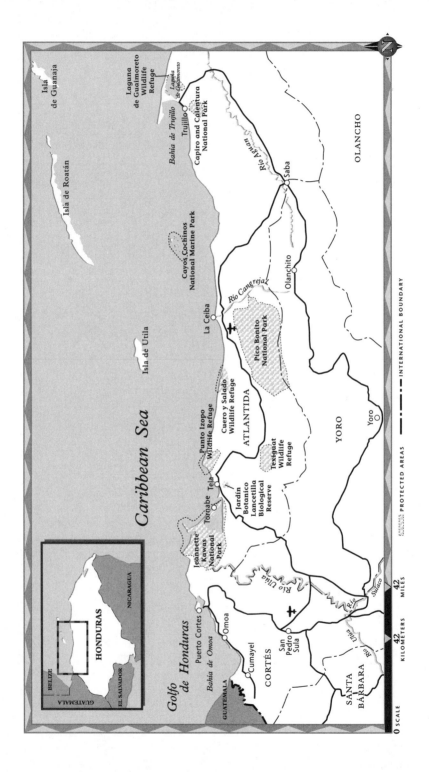

CHAPTER 5

Paradise Discovered:
The Caribbean Coast

The north coast of Honduras, stretching 750 kilometers (466 miles) from the border of Guatemala in the west to Nicaragua in the east, consists of alternating white-sand beaches, mangrove forests, untamed rivers, and rocky cliffs overlooking the clear blue water of the Caribbean. Just inland, high mountains cloaked in clouds harbor hundreds of exotic species, the very inaccessibility of the land serving to protect the habitat.

Until a few years ago, Caribbean Honduras was almost completely unknown to outsiders. Anyone who visits the beaches lining the crescent bays of Tela and Trujillo, or rafts the Cangrejal River outside of La Ceiba, knows that this coast of Honduras is ripe for mainstream discovery. Indeed, small hotels are popping up, transportation and guiding services are improving, and prime real estate is being gobbled up by domestic, Mexican, U.S., and European speculators. In ten years the coast will surely be transformed, either by the tourist industry or by big business' plans for expanded palm-oil and banana plantations, oil refineries, and *maquila* factories.

Honduran environmentalists are among tourism's most avid promoters. They recognize the industry to be a powerful incentive to their countrymen to preserve their resources for long-term success, rather than exploit them for short-term gain. Tourism, however, brings problems as well as solutions. A network of North Coast environmental groups is working hard to develop and regulate tourism so that it will not destroy fragile habitats or traditional cultures as it brings in funds to preserve nature.

Come see the Caribbean coast of Honduras now. Later, you'll be able to say you saw it in the good old days. And by contributing needed income to the local economy, you'll be able to help preserve this slice of paradise. In this chapter, the attractions of the North Coast will be covered geographically, starting at Omoa in the west and ending with Trujillo in the east.

VISITOR INFORMATION

Tela, located 50 kilometers (31 miles) east of San Pedro Sula, is a sleepy little town with pastel buildings and a pretty Parque Central. The friendly, multiracial people of Tela are bracing for a major boom in tourism, but for now the surrounding beaches and forests are still uncrowded. From the hustle and heat of San Pedro or the hassle of the airport, head east to the coast. After passing through banana and African palm plantations, take a left at Tela, leaving the coastal highway to discover what was once the unofficial capital of the "banana republic" run by the United Fruit Company.

The center of town is Tela Vieja (Old Tela), which surrounds the bustling Parque Central. The newer part of town is the western side, also known as Tela Nueva. The beaches are cleaner across the river near the Villas Telamar. From either side of town, to the east and to the west, white-sand beaches stretch to the horizon.

Though Tela's past was tied to bananas, its future lies in its beaches. When United Fruit, famous for the Chiquita brand, moved its headquarters to Lima, closer to San Pedro Sula, in the early 1970s, the town nearly died. Its economy was saved by busloads of domestic tourists coming to Tela each weekend to relax on the 50 kilometers (31 miles) of white-sand beach that line Tela Bay. Its location at the midpoint between the peninsula of Punta Sal to the west and Punta Izopo to the east brought the city to the attention of a group of developers who, in the late 1970s, saw Tela as a perfect base for a large, modern resort. Partly because of the political instability and a less-than-welcoming military government, the investors instead headed to Mexico and built Cancún. In Tela, it is still possible to imagine what Cancún must have looked like before it became a Times Square for condo time-share salesmen and drunken college students on spring break.

The word is out about Tela once again. The Tela Bay Development Project is getting ready to build a master-planned resort with 1,600 low-rise hotel rooms on 120 hectares (288 acres) in the buffer zone of Jeannette Kawas National Park. A Canadian firm, the Malwood Development Company, is investing $15 million in seed capital, expecting eventual corollary investments of $350 million. Other plans include an expansion of the tiny local airport, and construction of golf courses, marinas, more hotels and condominiums, two beach clubs, a "water fun park," and an equestrian club.

The main local NGO, PROLANSATE, is challenging the developers every step of the way. PROLANSATE welcomes the influx of environmentally oriented tourism but is attempting to limit its scope so as not to destroy the wildlife, mangrove habitat, beaches, and coral reefs that are Tela's chief attractions. In 1999 PROLANSATE lost a battle with the oil giant Petrotela, which decided in its deep wisdom to build a short oil pipeline from the main pier, through town, to a small refinery located next to the power plant. If the pipe ever leaks, it could spell disaster.

Garífuna dance troupes perform regularly at the Villas Telamar and sometimes at other area restaurants, but for the most fun, try to get invited to a party at one of the nearby Garífuna villages such as La Enseñada, El Triunfo de la Cruz, San Juan, or Tornabé. Check out the new Garífuna museum on Jose Cecilio del Valle.

Take care in Tela, especially after dark, and don't flash a thick wad of cash or expensive-looking watches or cameras. It is important to note that Tela has had a crime wave in recent years, generally involving men with machetes robbing tourists near but not directly in front of Telamar. It's sad to say this, but if you are on the beach stay near the guarded areas, and don't go on the beach at night, especially alone. There is probably just a small gang of perpetrators who will one day be apprehended. Most Teleños are extremely warm and friendly, but it's better to be safe than sorry.

James D. Gollin

Parque Central in La Ceiba

About 97 kilometers (66.5 miles) east of Tela, **La Ceiba** is a great place to dance to live music, a good base for visiting Cuero y Salado Refuge and Pico Bonito National Park, a white-water center. It's Honduras's third-largest city, and it's known as the nation's party capital. San Pedrans, it is said, work hard and invest; Tegucigalpans play politics and take bribes; and Ceibeños like to party. Beachfront bars blast out live music 'til the wee hours and the beach is crowded with people from Tegucigalpa and San Pedro during national holidays, while the adult bars on the seaside strip offer what one friend referred to as "a little bit of Bangkok in Central America." Located on the coast just opposite the Bay Islands, surrounded by Pico Bonito National Park, Cuero y Salado Wildlife Refuge, and the Cangrejal River, La Ceiba has become a mini-Mecca for ecotourists and adventure travelers

The town itself is nothing spectacular, a typical Honduran town with a pleasant Parque Central and a beach too dirty for foreign standards, until you get a bit away from town center. Its charm lies in the beauty of its surroundings and the liveliness of its people. La Ceiba has long been a center for Standard Fruit (Dole). The influence of the gringo banana-men and sailors, regular boat transport to New Orleans, and the proximity of the Bay Islands have led to a large bilingual population in La Ceiba, especially among the middle and upper classes. Don't be surprised to meet Ceibeños who have gringo last names or greet you in perfect English.

Avenida República and Avenida San Isidro, flanking the Parque Central, have enough travel agents, banks, hotels, and fast-food joints to satisfy your every need before you head out to explore the surrounding natural attractions.

Learning Spanish? La Ceiba is home to the Centro Internacional de Idiomas (440-0547, e-mail: cii@tropicohn.com). The school can arrange volunteer programs for students interested in environmental issues. Students engage in one-on-one practice with Honduran instructors, and home stays are available.

The USHA Metaphysical, Natural Cure Center (on the Ceiba-Jutiapa Highway at Kilometer 225, 30 minutes from La Ceiba) offers natural hot springs, therapeutic treatments, and vegetarian cuisine. The center's director, Dr. Sebi, has 20 years of experience treating physical and mental diseases. It's located.

While there is a white-sand beach all along the shore in front of La Ceiba, it's best not to swim near such population centers because of inadequate sewage disposal. Be careful where you swim! Take the coastal highway east for 5 kilometers (about 3 miles) to Boca Vieja and head out to Playa Perú, where you can sunbathe, swim, rent hammocks suspended under *palapas,* and order cold beer and hot food from vendors, all at reasonable prices.

At present there is very little organized cycling in Honduras, but the beauty of the rough terrain lends itself to mountain-biking road trips—and it's only a matter of time before the international outfitters start running trips to the area. For now, you can explore on your own. If you have mechanical trouble, don't worry. Cycling is a common means of transportation on the coast, and bicycle mechanics can be found anywhere.

A word of warning: If you are riding on the pavement and a car or truck honks a friendly warning, immediately steer off the road. On a bike, you never have the right of way. Another warning: Women wearing Lycra should not ride alone unless they want to start conversations all along their route.

For a wonderful excursion to a nearby waterfall, take the highway 8 kilometers (about 5 miles) east of La Ceiba to the Puente Río María, the bridge over the María River. Take the road inland and leave your bike at the last hut before the trail ends, then hike in to a gorgeous waterfall with a great place to swim. Alternatively, get a ride up the Cangrejal to the town of Las Mangas and coast back down the dirt road toward town, stopping to swim a half a dozen times along the way. You can rent bikes at Bar El Canadiense on Avenida 14 de Julio y 1a Calle.

Trujillo Bay is one of the great untapped tourist sites of the Caribbean and a great place for swimming, hiking, or just relaxing. Its 60 kilometers (37 miles) of white-sand beach stretch from Puerto Castilla at the tip of the Cabo de Honduras all the way to the historic town of Trujillo and beyond, to the Garífuna villages of Barrio Cristal and Santa Fé. In 1502 Columbus sailed into the bay, landed at Trujillo, and offered a mass in thanks for his safe passage. It was the first time he set foot on the American mainland.

Trujillo was the first capital of Honduras, founded in 1525 by Juan de Medina, and became a major port for gold and silver ship-

Coastal view near Trujillo

ments back to Spain. Pirate Henry Morgan successfully sacked the town. But American mercenary William Walker, after being deposed as President of Nicaragua, made the mistake of seizing Trujillo in 1860 in an attempt to foment another Central American revolution. After miserable battles in nearby swamps, Walker surrendered and was executed by a firing squad. His body still lies in the Trujillo cemetery; any local can point out the spot. American short-story writer O. Henry (William Sidney Porter), on the lam from the law, hid out in Trujillo in the late 1890s. He later wrote of the place, fictionalized as Coralio in his book *Cabbages and Kings,* in which he describes Trujillo as a "vacuous beauty lounging in a guarded harem . . . a little pearl in an emerald band."

During World War II the Allies based their reserve warships and transports in Trujillo Bay, out of harm's way. More recent gringo interlopers include Ollie North, who hung out at the Bahía bar while plotting the Contra war against the Sandinistas in the mid-1980s. American soldiers with guns strapped across their bare chests still drink at the Bahía, their helicopters parked nearby. One, his chopper sitting on the runway, was recently overheard radioing his base at Palmerola that the weather would prevent their returning until morning. Next door, retirees from the southern United States laid plans to set up a casino on Swan Island that would keep out the riffraff. More familiar is the spectacle of 65-year-old gringo men cavorting with 14-year-old local girls. "This place," a local Peace Corps volunteer summed up, "is a magnet for freaks." Perverts and pederasts should know that Honduras has recently strengthened its laws and enforcement. Consenting adults are free to develop friendships and romance, but the kids are off limits.

Trujillo consists of the main town, a cluster of hotels lining the airport runway a few miles to the east, and the Garífuna village of Barrio Cristales just to the west. All three are lined up along the quietly lapping, protected waters of Trujillo Bay, and all offer a collection of reasonable bars and restaurants.

Garífuna culture is a definite plus for Trujillo. While in a Garífuna neighborhood, you might want to try their herbal white lightning, *gifiti,* which they claim has aphrodisiacal qualities. In Barrio Cristal, visit GariArte (434-4207), a shop run by Ricardo Omar Lacayo that sells Garífuna artifacts such as drums and carvings.

THE TRUJILLO REFINERY

Trujillo boasts what might be the best undeveloped deep-water port in the world, and therein lies its problem.

FUCAGUA's main struggle consists of opposition to a Kuwaiti-backed international consortium that took a 30-year lease on a plot of land near Puerto Castilla during the Callejas administration. The plan is to build a $1.8-billion oil refinery— the largest in Central America, scheduled to produce 150,000 barrels a day. Trujillo's well-sheltered deep port and lax Honduran laws permitting single-hulled supertankers make the site an ideal place to rake in profits. Production would meet all of Honduras's domestic demand and also provide for exports to the rest of Central America. The highly mechanized petrochemical plant would employ 5,000 people for six months during con-struction and then only 300 full-time workers, mostly as janitors and watchmen.

The refinery project is supported by Tegucigalpa politicians, some of whom are rumored to have been personally enriched by the Kuwaiti investors or promised lucrative construction contracts. But the local population, once mixed in its response, is now nearly united in opposition. Daniel Regalado, ex-Honduran Ambassador to Singapore, joined FUCAGUA members and local teachers in whipping up a frenzy of opposition to the project, capped by a 1994 visit by the Greenpeace ship Rainbow Warrior *and a chil-*

There you can buy premixed bags of Palo de Hombre, Contrigo, Quacu, Chenirud, Romero, and Pimienta Gorda. When you get home, add rum to make your own *gifiti*. GariArte is located a half-block south of the Calle Principal, 1 block west of the bridge lead-ing to Trujillo. Ten kilometers (6.2 miles) west is another Garífuna village, Santa Fé, famous for the fresh fish served at El Caballero restaurant downtown.

dren's march for nature. Most Trujilleños are now convinced that a single oil spill would destroy their future, which they see as linked to tourism and retiree-related income. Acid rain from the plant would damage Capiro and Calentura and perhaps even drift as far as the Río Plátano Biosphere Reserve. While President Callejas supported the project, President Reina's Environmental Secretary, Dr. Carlos Medina, denied it the necessary environmental permits, and the project died in 1995.

But in early 1997, Reina reorganized his government, assigning responsibility for environmental affairs to the Ministry of Natural Resources, run by Jeronimo "Super Chombo" Sandoval. Super Chombo accused environmentalists of being opportunists seeking money from gringos to obstruct progress, and the refinery project surfaced again.

The Fundación Fasquelle called a press conference to point out that in 1996 Honduran ecotourism earnings reached $150 million—a number exceeded only by long-term hard-currency earners like coffee and bananas. According to National Geographic *and* Newsweek *articles cited at the conference, Puerto Vallarta brings in $300 million a year and Cancún $2 billion—representing potential revenues put at serious risk by a highly polluting refinery on the white sands of Trujillo Bay. Reina's plan was thwarted, but pressure to build at Puerto Castilla is sure to resurface.*

Trujillo's NGO acronym is FUCAGUA, the Foundation Capiro and Guaimoreto. The foundation was created in 1992 when the Capiro and Calentura National Park and the Guaimoreto Lagoon Wildlife Refuge became part of the protected areas system of Honduras. Freddy Matute, executive director of FUCAGUA, maintains the main office next to the Cine Bahía and can be reached at 434-4294. FUCAGUA's membership consists largely of the local schoolteachers, so if you go to their office you're sure to learn something.

If you like adventure, or you're flat broke, and want to get to La Mosquitia from Trujillo, take a 1 p.m. bus from Tocoa to Sangrelaya. The nine-hour trip costs 76L. Spend the night in a modest *hospedaje* in Sangrelaya, then walk three hours on the beach and through a thick forest to Palacios. Alternatively, boats leave nearly every day from Trujillo to Palacios, taking 12 hours and charging $7 to $8. You can also take a 20-minute ride in a plane for only $15.

Tela is easily reached from the airport or town by regular buses (90 minutes) along an excellent road. Buses from San Pedro Sula and La Ceiba arrive at a terminal 2 blocks east of the main square in Tela. A special train makes regular runs along an old banana-company rail line, ferrying tourists through the town of La Ceiba and out to the beach at Playa Peru. The train's schedules have been irregular of late, but inquire while you are in La Ceiba. It's a nice way to get around. There are also good beaches and food at the nearby Garífuna communities of Sambo Creek and Corozal.

La Ceiba also has the best domestic air transportation connections in all of Honduras. Daily flights leave for San Pedro and Teguz; for all three Bay Islands; and for Trujillo, Palacios, and Puerto Lempira. If Isleña doesn't have a flight when you want, try Sosa, Caribbean Air, or a handful of tiny companies that fly into the Mosquito Coast. Tourist buses are double the price of regular buses but a lot more comfortable, and they leave regularly for Trujillo (2.5 hours) and Tela (1.5 hours). Boats leave regularly for the Bay Islands and destinations down the coast.

NATURE AND ADVENTURE SIGHTS IN TELA

Jeannette Kawas National Park (Punta Sal)

The Parque Nacional Jeannette Kawas (PNJK), formerly Punta Sal, consists of a nuclear zone (where officially no agriculture is allowed) of 500 square kilometers (193 square miles) surrounded by a buffer zone of 280 square kilometers (108 square miles), including a long, sandy beach accessible by car; the wildlife-rich Laguna de los Micos (Monkey Lagoon); Laguna El Diamante (Diamond Lagoon); and the

Village of Miami, near Jeannette Kawas National Park

peninsula of Punta Sal, tipped with coral reefs, shrouded with thick tropical forests, and dotted with a dozen tiny white-sand beaches.

Before visiting the park, stop at the PROLANSATE offices 2 blocks west of the Parque Central on Calle del Comercio. There's a small environmental education display, maps along the wall, T-shirts for sale, and a wealth of information about the park and plans for its further development.

The staff at PROLANSATE, like the population of Tela, is about half black (mostly Garífuna) and half mestizo. Tela is proud of its remarkably comfortable multicultural mixture, unheard of in most of Central America. In the office or at the park look for former PNJK director Juan Hernandez, known as "Manatee" because of his large size and affection for those lovable beasts. A tireless fighter for the environment, Hernandez admits that environmental considerations had nothing to do with the failure of early attempts to Cancún-ize Tela.

In Hernandez' view, had Tela been developed in the 1970s, today there would be no reef, no mangroves, no Garífuna culture. "Now, we know that development is coming. We have to be ready. This is

135

our work," he says. Hernandez has a view of ecotourism that puts him at odds with some hotel developers. "If the nuclear-zone wetlands are destroyed, ecotourism is a failure." And he's right: If the social situation and cultures of the coast are not protected, ecotourism will fail. PROLANSATE, along with Fundación Fasquelle out of San Pedro Sula and NGOs from Guatemala and Belize, participates in a Tri-national Commission of the Gulf of Honduras, attempting to develop a sustainable tourism model for the entire region.

About 50 to 60 people per day visit PNJK. Wildlife in the park includes pelicans, egrets, seagulls, vultures, and others, including a stunning 273 species of birds, 20 of which are endangered. At the tip of the peninsula, Doña Crisanta Andino serves fish lunches for around 35L, and there are plans for a visitors center. Typical personalized tours leave Tela at 6 or 8 in the morning, and include snorkeling over coral reefs, bird-watching near Laguna de Micos, hiking through the coastal rain forest, sunbathing on deserted beaches, and even swimming with the dolphins that like to leap in front of speeding boats. Most tours return by 2 p.m., when the water tends to get a bit rough.

On the edge of the park is the village of Miami, a collection of grass huts on stilts on a narrow strip of white sand separating the Caribbean from the brackish Laguna de Micos. The Garífuna residents of Miami will be happy to sell you coconut bread (called *pan de coco*), light meals, or even shots of their herbal medicine, a mandrake root–infused white lightning called *gifiti*. From Miami, you may be able to rent a canoe or boat to venture further into the park. Or you can just enjoy a day on Miami beach. There is no lodging in Miami, but The Last Resort has eight bungalows on the beach near Tornabé.

Some trails and small beaches in PNJK can sustainably handle only ten to 15 people per day. PROLANSATE is attempting to organize the local tour groups, but is meeting some resistance. "Why don't they spend the aid money they receive from abroad and build an environmental education center and some toilets out on the point?" asks Alessandro D'Agostino, owner of Garífuna Tours.

As is the case with most parks in Honduras, PNJK is a park with people living in it. In fact, there are 11 small communities on the coast and 36 inland, with a total population of approximately 19,000 people, overwhelmingly Garífunas, descendants of African slaves and

▲ Agua Caliente, near Copán (James D. Gollin)

▲ Shore vegetation, Central Honduras
(James D. Gollin)

▼ Scarlet macaw (James D. Gollin)

▲ Lobster diving in Honduran waters (James D. Gollin)

▼ Scuba diving in the Bay Islands (© Honduras Institute of Tourism)

▲ Sunset (James D. Gollin)

▼ Tegucigalpa (James D. Gollin)

▲ Miskito children in Wampu Sirpi (James D. Gollin)

▲ Independence Day, Caribbean
Coast (James D. Gollin)

▲ Copán ruins
(James D. Gollin)

▼ Oakridge, Roatán (James D. Gollin)

▲ White sand beach in Tela (James D. Gollin)

▼ Church near Parque Central in
La Ceiba (James D. Gollin)

▼ Ripe cacao fruit, the source of
chocolate (James D. Gollin)

▲ Close-up view of a lancetilla, a spiny palm tree (James D. Gollin)

Carib Indians. PROLANSATE is working to concretize their land titles both to protect their right to live in the park as long as they engage is sustainable economic pursuits and also to keep newcomers from swarming in to take advantage of the coming tourist boom.

Details: *Located 7 kilometers (about 4.5 miles) west of Tela, the park consists of 780 square kilometers (about 300 square miles) of coral-rimmed beach, thick forests, and calm lagoons. The park is open from dawn to dusk, and entrance is 10L per person, $10 for foreigners. The easiest way in to the park is to drive to the main highway and take the four-lane road (obviously made for tour buses of the future) to the tiny town of Tornabé, where the four-laner melts away to a one-lane dirt track amid the lazy palm trees and the shacks of the Garífunas. Continue on to the left on foot, by car, or in the back of a pickup-truck taxi to the town of Miami, where the road stops. Here you can hop a boat or rent a canoe and head into the park.*

Lancetilla Botanical Gardens

In 1925, American explorer and pioneer tropical botanist Wilson Popenoe was given the task of setting up an experimental garden somewhere in Honduras where fruit trees and ornamentals from around the world could be cultivated and eventually brought to market for the greater good of the United Fruit Company.

He started with 900 acres 1 kilometer south of Tela, which he named Lancetilla after a spiny palm tree endemic to the area. Popenoe introduced Asian exotics such as durian, litchi, rambutan, and mangosteen, as well as hundreds of varieties of banana, cacao, edible nuts and spices, hardwoods, and flowers. Popenoe's garden has now gone wild and grown to include 41.5 square kilometers (16 square miles) of interpretive trails winding through more than 636 species (including 392 genuses and 107 families) of plants. Some form of exotic tropical fruit is always ripe in Lancetilla, and orchids and other flowers are always blooming. More than a showcase of Honduras's diversity, the park boasts the world's largest collection of Asian fruit plants. Today, the park is managed by the government agency ESNACIFOR.

While Jeannette Kawas National Park receives almost 5,000 visitors per year, Lancetilla receives ten times that number, many of them schoolchildren. Local tour agencies such as Marimar, Bahia

THE TRAGIC TALE OF JEANNETTE KAWAS

PROLANSATE, the Foundation for the Protection of Lancetilla, Punta Sal, and Texiguat, was founded by concerned Teleños in 1992. The figure driving the group was a fearless woman by the name of Blanca Jeannette Kawas Fernandez. As the head of an important local real-estate family, Kawas had both a social status and the personal magnetism that allowed her to storm into a colonel's office or fly to Tegucigalpa and pound on desks in cabinet offices when the natural wonders surrounding her beloved Tela were threatened.

On February 6, 1995, Kawas sat in her dining room, chatting with her assistant Marcial Bueno about the success just two days earlier of a protest march opposing the development of a new palm-oil plantation in Punta Sal National Park. At 7:45 p.m. two men approached the well-lit window of her home, slipped a 9-millimeter pistol between the slats of a wooden blind, and fired twice, killing her instantly. They then leapt into a waiting beige Toyota pickup truck and sped off.

Does anyone know who killed Kawas? Many believe that, like Chico Mendes, the Brazilian activist, she was killed by agents of the cattle barons who are cutting rain forests to expand their pastures. Others have blamed a local army colonel who had recently claimed title to 265 acres of coral reef and rain forest at the tip of a peninsula in Punta Sal National Park, land perfect for a major resort development. Kawas opposed the colonel's land grab. Still others point the finger at San Alejo African Palms, the palm oil–extracting subsidiary of the United Fruit Company. San Alejo's oil-extraction plant, located within the buffer zone of Punta Sal park, dumps waste materials into a river that flows into the once-pristine Monkey Lagoon. When fish and birds in the lagoon began to die, Kawas went on the warpath and attempted to close the plant.

Another suspect is the National Union of Campesinos (actually a cooperative of palm oil–plantation owners), which was trying to expand into the park, taking advantage of a recent presidential decree allowing poor campesinos to plant crops in Honduras's protected areas.

Finally, there is Plypsa, a timber company with a major sawmill and plywood factory just east of Tela that had been cutting tropical hardwoods in the Toloa Mountains above Punta Sal. They had a concession to cut 2,500 cubic meters of tropical hardwoods in that fragile area and were rumored to have taken out much more. Deforestation led to siltation in the rivers leading into Punta Sal. When the concession was expanded to 15,000 cubic meters, Kawas pounded on desks. COHDEFOR, the Honduran Forestry Service, reluctantly revoked the concession.

About a third of Tela's population of 35,000 turned out for Kawas' funeral and listened as priests, politicians, and environmental activists called for justice. The FUSEP (Public Security Force) declared that they had strong leads and would arrest the culprits within days, but the killers have not yet been apprehended.

In the wake of Kawas' death, Punta Sal, the prime natural attraction of Tela, was renamed Jeannette Kawas National Park, and representatives of 50 Honduran environmental groups met with COHDEFOR Minister Rigoberto Sandoval to demand that the government take responsibility for protecting Honduran parks and reserves.

Kawas has become something of a martyr, and her loss is still keenly felt in Tela. Be delicate in any discussions about her fate.

Azul, and Garífuna Tours organize trips to Lancetilla, or you can hop a taxi and go on your own. The entrance to the gardens is from the main highway, just to the west of the main turnoff for Tela.

Guides can be hired at the visitors center near the park entrance, typically leaving every half-hour. Or you can wander by yourself through cathedral-like stands of giant bamboo and the central arboretum zone, which houses exotic species that look like something out of a science-fiction fantasy. The rather crowded arboretum area is seen as a sacrifice zone by local environmentalists, but the nearly deserted trails lead deep into the park. Follow a path to the swimming hole on the Río Lancetilla for a refreshing swim, and bring water with you—you may stay longer and wander farther than you expect.

Once, after striking up a conversation with a campesino named Leopoldo who lives in the park, we mentioned that we loved the fruit of the mangosteen, then out of season. Leopoldo grabbed his machete, waved his hand, and took us on a two-hour hike up past waterfalls and over a mountain to a microclimate where a mangosteen tree was already bearing ripe fruit.

Details: Located 1 kilometer (.6 mile) south of Tela, Lancetilla comprises 41.5 square kilometers (16 square miles) of both carefully tended and completely wild botanical gardens. It is open from 7:30 a.m. to 3:30 p.m. daily, but overnight guests can stay at a large dormitory. Admission is 5L for Hondurans and $5 for foreigners.

Punta Izopo

To the east of Tela is Punta Izopo, 115 square kilometers (44 square miles) of tropical forests, wetlands, and mangrove forests. The white-sand beaches and rocky point are similar to those of Punta Sal, and well populated with migratory and coastal birds. If Jeannette Kawas National Park ever becomes too crowded, Punta Izopo will become increasingly attractive to environmentally oriented tourists who like things a little wild. Inland, the Texiguat cloud forest is still a diamond in the rough, with too few visitors to count.

Near Punta Izopo, a new resort development has invested millions of lempiras in moving earth, building cement structures, and attempting to create a marina that would fundamentally change the delicate ecosystem. As of late 1996, construction had been stopped by a demand for an Environmental Impact Study according to newly formulated Honduran environmental laws, but Punta Izopo is definitely an endangered site.

African palm production is also booming in the area. Plantation developers first drain wetlands with networks of canals, then plant monocrops of the oil-producing palm species, destroying all local flora and fauna. Honduran multimillionaire Miguel Faucusse plans to build a huge network of plantations in the area between Punta Izopo and Cuero y Salado, near La Ceiba, destroying what is now a natural biological corridor. Faucusse, sometimes referred to as "the Conquistador," is also investing heavily in palm plantations in Cuba. Palm oil, in addition to providing an extremely high cholesterol cooking oil and margarine, is a major ingredient in many soaps and other products.

Details: *Punta Izopo is a 115,000-hectare (284,050-acre) peninsula, framing Tela Bay to the east and paralleling Punta Sal peninsula to the west. It is open from dawn to dusk, and so far has no organized admission charge. Punta Izopo is most easily accessible from the Garífuna village of Triunfo de la Cruz, 15 kilometers (9.3 miles) east of Tela. By car, take the*

Bailey bridge plaque

141

THE ROAD FROM TELA TO CEIBA

The 96.5-kilometer (60-mile) stretch between Tela and La Ceiba is quite pretty, winding a bit inland from the coast, through rolling hills dotted with small villages. Inland, the Cordillera Nombre de Dios rises about 2,438 meters (8,000 feet) above sea level, about 1.5 to 8 kilometers (1 to 5 miles) from the sea. With all the precipitation in those mountains and that intense vertical drop over such a short horizontal run, it is small wonder that this part of the Caribbean coast features the largest network of crystal-clear waterfalls in Central America. Access is easy. Inquire about paths at the local villages. Be courteous, and dress a bit conservatively (women should wear sundresses over their bathing suits); the locals are not used to foreigners. If possible, hire a young man to act as your guide up to the waterfall zone, giving him a tip of a few dollars.

In the past the road from Tela to La Ceiba has been in a profound state of disrepair, with bridges regularly wiped out as storms bring water from the cloud forests down to the sea, especially because local builders pull gravel for construction from the riverbeds, increasing the potential for erosion.

Once, driving at night, I came upon a truckload of dirt piled in the road ahead. The bridge, it seems, had recently collapsed and the pile of dirt was the only indication of the danger ahead. The rented car ran up the dirt pile, launched into the air, and landed safely on another dirt pile. A pontoon bridge had been set up a hundred yards farther inland, but this was nearly invisible at night.

In 1997 culverts and diversions were installed to channel storm water past the coast road, final paving and improvements were completed, and the road became a joy to travel— until Mitch arrived in 1998. At present, some of the bridges are out, replaced by pontoons or temporary Erector set–like "Bailey" bridges. So proceed carefully.

*turnoff for Club Marbella to the end of the road, then go on into the park
by foot. From there, the best way to explore the lagoons is by canoe.*

NATURE AND ADVENTURE SIGHTS IN LA CEIBA

AMARAS

AMARAS is probably the Honduran environmental NGO with the
most attractive acronym. Besides meaning "you will love" in Spanish,
AMARAS stands for Associación del Medio Ambiente y Rehabilitación
de Aves Silvestres (Environmental and Wildlife Rehabilitation Center)
and is a center for the rehabilitation and release of wild birds. And
doesn't AMARAS sound a lot better than FUPNAPIB or FUCSA?

Bilingual signs on the main trail tell the story of a pet market
in the United States and Europe that thrives on parrots, macaws,
and other rain-forest birds that are captured illegally in the wild.
Typically, hunters kill adult birds and capture the young, often
drugging them, stuffing them in shipping tubes, and smuggling
them out to middlemen in the North. Under pressure from local
environmentalists and the Humane Society of the United States,
Honduran customs agents began enforcing the law that prohibits
the hunting of these birds. But what could they do with dazed,
drugged, perhaps injured young birds seized at the airport? In the
wild, they would not last a day. AMARAS was formed to care for and
rehabilitate these birds. Over the last two years, approximately 100
birds have been released in small family groups into Pico Bonito
National Park and Cuero y Salado Wildlife Refuge. Those too
injured to survive in the wild are visited by more than 1,000 schoolchildren who come to AMARAS each year as part of an environmental education program funded by El Marranito, the La Ceiba
sausage company.

Visitors to AMARAS can get close to the unbelievably beautiful
scarlet macaws, green parrots, toucans, hawks, and motmots. But
direct interaction with birds destined for release is discouraged by
the AMARAS staff. The social birds, if overaccustomed to human
company, will fly to neighboring campesinos' homes and wait to be
fed after their release into the wild. The campesinos, more often
than not, will clip a wing and be glad that fortune sent them a new

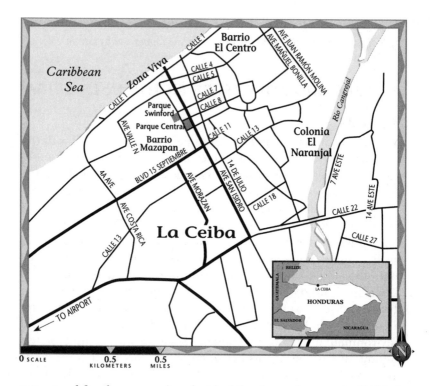

pet—good for the campesino, but bad for the endangered wild-bird populations.

While about 1 hectare (approximately 2.4 acres) is dedicated to the bird rehabilitation center, the rest of the 87-hectare (215-acre) agro-ecological farm is dedicated to for-profit environmental reforestation, including small plantations of tropical hardwoods such as mahogany, teak, rosewood, and San Juan, interplanted so as to provide habitat for local fauna. Farm owner Pepe Herrero has also planted dozens of hectares of former cattle pasture with native trees, planting pepper vines at the base of each. The resulting organic green and black peppercorn crop pays for further reforestation and provides a duplicable model for the conversion of pasture back into forest. The plantation is appropriate, productive agroforestry land use, particularly in the park's buffer zone.

Details: *15 kilometers (9.3 miles) from La Ceiba on the main coastal highway, or 5 kilometers (3 miles) west of the airport. AMARAS itself is a*

1-hectare (about 2.4-acre) center set in the midst of an 87-hectare (215-acre) agroecology center. A 10L entry fee is charged at the gate. Bilingual signs allow for a self-guided tour, or contact The Lodge at Pico Bonito (441-0583) or FUPNAPIB on the second floor of the Jet Stereo Building (443-3824) to arrange a visit.

The Butterfly Museum

More than 5,000 incredible butterflies and moths—some as big as your hat—are displayed in this air-conditioned museum run by Robert Lehman. The establishment is a testament not only to the creatures' beauty but also to the fragility of their habitats. The museum serves an educational role in the protection of Honduras's parks and reserves, has hands-on exhibits for children and adults, and shows bilingual (English-Spanish) videos. Lehman conducted a ten-month survey of the butterflies in La Muralla National Park. Some of the butterflies are found here, and he created three butterfly/insect boxes with an illustrated book that are on display in La Muralla's visitors center. A similar project is underway for Pico Bonito National Park.

Details: The museum is near the La Quina hotel, at Colonia El Sauce, 2 etapa, Casa G-12; 42-2874. Admission is 20L. Hours are 8 a.m. to noon and 2 to 5 p.m. Monday through Saturday. The museum is closed Wednesday afternoons.

Cuero y Salado Wildlife Refuge

The 14 square kilometers (5.3 square miles) of tropical wet and mangrove forests that make up the Cuero y Salado Wildlife Refuge and the estuaries of the Cuero and the Salado Rivers comprise the largest manatee reserve in Central America.

Manatees—tuskless, walrus-like sea cows—are big (weighing in at up to 1,000 pounds), cute, harmless, and terribly endangered. Easy to catch in nets and as tasty as pork, manatees have long been preyed upon by local fishermen, but the mammals' tendency to loll just beneath the water's surface to catch the sun has made them frequent victims of a more modern threat: motorboat propellers. As with many species, though, the greatest threat to the manatees is probably the loss of the pristine habitat they need to survive.

Manatees, like rather plump canaries in extremely wet coal mines, live where freshwater streams and rivers meet the ocean. They

James D. Gollin

Picking coconuts in Cuero y Salado

are herbivores, happily munching on bits of seaweed and grasses, and are highly sensitive to even minor changes in the environment. Sediment in the water caused by upstream deforestation or agro-chemicals washing into streams from banana, pineapple, or palm-oil plantations will kill off the manatee as surely as a speedboat's motor. At present, manatees range from Cuero y Salado all the way to Jeannette Kawas National Park near Tela, but the nearly inaccessible bio-corridor of wild marshes and estuaries that link the two wildlife preserves may soon be canalized and drained by several African palm plantation owners. In the meantime, come to Cuero y Salado early in the morning or at dusk and visit with the endangered manatee while you still can. Be aware that the creatures are shy, and sightings are by no means assured.

After a few hours in the estuaries, wander down to a white-sand beach where the rivers meet the sea. This area is a coconut planta-tion, still officially owned by Standard Fruit. A local boy might offer to climb a tree and poach a fresh coconut, but be aware that poaching Standard Fruit's coconuts is against the rules. Camping is allowed for

10L per person, and locals will be pleased to cook you dinner for a reasonable fee.

Standard Fruit Company, famous for the Dole brand, still owns land around Cuero y Salado, where it grows and harvests coconuts. Despite its reputation in the history books, Standard Fruit has been quite supportive of FUCSA, often matching local donations lempira for lempira. While relations with the banana giant are smooth, problems persist with cattle ranchers, including one neighbor who took down a fence and burned 60 hectares (148 acres) of the refuge to provide additional grazing for his cows before a court order slapped him in jail and forced him to withdraw. African palm growers such as Caicesa, a subsidiary of Standard Fruit, have gradually transformed 3,000 hectares (7,410 acres) of the buffer zone into palm plantation.

Getting to the refuge is half the fun. Start from the town of La Unión, 30 minutes west of La Ceiba, and head along the railroad tracks toward the sea. If the train, which as of this writing still belongs to Standard Fruit Company and not the refuge, is not disposed to ferry ecotourists, local boys will push and pole you along the flat track in a pushcart called a *burra*. While you may want to help pole yourself, acting like a terrestrial gondolier, do give the boys 80L for their efforts. It's hard work and the boys will break a sweat, causing some people to fret about exploitation of children. Remember that 80L is three times the daily minimum wage for an adult. The kids and their entire families can eat for days on one good tip. Prices for the *burra* ride and guided boat tours, and the park entrance fee, change from time to time; check with the refuge office for details. More than 70 families live in the reserve, and responsible tourism is generating both income and a reason to help conserve the wilderness here.

Once in the refuge, motorized skiffs and canoes are available for tours of the complex network of estuaries. Local guides, trained by the RARE Center, will bring you to the best spots to see howler and white-faced monkeys, iguanas, caimans, alligators, dozens of species of bird and, of course, the largest population of manatees in Honduras, estimated at around 50.

Details: *33 kilometers (about 43 miles) west of La Ceiba, between the Cuero and Salado Rivers, this 14,000-hectare (34,580-acre) refuge is home to a significant manatee population. Fees are $10 for foreigners, 10L for* *locals. For more information, contact the FUCSA environmental group in La Ceiba, 443-0329, e-mail: fucsa@tropicohn.com.*

Pico Bonito National Park

With 1,500 square kilometers (about 570 square miles) of nearly virgin rain forest and cloud forest, Pico Bonito is the largest national park in Honduras, and one of the most beautiful. Due to the steep slopes of the mountains in the Nombre de Dios, the park's nuclear zone is almost inaccessible, but the buffer zone can be reached through the river valleys of the Cangrejal, the Armenia Bonito, the Danto, or the Zacate.

There are various relatively easy ways to enter Pico Bonito's vast wilderness. The first is to follow the route used by the rafting tours that run the Cangrejal River. Drive, hike, or hop on the occasional bus that plies the Yaruca route up a dirt road on the eastern bank of the river, just to the east of town. The river forms a natural park boundary. If you want to reach Pico Bonito on your own, find a place with no rapids and simply swim across. But take care that you are not swimming near one of the many rapids. And before taking a hike to one of the many waterfalls visible from the road, check with a local guide for good instructions or ask at Expatriates Bar and Grill for advice. Ríos Honduras (see Guides and Outfitters, below) always includes a short hike in Pico Bonito as part of its Cangrejal day trips.

In the past, most organized tours to Pico Bonito headed to the visitors center co-managed by FUPNAPIB (Pico Bonito National Park Foundation) and CURLA, a local public university. As of publication date, post-Mitch road damage and politics at CURLA complicated this route in, so ask around before trying the following instructions. Take a bus to the community of Armenia Bonita, 5 kilometers (about 3 miles) in from the main road, taking a left just west of the Air Force base attached to the airport. The park's campground *(campamento)* is 5 kilometers farther on a four-wheel-drive road. You will pass a guard post that will charge you 20L to visit or 50L to spend the night, though prices for foreigners may be rising soon. Guides can be arranged through the FUPNAPIB office at 443-3824, or sign up with a tour agent. Nearby is the fortress-like B&B Noa Noa, containing a half-dozen rooms and run by a German-

GREEN WOOD PROJECT

At The Lodge at Pico Bonito, check out the beautiful wood furniture around the poolside bar. The furniture was made by local craftsmen with the help of the Vermont-based Good Wood Alliance. The project, launched in 1993 in the Pech Indian village of El Carbón, brings North American woodworkers skilled in low-tech woodworking methods to Honduras to teach local artisans how to create Appalachian-style chairs and other furniture from sustainably harvested forest products. The primary wood used for the furniture is cola de pava (tail of the turkey), an abundant local wood that not only resembles cherry in strength and density but also regenerates rapidly from cut stumps. Construction methods rely on traditional hand tools and innovative uses of non-timber forest products, such as bark and vines. No glue or nails are used. Furniture is sold locally and can be shipped for a reasonable charge. Ask for details at the lodge, or at the regional COHDEFOR office located near the airport on the road to Tela. In the United States, contact Scott Landis, Green Wood Coordinator, 80 Academy St., South Berwick, ME 03908; 207/384-0062, fax: 207/384-0063; e-mail: scottl@ttlc.net.

Czech family. The place is clean and secure, heavily populated by guard dogs.

The third and probably the most rewarding way in to Pico Bonito is through the new ecoresort The Lodge at Pico Bonito, about 7 kilometers (4.3 miles) beyond the airport. Call the lodge (800/524-1823) in the United States, or 441-0583 in Honduras) for information about hikes and tours. Half- or whole-day trips with bilingual local guides and naturalists should be available. Group size is a minimum of two and a maximum of eight, and trips are highly specialized according to skill level and interest. Attractions include excellent bird-watching (over 180 species identified in the area), swimming under waterfalls, and hiking on trails up the river valleys into the thick of the jungle.

The lodge is set in 100 acres of former cacao plantation and forest at the edge of Pico Bonito's buffer zone and is a wonderful place to spend a day. Or a week.

There are plans for a new visitors center a bit further west than The Lodge at Pico Bonito, at the Rio Zacate. A series of extraordinary waterfalls, with swimming holes beneath them, are easily reached by road and well-built paths, but FUPNAPIB is still raising funds to build the center nearby. If you swim at the lowest of the waterfalls, don't be surprised if a carful of evangelists shows up to baptize a new born-again member.

Only seven expeditions have made it to the 2,434-meter (7,985-foot) peak of Pico Bonito, a trek for the truly adventurous. A record was set in 1992 by a group of Peace Corps volunteers that included Kent Forte and local Ricardo Fito Steiner. The group hacked their way up through the dense cloud forest, hung soaking-wet hammocks from tree trunks, and made it to the summit and back in eight days. In 1998, guides Jorge Salaverri and German Martinez made it in six days. Care to try and break the record? A volunteer program now exists to maintain trails and upgrade the park. Contact the FUPNAPIB office (443-3824) in La Ceiba to apply. A minimum three-week stay is required. The facilities are spare; bring a mosquito net, rain gear, and food to cook for yourself in the crude cooking facilities at the visitors center.

Details: *Looming behind La Ceiba in the Nombre de Dios mountain range, this 150,000-hectare (370,500-acre) park is the largest in Honduras. Entrance fees are 10L. For more information, contact Fundación Parque Nacional Pico Bonito (FUPNAPIB), 443-3824, e-mail: fupnapib@tropicohn.hn.*

Tropical Butterfly Farm and Gardens

The Tropical Butterfly Farm and Gardens, one of La Ceiba's newest attractions, features gardens that encompass 20 hectares (50 acres). Visitors receive a guided tour, often led by owner Robert Gallardo himself. The farm includes the enclosed Butterfly House, home to "owls," morphos, and longwings. The Caterpillar House is next on the list. Larvae are reared to their pupae stage and are then shipped to butterfly houses all over the world. Inside you have the opportunity to touch larvae (if you'd like) and you might even see butterflies hatch. Robert Gallardo is also an avid birder, and other activities include bird-watching on trails through the jungle, where more than 160 species have been recorded, including the ornate and black-and-white hawk eagles, the royal flycatcher, and manakins. You may also see the local Garífunas pound on drums and dance the *punta*.

Details: *Located on the property of The Lodge at Pico Bonito, west of town at the edge of Pico Bonito National Park.*

NATURE AND ADVENTURE SIGHTS IN TRUJILLO

Capiro and Calentura

Dominating the landscape behind Trujillo are the peaks of Capiro and Calentura, rising 1,250 meters (4,101 feet) seemingly directly out of the ocean. Some 6,100 hectares (15,067 acres) of lower montane rain forest surround a small cloud forest near the summit. The park was founded in 1991, largely to protect the water supply for the 40,000 residents of the Trujillo area. Monkeys, toucans, and jaguar abound in this forest,

Rafting on the Cangrejal River

151

THE CANGREJAL RIVER

The Cangrejal is one of Central America's most accessible and beautiful rivers. Flowing from the depths of Pico Bonito cloud forest down to the Caribbean, the 32-kilometer (20-mile) river provides regular excitement for hundreds of whitewater rafters—many of whom day trip in from the islands—and kayaking aficionados who, having made the pilgrimage, spend months running relays up and down the river. The rapids of the lower Cangrejal are in the Class III to IV range, easy to moderate. Farther up the river are Class IV, V, and, during floods, even VI (i.e., unrunnable) rapids, depending on the rains. Generally, the river is highest from September to January and lowest from March to June, but it is runnable almost every day of the year. The water, pure and clear, is free from the nasty tropical diseases that infest rivers that run through rangeland or heavily populated areas.

Locals drive, bicycle, or catch a bus up the dirt road that parallels the Cangrejal's east bank. This road once snaked over the mountains to Olanchito, but since the new paved highway opened, the Carretera Vieja (Old Highway) has become a dead-end. Go 32 kilometers (20 miles) up, past a Korean-owned maquila *factory, and beyond, to one of the sand and gravel beaches protected by FUPNAPIB and FUCSA. Why protect a beach? Because unscrupulous building contractors like to drive their dump trucks down to the riverbank, load up on building*

easily reached from Trujillo on the road that passes the Hotel Villas Brinkley. The road was built by the U.S. military for $3 million to install and service a radar station at the summit during the Contra wars of the 1980s. The radar, built and manned by the Drug Enforcement Agency, was said to be able to track small boats and planes up to 250 miles out to sea. Following some arcane cost-cutting logic, the radar was disassembled and the installation abandoned a few years later.

materials, and leave gaping holes that not only ruin the aesthetics of the river but cause rapid erosion during major rains, taking out riverside roads and even bridges.

In the early 1990s, developers attempted to dynamite the rock formations that channel the upper Cangrejal—they needed rip-rap for a jetty at La Ceiba's new port. To prove that the river is worth more in its natural state than as a quarry, FUCSA invited watershed management experts Professors Carlos Rivas and Hernán Solis up from CATIE (Centro Agronomico Tropical de Investigacion y Ensenanza—Tropical Agriculture Research and Higher Education Center) in Costa Rica, who testified to the Honduran Congress that the rocks in the river dissipate the energy of storm runoff. The dangers of erosion in rivers with steep sides are extreme. In 1974, for example, at Choloma near San Pedro Sula, deforestation caused the riverbanks to slough off during Hurricane Fifi, forming a temporary mud dam that blocked the river. When the dam burst, hundreds of lives were lost. Offering a carrot of profit in addition to the stick of erosion, local environmentalist Pepe Herrero invited rafting expert Dick Eustis down from Colorado, and a small ecotourism boom developed.

Ríos Honduras, formed in 1992, ran the river daily during the high season (November through March) for two years and now has a permanent presence in La Ceiba, running the river throughout the year. Ríos' success has spawned a number of imitators.

A visitors center at the start of the road is maintained by FUCAGUA, providing information, two interpretive trails, and a 30-minute rain-forest medicinal trail tour.

At the peak of Calentura is the abandoned radar station and a radio tower used by Motorola, COCESNA (Central American Air Traffic Control), and Standard Fruit Company. FUCAGUA hopes to collect rent from the above to supplement ecotourist income and

James D. Gollin

Cangrejal River farmhouse near Las Mangas

make the park self-sufficient in the near future. Bungalows near the radar station should soon be available for overnight stays, allowing an early morning view of the entire Trujillo Bay and, in the other direction, the fertile Río Aguán valley.

Capiro and Calentura is the source of 13 rivers. Threats to the park include illegal logging, cattle grazing, and slash-and-burn agriculture by campesinos migrating up from the deforested south. Seventy percent of Trujillo's population is under 18 years of age. The U.S.-built road encourages logging, and COHDEFOR's enforcement of a ban on logging is intermittent. On the far side of the park are the Cuyamel caves. It's best to go with a tour guide because equipment is needed to explore the cave system.

In the valley between the peaks of Capiro and Calentura, five waterfalls congregate into pristine pools and a gorgeous swimming hole at the source of the Río Negro. From the Parque Central, head east to the stadium, take a right, then walk for 15 minutes up to the end of the dirt road. From there, follow the pipes up on a path to the right. The forest is filled with parrots and other birdlife as well as monkeys. The trail ends at a small dam that provides drinking water for all of Trujillo. Be polite and swim below the dam.

Details: This 6,100-hectare (15,067-acre) park is located directly behind Trujillo. The 10-kilometer (6.2-mile) walk up 1,127 meters (3,700 feet) takes about 3.5 hours and the return trip around 2.5 hours. Thanks to the hard work of the U.S. Army, the road is quite passable by sturdy vehicles. The 20-minute trip is best early in the morning before clouds form and obscure the magnificent view. For more information, contact the FUCAGUA (Fundación Capiro y Calentura y Guaimoreto) office, 434-4294.

Guaimoreto Wildlife Refuge

To the east of Trujillo, the 7,000-hectare (17,300-acre) Guaimoreto Wildlife Refuge consists of a brackish lagoon surrounded by mangrove swamps, spawning ground for much of the marine life in the area. It's also a good locale for birding. Of the park's 7,000 hectares, 4,000 are water.

Red snapper and shrimp have been overharvested in Trujillo Bay, however, and fishermen are now catching them as they spawn in the lagoon. To make matters worse, the Japanese government is working with artesanal Garífuna fishermen, training them to catch more fish and freeze them for export to Japan. The Ministry of Natural Resources wants to give permits to a Japanese company to build a processing plant that would likely result in the devastation of the local fishery.

Beyond Guaimoreto, toward the tip of the Cabo de Honduras, **Puerto Castilla** has a great old hospital built by the Standard Fruit Company and a housing complex that was once home to banana-company executives. In the other direction, on the road toward Tocoa, you might want to stop at the **Hacienda Tumbador,** a crocodile farm, or visit the natural hot springs at **Agua Caliente** (take a right at the Praga restaurant about 10 kilometers [6.2 miles] from town).

Details: To reach Guaimoreto, take a bus toward Puerto Castilla, get off at Puente Viejo, and take the dirt path to the adobe house, where you can rent a heavy cayuco (canoe) for 30L per day. You can also arrange for a lesson in Garífuna cooking or fishing here. The best time for bird-watching is early in the morning. Turtle Tours (44-4444) will transport you and take you out in fiberglass canoes for $15.

GUIDES AND OUTFITTERS

Garífuna Tours, based in Tela (448-2904), operates one of the most tourist-friendly excursion companies in Honduras. There's almost no place in the vicinity where they don't take travelers, and it's very easy to book a day excursion to Los Micos, Punta Izopo, or Lancetilla. Transportation can be by motorized canoe, dugout canoe, or sea kayak. Eight-hour tours cost around $15. Their offices are a block east of **PROLANSATE,** just west of the Parque Central. Check out www.garifuna.hn for all their offerings. They also rent bicycles, a nice way to visit the nearby Lancetilla gardens. PROLANSATE (448-2042), the local NGO in charge of the park, with offices 2 blocks west of the Parque Central on Calle del Comercio, also offers tours around the area for a similar rate. Be aware that half-day boat trips are best started in the morning; the sea often gets rough in the afternoon. A third option is **Arenas Tours,** 991-3454, located near Autopollos al Carbon.

In La Ceiba, your best bet might be **La Moskitia Ecoaventuras,** Avenida 14 de Julio, Casa #125, across from the Parque Bonilla, La Ceiba; 442-0104, 441-1248, e-mail: mosquitia@laceiba.com. Owner Jorge Salaverri is part indigenous, knows his way around both the North Coast and the Mosquito Coast, and runs a highly professional outfit. They run day rafting trips to the Cangrejal and longer trips to the Río Plátano and the Tawahka reserve, as well as day trips around La Ceiba to Pico Bonito and Cuero y Salado.

Ríos Honduras takes bookings at the Caribbean Travel Agency on San Isidro, 443-0780; directly at 441-1985; or through the Rocky Mountain Outdoor Center in Colorado, 800/255-5784. This operation is the white-water pioneer in Honduras. The staff is highly trained, the equipment first-rate, the attention to safety and environmental issues impeccable. The day trips and longer excursions are not cheap—around $75 per day—but you get what you pay for. Ríos offers rafters and kayakers day trips on the Cangrejal; the Humuya near El Progresso; the Mame, toward Olanchito; and on other rivers throughout Honduras. Weeklong trips run the Sico in Olancho, the Plátano in La Mosquitia, and past the ruins of Copán. Some trips are for experts only; some are appropriate for beginners and include instruction.

A German-owned group, **Omega Tours,** 440-0334, e-mail: omegatours@laceiba.com, runs a great kayaking school with overnight accom-

A DAM FOR THE CANGREJAL?

A 1996 proposal to dam the Cangrejal for 100-megawatt hydroelectric power was overwhelmingly rejected by Ceibeños and communities in the watershed. In late 2000, however, a new large dam was being promoted, under pressure from the World Bank. Locals are pushing for a 50-megawatt high-head dam, which would divert only part of the river into pipes, creating energy from the drop in altitude rather than the pressure of water behind a fixed dam.

The dam would actually divert a significant percentage of summer flows for the upper 10 kilometers (6.2 miles) of the river, returning the water to the turbines in Las Mangas, which is above the principal commercial raft run. However, more experienced kayakers will lose the top section and its spectacular gorge (where the dam may be placed).

The high-head concept is undoubtedly the most environmentally and paddler-friendly option—short of no dam. The real issues are whether the project will be designed at a scale appropriate to the river's summer flows and whether management of the watershed will be considered from the beginning.

Typically, "bigger is better" attitudes and the fat contracts of big projects dominate planning, rather than technical studies and logic. In La Ceiba, local groups will exert pressure to force planners to complete the proper studies, averting— one hopes—a boondoggle or environmental disaster.

modations up the Cangrejal, including a small pool in which to learn your Eskimo rolls. In general, regardless of the company they work for, you can meet rafting guides at Expatriates Bar and Grill in the evenings.

EuroHonduras (443-0933 or 443-0927; e-mail: eurohonduras @caribe.hn) offers tours throughout the North Coast. As the name implies, their clientele is primarily European. They often subcontract their rafting clients out to Ríos Honduras.

For more information about protected areas around La Ceiba area, call or visit the FUCSA (443-0329) or FUPNAPIB (443-3824) offices in town.

In Trujillo, **Turtle Tours** (434-4431) is run out of the Hotel Villas Brinkley. Spanish, German, and English are spoken, although the office is sometimes closed. Operators offer half- and multiday tours to nearby reserves.

LODGING

In Omoa, **Acantilados del Caribe** (on the highway between Puerto Cortés and Omoa, 665-1403; $66) is the highest end of the Omoa hotels. It has well-equipped cabins, a private beach, boats, opportunities for diving, and a good restaurant. The hotel arranges visits to a nearby private ecological reserve called La Bambita. **Bahia de Omoa** (658-9076; $25) is recommended, and specializes in organizing sailing cruises. **Eco Rancho,** west of Omoa on the highway to Masca (556-6156; $80), comes recommended by many travelers. They arrange environmentally oriented outings in the area. **El Botin del Suizo,** on Omoa's beach ($3), suffered a fire but should soon be rebuilt, and the restaurant is open. Ulrich Lang's establishment is right on the beach and caters to backpackers.

In Tela, in the Tela Nueva neighborhood, you can stay at the **Villas Telamar** (448-2196), $50 for simple rooms, $350 for an entire house. As the former United Fruit Company executive housing compound, these are the most luxurious accommodations in Tela. The Last Resort is in the Garífuna village of Tornabé, just at the edge of Jeannette Kawas National Park (448-2545; $55). Its nine cabins in the Tornabé are a good base for catamaran trips to the Laguna de los Micos and the park. To the east of town, in Triunfo de la Cruz, is the new and upscale **Caribbean Coral Inn** (448-2942; $50 range). In addition to the hotels listed here, you'll find many inexpensive hotels located all along the beach, including **Sherwood** (448-2416, $32), **Cesar Mariscos** (448-2083, $45), and **Bellavista** (448-1064, $22).

Near La Ceiba, the best accommodations are at **The Lodge at Pico Bonito** (AP710 La Ceiba, in the United States 888/428-0221, locally 440-0388/89/91; e-mail: picobonito@caribe.hn; www.picobonito.com; from $95, kids free). The Lodge is the realization of a decade of work by ex–Peace Corps volunteer Kent Forte and hopefully is a precursor of more such well-built, environmentally sound hotels and resorts in Honduras. Set in 200 acres of forest to the west of the airport at the edge of Pico Bonito National Park, the cabañas are built largely from naturally fallen hardwood trees. The window blinds are carved from driftwood from nearby beaches. Paths through the woods connect 22 elegant bungalows to a restaurant and a small conference center. There are short hikes to waterfalls, bird-watching sites (including three observation towers), an on-site butterfly farm, and guided tours offered throughout the region. The restaurant, featuring a "Meso American menu," serves wonderful five-course meals to hotel guests and visitors.

Another eco-oriented hotel is the **Villas Rhina Club and Mountain Resort** east of town (443-1222, fax: 443-3558; e-mail: willarhina@honduras.com, www.honduras.com/villarhina, $37). Like The Lodge at Pico Bonito, they can schedule tours to local parks and protected areas, rafting, etc. Another welcome addition to the La Ceiba area is the **Caribbean Sands Hotel,** on the beach east of La Ceiba (443-0035; www.caribbean-sands.com, $80). It has 42 rooms with air conditioning, tennis courts, and even a three-hole golf course.

In town, **La Quinta** (443-0223, $40) has 113 rooms. No relation to the U.S.–based chain, this lodge offers the most upscale rooms in town for a reasonable price. Slightly cheaper are the **Caribbean King Hotel** (Avenida 14 de Julio and 7th and 8th Streets, 440-0789, $25), recommended by rafting guides; **El Colonial** (Avenida 14 de Julio, 443-1953; $20), which is simple, clean and well located in town; and **Hotel Iberia** (Avenida San Isidro and 5a Calle, San Isidro, 443-0401; $20). **Hotel Majestic,** on the beach just north of Colonia al Alambra (northwest of the Parque; $25) has rooms with air conditioning, private baths with hot water, cable TV, private parking, and good security. The owners are Garífuna.

The **Parthenon** is on the beach in town (443-0401; $30). Visitors should be warned that there is a significant hooker presence around the pool.

For those who want a more rustic atmosphere, head up the Cangrejal to the town of **Las Mangas,** which means "the sleeves," named for the confluence of two branches of the Cangrejal. The town is a pretty collection of adobe and thatch huts. The locals, used to kayakers, are quite friendly. Here, up to 12 people can stay in the tidy bungalows ($20 per cabin) run by the town's mayor, David Lopez. There is easy access to beautiful swimming holes and waterfalls as well as trails into Pico Bonito National Park (443-1847). You can make reservations at the office in the center of La Ceiba across the street from Café Verde. Another up-river option is **Omega Tours Jungle Lodge** (440-0334).

In Trujillo, **Hotel Villas Brinkley** (Barrio Buenos Aires, 434-4444; $35) is probably your best bet. Set back a bit from the beach, these colonial-style villas with Maya-inspired architecture are on a hill above town. The hotel often hosts conventions, so if you want to stay here it might be wise to make a reservation. It is also home to Turtle Tours (434-4431). **Christopher Columbus** is located off the runway by the town airport (434-4966; $55). Built by Arturo Alvarado, owner of Isleña Airlines, this hotel is expensive and painted an unfortunate shade of green, but does offer all the modern amenities.

Campamiento (434-4244) is a very comfortable rustic resort right on the beach about 4 kilometers (2.5 miles) west of town en route to the community of Santa Fé. Bungalows are around $30.

FOOD

For some reason, all restaurants in Tela seem to need an hour to prepare even a simple dinner. Order food before you're hungry, or you'll be starving by the time it arrives. Try **Luces del Norte,** 11a Calle y 2a Avenida NE, between the Parque and the beach. This seafood restaurant, open 6 a.m. to 10 p.m., also has a book exchange in downtown Tela. **Restaurante Garífuna** is located at the end of Jose Cecilio del Valle Street, near the river and next to the newly opened Garífuna Museum. Built in typical Garífuna architectural style, its specialties are local foods such as conch soup, yucca or cassava, and the tapado fried fish. **Tia Carmen's,** 1 block south of the Parque Central and 1 block from the beach has good, cheap food. Try the delicious *baleadas*, the Honduran equivalent of a burrito, for $2. For Mexican food, head to **Garibaldi,** on Avenida

Guatemala opposite the Banco Atlantida. Most of the hotels also have restaurants.

In La Ceiba, definitely stop by **Expatriates Bar and Grill,** Final de Calle 12a, Barrio El Iman, where Calle 12a dead-ends into Avenida 14 de Julio, a few blocks southeast of the Parque Central. This is the best place to eat, drink, and get useful information in La Ceiba. Make that in all of Honduras. Welsh-Canadian Mark Fluellon runs the bar, greeting regulars and doling out advice to travelers. He also carries 18 varieties of Honduran cigars behind the bar and, if you're not careful, you may wind up with a mixed box to take home. Maureen McNamara is the genius in the kitchen, serving up generous portions of grilled snook and snapper as well as chicken, burgers, ribs, and vegetarian burritos at reasonable prices.

The bulletin board at the back of the bar displays local news and information on rafting, diving, kayaking, and fishing trips, and has information of various houses and river- or beachfront cottages that rent for around $5 per night. Despite the name, most of the regulars are Hondurans, but Expatriates is also the favored watering hole for river guides and local environmentalists. The restaurant is upstairs over an air-conditioning store, but a large, thatched palapa roof is visible from the street. The restaurant is open from 4 p.m. 'til midnight; closed Wednesdays.

The other great restaurant in La Ceiba is **Ricardo's** (Avenida 14 de Julio y Calle 10a, 443-0458). La Ceiba has a long historical connection to New Orleans due to banana export, and you'll sense that connection when you try the Cajun-style blackened fresh fish. There is a salad bar, an air-conditioned room, and also a garden patio with hanging plants and a fountain.

There are also plenty of inexpensive places to eat, with great food and unusual names, such as Cric Cric Burger or Lady Burger & Car Wash Larry, on the beach. **Autos-Pollos,** on the highway to Tela near La Quinta Hotel, has inexpensive roast chicken with carry-out service, good food for a trip up the Cangrejal River.

In Trujillo, **Cafe Oasis,** across the street from Bancahsa, offers daily vegetarian specials, a book exchange, and an informative bulletin board. **Lempira,** at the Villas Brinkley Hotel, is an upscale restaurant with great views, a good spot for a romantic dinner. **Rincón de Amigos** is a good bar and hangout with a red-tiled roof, at the edge of the beach near town. Ask British owner John Thompson about the time he fell off a boat en route from La Mosquitia and swam for 24 hours until, near death, he landed at the beach in Plaplaya. **Jerry's,** also known as the Rogue Gallery, is owned by an expat and is well located on the beach just below downtown. Near the airport, **Chino's Bar** is a great place to sit in a hammock with a beer, or have a full seafood meal. The owners also rent oceanside cabañas nearby. **Gringo's Bar,** when last visited, kept monkeys in cages and birds with clipped wings to amuse the clientele. To the west, try the restaurant at **Campamento** or head on to the Garífuna village of Santa Fé, 12 kilometers from town, to dine at **El Caballero,** an outstanding spot for fresh seafood and great local ambiance.

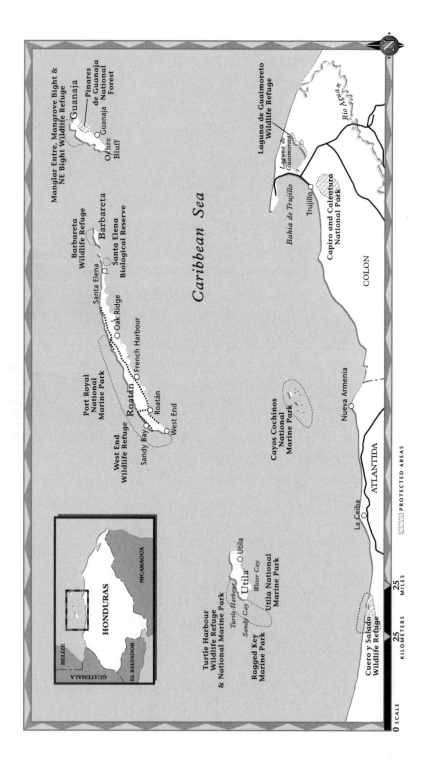

GUATEMALA
BELIZE
HONDURAS
EL SALVADOR
NICARAGUA

N

Turtle Harbour
Wildlife Refuge
& National Marine Park

Utila

Turtle Harbour

Sandy Cay

Water Cay

Utila

Ragged Key
Marine Park

Utila National
Marine Park

Cuero y Salado
Wildlife Refuge

La Ceiba

ATLANTIDA

Nueva Armenia

Cayos Cochinos
National
Marine Park

West End
Wildlife Refuge

Port Royal
National
Marine Park

Roatán

Sandy Bay

Roatán

West End

French Harbour

Oak Ridge

Santa Elena

Santa Elena
Biological Reserve

Barbareta
Wildlife Refuge

Barbareta

Manglar Entre, Mangrove Bight &
NE Bight Wildlife Refuge

Guanaja

Pinares
de Guanaja
National
Forest

Guanaja

Ohre

Bluff

Caribbean Sea

COLON

Bahía de Trujillo

Trujillo

Capiro and Calentura
National Park

Laguna de
Guaimoreto

Laguna de Guaimoreto
Wildlife Refuge

Río Aguan

SCALE

25
KILOMETERS

25
MILES

PROTECTED AREAS

0 SCALE

CHAPTER 6

Paradise under the Sea: The Bay Islands

Emerald gems in a turquoise sea, the Bay Islands of Honduras are the peaks of the Bonacca Mountain range, an undersea extension of the inland Merendon Mountains that loom behind San Pedro Sula. Already one of the premier scuba destinations in all of Central America and the Caribbean, the Bay Islands are growing rapidly in popularity. Lying 48 kilometers (30 miles) off Honduras's northern coast, they are a Caribbean outcropping of a Central American nation. In total, there are eight islands and 65 small cays (pronounced "keys"), comprising an oval chain. The islands' aggregate land mass adds up to nearly 150 square kilometers (58 square miles), most of it on the three principal islands of Roatán, Guanaja, and Utila. Culturally, ethnically, and linguistically, these islands are closely linked to other Caribbean islands, such as the Caymans, which lie just across the deep Cayman Trench.

Of course, very few people visit the Bay Islands just to see the Bay Islands. They are used primarily as a platform for the exploration of this hemisphere's most extensive coral-reef system. Stretching from the Yucatán down through offshore Belize to Honduras, the Great Maya Reef system is second only to Australia's Great Barrier Reef in size. It is the most extensive reef system in the Northern and Western Hemispheres.

Size, of course, is not everything. The important question is: How good is the diving? The answer: as good as it gets anywhere in the world. Rating the world's top dive spots from 1 to 5, the Bay Islands earn a definite 5 for visibility, beauty, and accessibility. From the tiny purple fishes that swim through your fingers to the sea turtles that lead you down through tunnels of multicolored coral to the massive walls, like living aquatic skyscrapers these "rain forests of the sea" are treasures of biodiversity. Like the Red Sea, the Barrier Reef, Bonaire, and a few other spots, the reefs that fringe the Bay Islands are on the must-see list of any serious diver. They may not have the diversity of coral species such as that found in the Indo-Pacific, but by Caribbean standards they are superb. And the Bay Islands are very user-friendly for all divers, from the complete beginner to the seasoned adventurer.

Shrimp boats in Roatán

James D. Gollin

Coral has long been both the boon and bane of these islands, protecting the pirate lairs by ripping the bottoms out of pursuing warships, providing refuge for aquatic life that has fed and sustained islanders for centuries, and, increasingly over the last decade, pulling in thousands of dive-oriented tourists. Coral-reef ecosystems are remarkably beautiful and complex, and at the same time almost impossibly fragile. For these reasons, and because fishing is the backbone of the non-tourist portion of the local economy, proper respect for the marine resources is high on everyone's agenda.

As in years past, the islands are currently home to aggressively entrepreneurial and strong-minded individuals, many of whom choose to be ship captains. In the olden days, many were pirates. In more recent centuries, they ran fishing boats. Now, many run dive boats and resort hotels. The islanders' fortunes have always been tied to the sea. Small boys who don't yet know how to tie their shoes can be seen in dugout canoes learning how to cross through the cresting waves to the flat water and paddle back to shore without flipping their craft. Their older brothers and fathers sign on as crew to the fishing, shrimping, and lobster diving fleets that regularly head out from French Harbour, Oak Ridge, and Guanaja. They fan out across the Caribbean, facing down hurricanes, risking their lives, pulling wealth from the sea.

Once beyond the horizon from home, boat captains from the Bay Islands wield power like little gods. If government rules prohibit the harvest of lobsters in certain months, captains might make port in Jamaica and sell the catch there. If diesel fuel is taxed excessively, others will send a tanker barge up to New Orleans and get their own supply. With huge amounts of illegal drugs passing through the region, largely on their way up from Colombia to the United States, many ship captains surreptitiously take on extra cargo or turn a blind eye to what goes on around them. Those captains, billfolds bulging with hard currency, suddenly have the capital to invest in a new boat or a dive resort, fueling the development of the most sophisticated tourist infrastructure in Honduras.

HISTORY

The distinct culture of the islands, of course, derives from its distinct history. Mainland Honduras was colonized by the Spanish five centuries ago. The heartland of Honduras followed a path of conquest, colonization, and independence pretty much in line with that of the rest of Central America. While Honduran nationalists making speeches under a statue of Francisco Morazán would protest such a statement, the fact is that most of those nationalists would feel more at home in the Ladino culture of Nicaragua or Guatemala than they would among the English-speaking, brown-skinned peoples of the Bay Islands. Bay Island culture is eclectic, a consequence of an eclectic history punctuated by encounters with several European, African, and Caribbean cultures.

In pre-Columbian times, the islands were inhabited by Paya Indians—related to the ancient Maya and to the present-day Pech of the Mosquito Coast. More than 50 archaeological sites have been excavated on the islands, many filled with artifacts such as "yaba-ding-dings," or clay figurines. If you've just got to see something called a yaba-ding-ding, head to the Roatán Museum, located in Sandy Bay at Anthony's Key Resort, where they are displayed along with copper beads and jade ornaments from that era.

Christopher Columbus landed on the island of Guanaja in 1502, naming it the Isle of Pines. He commented in his diary that the Bay Islands' tall trees might make a good source of spare masts and spars. Historians believe he landed just north of El Soldado beach on the west side of Guanaja where, in any case, a small monument commemorates his arrival. Columbus was quite pleased with what he saw, commenting "green, green, very green," but the friendly natives did not benefit from the sailor's pleasure. The islanders he encountered were enslaved by the Spanish and sent to Cuba and Mexico. By 1528, the islands were depopulated.

Having removed all the usable manpower, the Spanish abandoned the islands and the neighboring Mosquito Coast for centuries, concentrating instead on the gold- and silver-rich lands of the interior. The Caribbean served the Spanish only as a means of egress, a route for transporting their New World treasures back to the Old World. The fantastic wealth of precious metal that was pulled from the ground in mines around Tegucigalpa was usually shipped out through Trujillo. Sixteenth-century British, French, and Dutch buccaneers, eager to share in the abundance, began to lurk about the islands, hoping to catch a Spanish supply ship unawares. The single unifying theme of all buccaneer ships was their hatred of the Spanish.

The pirates also set up bases on the Mosquito Coast, on the far side of Trujillo. British privateers (buccaneers with an official charter from their respective governments, in this case mercenaries for the British Navy out of Jamaica) built permanent sites on the islands. In 1638 the British even established a fledgling colony on Roatán, manned by Puritans from Maryland who made a business out of exporting timber.

The early pirates and their descendants were joined by approximately 5,000 Garífuna, descendants of shipwrecked African slaves who had intermixed with Carib Indians. They arrived on Roatán in 1797, dumped unceremoniously on the shores by the British after an uprising on the island of St. Vincent; and were joined by English-speaking Cayman Islanders who migrated to Coxen Hole in the 1830s, and then by the various flotsam and jetsam of the Caribbean region. If you were wanted for a crime in Jamaica or you ran off with a Cuban man's wife, you could probably live out your days in the Bay Islands without anyone noticing or caring.

Ever ready to expand into a power vacuum, the British formalized their claim to the islands in the mid-19th century. In 1852 Colonel Philip Edmund Wadehouse, the governor of Jamaica, took possession of Utila in the name of Queen Victoria. Honduras issued diplomatic protests, as did the United States, but to no avail. A decade later, in exchange for Honduras's formal recognition of Britain's claim to British Honduras (later to become Belize), the islands were ceded back to Honduras. Not terribly pleased, over the next hundred years the English-speaking islanders proceeded to ignore the mainland whenever possible.

Nothing stands still in the Bay Islands, where each year brings another spurt of growth. Once sleepy, backward, English-speaking islands off a little-known Central American republic, the islands have been transformed over the last two decades. It is as if a giant tugboat were pulling them away from mainland Honduras and toward the Bahamas or the Virgin Islands. Pioneer divers drifted to the Bay Islands in the 1980s. Dive magazines, not far behind, began flagging the Bay Islands as their number-one pick for Caribbean dive vacations. As the sport broadened, risk-loving adrenaline junkies were joined by pale-skinned, desk-bound professionals on one-week winter vacations; by grandparents who toy with scuba but prefer to snorkel; and by sunbathers ever happy to loll on a West End beach sipping rum drinks while their diving friends build up nitrogen and play with gear. More recently still, the Bay Islands have been invaded by North American retirees and seasonal "snow geese" from Canada who snap up condominiums and seaside lots at prices that seem to double every few years. A 1999 population estimate is 26,000 on Roatán alone.

Rather than market themselves as a part of Honduras, early dive resorts advertised as if they were located on an island nation called Roatán. During the first decade of growth Honduras made the pages of guidebooks as a choice destination. Before, it had been mentioned only as a place to catch a connecting flight. As tourism spread from Roatán to the neighboring islands of Guanaja and Utila, resorts began to describe themselves as being located in "The Bay Islands," still not mentioning that the Bay Islands are a part of Honduras. In fact, the Open Road guide to Honduras is entitled *Honduras & Bay Islands*, as if the one is not a part of the other. The Bay Islands, like the Mosquito Coast, definitely are a part of Honduras—but they are as different from Tegucigalpa as Maui is from Manhattan.

THE REEF

The United Nations declared 1997 the Year of the Reef, and most coral-reef activists were overjoyed. Coral reefs, the marine equivalent of tropical rain forests, are restricted to a tropical belt around the world between 30 degrees north and south latitudes. Incubators for marine life, these reefs are key spawning grounds for fish and habitats for lobster and crabs. The reef itself, or, to be more specific, the surface of the reef, is a living thing that sits on top of the skeleton of its ancestors. Each generation adds a new layer of life. Within a tiny area, there may be scores of species of coral, dozens of species of fish and, on the microscopic level, thousands of other forms of life. The complex interaction of all of these species in a zone of such intense biodiversity involves thousands of organic compounds, from natural antibiotics that fight off diseases to sexual attractants, some of which are already working their way into modern medicine and biotechnology.

The colonies of marine organisms that we call coral reefs are under tremendous pressure. According to Sea Grant College, 10 percent of the earth's reefs have collapsed. Reef activists warn that we risk much more serious losses in the next 20 years. Much of that destruction is due to industrial and agricultural pollution, to inland deforestation and resultant siltation, and to generalized human population growth in waterfront areas. The first warning sign is a phenomenon known as coral bleaching. When changes in water temperature, salinity, or nutrients are provoked by natural and human causes, the little symbiotic algae cells called zooxanthellae are expelled by the coral, which loses its pigment. Scientists can't yet explain exactly why. The bleached coral can be caused by an interruption of natural water currents that, in turn, is caused by waterfront construction; by cycles of deforestation, erosion, and siltation; and/or by the spread of effluent from agro-industry or unprocessed human sewage. If water conditions return to their original state, coral bleaching stops and coral color and health return as well. If the natural current interruption continues, the coral dies.

In addition to systemic threats like bleaching and siltation, coral reefs are threatened both directly and indirectly by the rise of diving as a sport. Direct threats come from poorly trained or unsupervised divers who bump into coral with their tanks or fins, breaking off pieces and rendering the entire colony susceptible to disease or predation by coral-eating organisms. Unthinking dive-boat captains who drop anchor over a pretty spot, rather than tying up to previously installed, carefully anchored buoys, destroy many beautiful areas. Many types of coral can be killed simply by the careless touch of a human hand that strips them of an invisible but protective layer of slime. Reefs are killed indirectly by resort construction and inadequate processing of dive-tourist sewage. Also, many divers and other tourists purchase jewelry and other souvenirs made from coral, which is just as bad as killing the coral directly. If you are insensitive enough to purchase any jewelry made with endangered black coral, be aware that U.S. customs may well seize it.

So why do coral-reef activists feel that divers are their natural allies? If you've ever dived in a place like the Bay Islands, you probably already know the answer. To float weightlessly in warm, clear water over and through an impossibly beautiful coral reef, surrounded by multicolored fish of every shape and size, is a profoundly moving experience. Thousands of people come to diving for the adventure, but stay for the experience, developing an almost religious appreciation for the indescribable complexity and beauty of the reef systems.

The Berkeley-based **Coral Reef Alliance** (510/528-2492, fax: 528-9317; e-mail: coral@aol.com) is a network of divers who have chosen to help protect the reefs they have come to love. Members take a pledge to protect the coral and can sign up for voluntary coral monitoring programs in the areas in which they dive. **Reefkeeper International** in Florida (305/358-4600, fax: 305/258-3030), is involved in directly confronting construction or pollution that will

MANGROVES AND DEATH

Not long ago, the swampy mangrove forests that once belted many parts of the islands were rapidly being dredged or burned and filled to create new waterfront land for resorts, at significant environmental costs. The complex network of mangrove roots, mud, saltwater, and freshwater forms a perfect nursery for myriad sea creatures, and the mangroves and reefs, the open channels and lagoons, the mud flats and white-sand beaches are all part of an interrelated network of life that if disturbed in one zone will affect all the rest.

This lesson has been learned—or should have been learned—when Albert Jackson built his Fantasy Island Resort. Jackson owns a dredging company and so, at little immediate cost, set about building two large jetties to protect the white-sand beach in front of his luxurious hotel. The jetties cut off the natural flow of water through the area, created siltation, and ultimately killed much of the reef in front of the resort.

The boom in tourism creates constant pressure to fill in the mangroves and build hotels. As the waterfront develops, locals are forced to move back into the hills, to the forests that once covered the centers of the islands. As the inland populations grow, more trees are cut. When rain falls on deforested land, the soil erodes. Erosion ruins agricultural land, kills the reefs, and threatens the underground aquifers that provide drinking

destroy reefs, such as the cruise-ship dock that destroyed much of Paradise Reef off Cozumel, Mexico, but resulted in an embarrassing court ruling that might well protect other reefs from cruise ships.

In short, much like ecotourism in the rain forest, responsible divers can mitigate most of the damage they can potentially cause. Like rain-forest ecotourism, diving is an excellent forum for public education and activist development around coral-reef preservation *water to tourists and locals alike. Recent studies reported in* Coconut Telegraph, *Roatán's monthly magazine, indicate that not only are many wells on the island drying up, but some are also now contaminated with fecal chloroform.*

Despite the population increase, Roatán maintains its wilderness in the north, where red mangroves still line the bights and bays (a bay is shaped like a teardrop; a bight is shaped like a U). Much more of the island was once lined with red mangroves, but islanders cut them down to extract a red dye from the bark for use in tanning leather. In the 1960s, taking the bark from the trees for sale to the mainland was prohibited. Along the shoreline, thrusting up from the mud and brine, are forests of black mangroves, their leaves often encrusted with sea salt.

White mangroves, which need a more solid foundation, are less common, though Palmetto Bay Plantation features the spectacular sight of a fluorescent green ground cover growing underneath a large grove of them. Another interesting tree still found is the buttonwood, whose lumber (purportedly so solid that it sinks in water and will never rot) was used in the past for stilt houses. The buttonwood is a "walking tree," which extends its roots and, over time, appears to have moved. Of course, if you don't have a hundred-year attention span, you'll have to use your imagination.

issues. A good dive program, like any ecotourism operation, should have a strong educational component, responsible supervision to keep both divers and the environment safe, and information for those who are interested in opportunities to help preserve coral reefs. If you want to visit the reefs, remember that you are a guest in a very fragile environment. Never touch the coral with any part of your body or equipment unless a responsible dive master shows you how to touch which types of coral. If you're tired, float. If you can't maintain "neutral buoyancy," take a class or stay away from the coral. Never stand on a reef. In picking accommodations, whether they be $4 per night or $400, avoid those that are built on former reef or mangrove forests or that discharge raw sewage or other pollutants into the water. In sum, yes, go ahead and dive. Enjoy it. Just make sure that you are not part of the problem.

VISITOR INFORMATION

Each island has a different character. Roatán has the most sophisticated infrastructure, the best hotels, and the best nightlife. Guanaja is the least affected by tourism and the farthest removed from the coast, a place where visitors are still treated like family. Utila is the bargain island, perhaps the cheapest place to get dive-certified on the globe. Cayos Cochinos, technically not a Bay Island but nevertheless covered in this chapter, has only one resort and is a great place to seclude yourself amid the sea, sand, and coral.

Throughout the year, island temperatures are relatively stable, between 77 and 84°F. Even when it's hot, the trade winds bring cool relief. Rainfall exceeds 2 meters (6 feet) per year, and the heaviest rains fall between October and January. Regardless of the weather up above, the reefs are always beautiful and warm, but excessive rainfall and hurricanes can affect underwater visibility for a few days.

For many travelers, the Bay Islands are the introduction to Honduras. If you've made it this far, by all means visit the mainland. It's just a 15-minute, $20 plane trip away. Combine a trip to the islands with a white-water rafting adventure on the Cangrejal, a hike through a cloud forest, or a visit to Copán Ruins. Don't miss this opportunity. As wonderful as the Bay Islands are, they are only the best-known, most-visited part of a land of many such wonders.

On Isleña Airlines, its parent TACA, and its smaller competitors, Sosa and Rollins, there are as many as a dozen flights a day from La Ceiba to Roatán, half a dozen flights from San Pedro to Roatán, and a few daily flights to the other islands. The short hops take around 15 minutes and cost around $20. A round-trip flight from San Pedro Sula to Roatán costs $120. Flying from island to island is a bit harder. If on Guanaja, for example, you may have to pop back to La Ceiba for a connecting flight to Roatán, depending on the time and day you want to fly. Schedules change regularly, flights are often late and sometimes early, and additional flights are generally added if there are people ready to pay to fly.

The old international airport at Roatán was a bit of a joke, with a rickety terminal and a control tower intentionally built into a hill. With limited control-tower capacity, large planes flown by foreign carriers could not land on the island, giving a great competitive boost to SAHSA, the now-defunct Honduran airline. More recently, the tower's capacity has been brought up to international standards, the new terminal has opened, and Roatán is open for business. Roatán also receives jets nonstop from Miami every Sunday, and there are plans to increase the nonstops from Houston and New Orleans. There is a weekly nonstop from Milan, Italy. Be aware that if you buy a ticket for a flight from San Pedro Sula to any of the Bay Islands, chances are that you will change planes in La Ceiba even if they don't mention that fact. The airstrips of Guanaja and Utila are too small to receive larger planes and jets.

Note that immigration theoretically requires passengers who fly into Roatán's airport to have round-trip tickets. If you have a one-way ticket, you may be obliged to purchase a return ticket in order to pass through immigration. There are stories about officials hassling people who look like hippies. Also note that camping is illegal and discouraged on the island. If you are carrying a lot of camping gear, make sure the name of a hotel where you plan to stay is on the tip of your tongue.

Passenger and cargo boats head out from La Ceiba to the islands nearly every day. The trip is worthwhile for those who really like boat trips, as the plane trip is fast, easy, and reasonably priced. You can take a boat from La Ceiba to Roatán for $12 one way or to Utila for $15. However, if you want to take a boat from Roatán to Utila, you'll probably have to go back to La Ceiba first. If you are really into boats, call Roatán Charter at 800/282-8932, fax: 352/588-4158, and ask

SAND FLIES

Called "flying teeth" by tourists, tiny, mosquito-like sand flies can ruin your trip to the islands if you are careless and unlucky. The little devils live and breed on sandy beaches but they hate wind, so you are most endangered if sunbathing on, say, Roatán's West End on a windless day. Also called no-see-ums, there are actually three different species of sand flies; all are found throughout the Caribbean, and all three are biting nuisances. One feeds only at night, another feeds only at dusk and dawn, and another feeds only during the day. Females drink blood (they need the protein in order to lay their eggs and must have a blood meal before laying each clutch), while males feed on plant juices.

If your lodging has a ceiling fan and there is a breeze coming through the screens, you should have no problem. If the owner of your beachside bungalow or restaurant pays someone to rake the nearby beach regularly, upsetting the sand fly breeding cycle, you'll have no problem. If you lie unprotected on a beach that has not been raked, you might wind up with a few hundred red welts that itch enough to keep you awake at night. Various repellents, from Avon's Skin-So-Soft to cactus juice, citronella, tea-tree oil, and other products, work well for different people. The surest bet is to use DEET (the active ingredient in Off and Cutter), though DEET is said to be toxic and is strong enough to melt synthetics. The point is that you must cover yourself with something every day, and after every shower or long swim. If you're bitten, try a topical hydrocortisone cream and an antihistamine such as Benadryl to alleviate symptoms so you can get some sleep.

about renting a sailboat. Pick it up in La Ceiba and head out to the islands with the power of the wind.

ROATÁN

Roatán is the largest and most developed of the islands, the only one with a real road. Getting around is easy. You can take a shared taxi, rent a car, or be ferried around by the courtesy vans owned by the major hotels. On the other hand, once you get to your hotel you probably won't want to move around very much, except by boat and underwater.

In 1980, the total permanent population of Roatán was estimated to be about 10,000 people, but that number skyrocketed to an estimated 26,000 in 1999, not counting tourists. The original 10,000 were almost entirely English-speakers, either light-skinned or dark-skinned or anywhere in between, while many of the recent arrivals are Spanish-speakers from the mainland. The

James D. Gollin

Flying in to Roatán

177

island used to be predominantly English-speaking, but the influx of mainlanders is tipping the scale toward Spanish. Most of the newly arrived "Spaniards" live in the Los Fuertes neighborhood outside French Harbour. Traditionally, the towns of Corozal and Jutiapa are mostly Spanish-speaking. Almost everyone working in the tourist industry speaks some English, though most taxi drivers are "Spaniards." The Bay Islands accent is similar to that of the Caymans, a lighter version of the sing-song Jamaican dialect. If you can't understand what someone says, smile and ask them to repeat it.

The Cuba-shaped island is 40 kilometers (25 miles) long and only about 3 kilometers (1.8 miles) wide, with a ridgeline forming a central spine some 235 meters (771 feet) above sea level. The hills are covered with pine and oak trees and thick tropical undergrowth.

Roatán has banks, supermarkets, photo supply shops, a new mall built by Albert Jackson that includes a movie theater, and even a bit of nightlife—more so than the other islands. But people don't come to Roatán for the nightlife. They come because the green island, fringed with coral reefs and white-sand beaches, is drop-dead beautiful. Further, despite its newfound popularity, the island maintains its charm. People are friendly and helpful, in a non-hurried island way.

NATURE AND ADVENTURE SIGHTS IN ROATÁN

Coxen Hole

Named after pirate John Coxen, Coxen Hole is on the western part of the island's south shore and just a few kilometers from the airport. Sometimes called Coxen's Hole, it's a lively village, with little bars and restaurants, and the best place for banking or shopping but not a great place to spend the night. In Coxen Hole, as in any town on the islands, be aware that municipal water and electricity utilities often shut systems off from around 11 p.m. until dawn. Many resorts have their own generators, but smaller hotels in town may not. Before you pay extra for air conditioning, make sure that you can use it while you sleep.

ENTER THE COUSTEAU SOCIETY

If you stop by El Faro hotel in French Harbour you might well run into Claude Buffet, project manager of the Cousteau Society, or up to 50 other foreigners who have taken up temporary residence there. In nearby offices, the Cousteau Society team is working with 60 Hondurans on a project to identify pollution sources on land and their effects on coral reefs, sea grass, mangroves, and artesanal fishing. Under the auspices of the Environmental Project for the Bay Islands, paid for by the Honduran Institute of Tourism and the Inter-American Development Bank, Phase I involves diagnostics and evaluation, Phase II will select particular areas in need of protection, and Phase III will develop management systems for the protected areas.

Officially, the entire sea around the islands is a giant marine reserve, but in practice only the West End/Sandy Bay area of Roatán, Port Royal, and Turtle Harbour on Utila are well protected at present. Italians are in charge of water treatment and sewage and the Spanish are clearing up land title issues, but the French, under the direction of Buffet and the Cousteau Society, get the fun job of monitoring and protecting the coral. They divide the ocean floor into subsegments and at six sites around the islands regularly monitor the size and health of coral, fish, and sea grasses, meticulously measuring, weighing, and testing. So far, there seems to be a bit of algae growth from leaking septics, but overall the ecosystem is in good health. On Guanaja there is concern that the mass death of the mangroves caused by Mitch might lead to sedimentation, and observers are monitoring the situation carefully. A U.K. organization called Coral Cay Conservation, led by William Bradley, has developed a volunteer dive program on Utila. Call 455-5185 for details.

One good place to visit in Coxen Hole is the headquarters of the **Bay Island Conservation Association** (BICA) in the Cooper Building. BICA was formed in 1990 by islanders interested in preserving the local natural resources. BICA plays a strong role in local education efforts and has increased environmental awareness. In particular, they have a program for schoolchildren that promotes pride in the island ecosystem under the motto "Wild and Free." Pick up a Wild and Free button while in the office, or a BICA T-shirt for $12, a guide to the more than 120 bird species on the islands for $5, and other books and materials on environmental matters.

BICA members are also involved in organizing community-wide activities such as beach cleanups. BICA also manages the Sandy Bay Marine Reserve, which protects more than 3.2 kilometers (2 miles) of coral reef around Anthony's Key Resort. The marine park is their priority project. They also run two or three guided snorkeling trips a day, generally in the Sandy Bay area. Ask for Carmen Cartagena at the Sandy Bay BICA office near Tino's Dive Shop, or call or fax the main office (445-1424).

BICA has received funding from the USAID-supported Fundación Vida. It also works jointly with the RARE Center for Tropical Conservation to promote the protection of natural resources by focusing on a particular yellow-naped parrot found only on the Bay Islands, "symbolizing the beauty, purity, and freedom of our islands." The goal of the project is to instill local pride in and encourage protection of the environment by educating locals about their natural resources. For information, contact Cheryl Galindo or Irma Brady at BICA in the Cooper Building in Coxen Hole; call or fax: 445-1424.

Another interesting stop, upstairs in the Cooper Building, is the office of the *Coconut Telegraph* (445-1660, fax: 445-1659; e-mail: cocotel@globalnet.hn), the colorful magazine of the Bay Islands. Though an important sponsor of cultural events and a champion of environmental causes, the magazine is published somewhat irregularly. The office provides a good information hub.

Your most important stop in Coxen Hole might be at the **Casi Todo** (Almost Everything) bookstore and **Que Tal? Cafe,** (445-1944 fax: 445-1946; e-mail: quetal@globalnet.hn and casitodo@globalnet.hn), sharing space upstairs in what appears to be a large house at the *"triangolo"* where the road from downtown Coxen Hole meets the main highway toward Sandy Bay. Expat Averyl Muller sells specialty coffees, great food, and baked goods; has a new and used bookstore with trading and local-interest sections; and runs a great travel and tour agency. You can even buy airplane tickets here. He's open Monday through Friday from 8:30 a.m. to 4:30 p.m., Saturday 'til noon.

Bancahsa Bank has offices nearby, at the center of "downtown," and you can get cash advances on your VISA card. Bancahsa is open from 8 a.m. to 11:30 a.m. and from 1 to 4 p.m. Monday through Friday, and open Saturday morning. Note that there is no bank in West End. For shopping, the biggest supermarket on the island is **Casa Warren** on the main street, where you can pick up supplies ranging from groceries to roasted chickens to Huggies diapers. Nearby, **Yaba Ding Ding** and **Coco Loco** are among the souvenir shops.

A new addition to Coxen Hole is the **Cruise Ship Pier** where first one, then two, and now four times weekly cruise ships arrive, disgorging 1,500 or more tourists to day trip on the island, then picking them up at night before sailing off to the next destination. The cruise-ship passengers—well-heeled, demanding, temporary—are changing the face of tourism on Roatán, as they provide an incentive for tour operators to get fleets of air-conditioned buses and for restaurants to be able to serve 500 for lunch. Operators include Premier out of Ft. Lauderdale, Norwegian out of Houston, and Commodore out of New Orleans.

Details: There is really only one main street in town, ending at the water. Halfway down on the left is the Cooper Building. There are three main exits from town to the main road: "El Triangolo" toward Sandy Bay, "Arco Iris," and "Airport" to the east.

French Harbour

Ten kilometers (6.2 miles) east of Coxen Hole is French Harbour. Unlike Sandy Bay and the West End, French Harbour is a busy working town, with fleets of fishing boats heading in and out. Unlike Coxen Hole, French Harbour has some charm. If you prefer a little bit of reality in your Paradise—you want to walk past churches and playing schoolchildren on your way from beach to restaurant—you might want to stay at French Harbour. In any case, many people come to French

James D. Gollin

The recompression chamber near Anthony's Key Resort

Harbour at least once during their stay in order to eat at **Gio's** restaurant, where the wall by the bar is plastered with photos of every Honduran President, U.S. senators, and stars such as Julio Iglesias, all of whom show up in their yachts and ask where to get a great meal. Alas, the French Harbour Yacht Club, a long-time local institution, and the Buccaneer Hotel both recently closed down, perhaps because more tourists are heading for the resorts at the West End.

The coral in the French Harbour area is just as beautiful as the reefs of the West End. In fact, the coral is nearly perfect throughout the Bay Islands. If the wind is coming from the north, kicking up the seas around Anthony's Key Resort and West End, the water around French Harbour should be calm. If it's stormy at French Harbour, head across the island. If you've booked ahead, don't worry about it. The dive boats can make their way around the island to the calm water.

Details: From the airport, it's a 15-minute ride past Dixon's Cove, Brick Bay, and Los Fuertes to French Harbour, and most of the resorts such as Fantasy Island and CoCo View are a few minutes further. Like Coxen Hole, French Harbour really has only one main road skirting the harbor, with a few entrances out to the highway. You can't get lost for long.

Oak Ridge and Beyond

Each year, developers carve another road through the hills and open up another breathtakingly beautiful bay or two to resort or residential development. Twenty-two kilometers (13.6 miles) east of Coxen Hole is the port of Oak Ridge, a great place to come if you want to get away from the resort atmosphere. Oak Ridge is a working town, and the industry is not tourism but fishing. At the **Reef House Resort** ($120 per person, all-inclusive; 800/328-8897, fax: 210/341-7942), the reef is just outside your door and the dive boat can take you farther east to fantastic dive sites or for picnics on deserted islands. Sources warn that waste flushes directly into the ocean. On the north shore, across the island from Oak Ridge, is the Garífuna community of Punta Gorda. From there you can hike through the protected watershed of the **Port Royal Park and Wildlife Reserve** to the ruins of the British fortifications at Port Royal. The reserve is formed by the largest contiguous portion of pine (*Pinus caribaea*, var. *Hondurensis)* in Honduras. The trip is easier done by boat.

Paya Bay can be reached by a well-maintained dirt road heading east from the Oak Ridge–Punta Gorda detour. A large terrace overlooks the deserted beach and there are eight Victorian-style bungalows. Come for a meal and a swim and inquire about an overnight stay.

Beyond Port Royal, at the eastern tip of Roatán is the tiny island of Santa Elena, also known as Helene, and 3 kilometers (about 1.8 miles) beyond that is Barbareta, a 5-kilometer-long isle protected as the **Barbareta Marine National Park.** In the park are the Diamond Rock rain forest, mangroves, and, of course, beautiful reefs. The 480-hectare (1,200-acre) island is the fourth largest of the Bay Islands, and has one resort, the Barbareta Beach Club

Details: The road as far as Oak Ridge Harbour is good, but if you take the turnoff for Punta Gorda, Paya Bay, and points east, be prepared for a rougher ride and fewer services.

Sandy Bay and AKR/RIMS

About 6 kilometers (3.7 miles) west of Coxen Hole, on the island's north shore, is Sandy Bay, a prime spot for scuba diving. There are about a half-dozen dive resorts in the area, but if you are on a budget you might want to continue on another 5 kilometers (3 miles) to West

End, where there are more choices. If you have the funds, consider staying at **Anthony's Key Resort,** known as AKR. If you don't stay there, make sure to come visit. It is, in many ways, the perfect place to dive.

Julio Galindo, owner of AKR, understands that environmentalism is good for business. In 1989 he bought a patrol boat and hired local spear-fishermen to protect a 3.2-kilometer (2-mile) section of reef adjacent to his resort. The explosion in reef life was so remarkable that, in 1993 a 17.6-kilometer (11-mile) section along the West End of Roatán was declared a marine park, and more locals were hired to patrol the area and prevent poaching. "My dream is to convince these guys that we can make more money by showing the turtles, lobsters, and groupers to sport divers day after day than by killing and eating them once," says Galindo. This diver-friendly idea is currently being expanded throughout the entire Bay Island chain of Roatán, Guanaja, and Utila as part of the internationally financed Bay Islands Marine Park discussed above.

At AKR, hotel owners Julio and Cheryl Galindo and their sons, Julio Jr. and Samir, who now actually manage the resort, provide an environment well suited for both education and relaxation. Mangroves and intricately weathered coral line the coast, separating 56 simple but elegant bungalows, 16 air-conditioned, most on stilts above the water. Some of the units are on a small island, Anthony's Key. There are a sandy beaches on the coastline and keys, but AKR isn't the place to go just to sun-worship and read the latest mystery novel. AKR markets the ever-present environment. In addition to the all-inclusive diving packages that most visitors purchase, there are also opportunities for snorkeling, kayaking, and horseback riding on the beach.

Most people come to dive, of course, and the diving could not be easier. Included in the cost of the dive packages, which run from $775 to $975 per week, are all meals and three boat dives per day, as well as night dives, dolphin dives, and other activities. Avid divers have their choice of a number of AKR's dive boats, which head out to different locations. The dive-site schedules are clearly displayed. As on the other islands, prime dive sites have been given wildly descriptive names, such as "Enchanted Forest" and "Bear's Den." Needless to say, there are neither trees nor bears underwater, but every site surrounding the Bay Islands offers first-class diving. Some are better for sponges, while others have a magnificent variety of tiny fish. Some are interlaced with caves, chutes, and tunnels; while others are home to sea turtles. If you want to see it all, stay with one boat as it makes the rounds. All Bay Island sites have buoys safely affixed to the reef so your dive boat will not have to drop anchor.

Started as a modest attempt by the Sandy Bay community to protect their coral reefs, the 4.2-square-kilometer (2.6-square-mile) area from Lawson Rock on the east to Gibson Bight on the west was officially designated a protected area in April 1989, becoming the first marine reserve in Honduras. With the support of local residents, the West End Marine Park received formal protection on August 1, 1993. The **Sandy Bay West End Marine Parks** now include a 13-square-kilometer (5-square-mile) area of coral reef that extends from Lawson Rock on the east around the southwest tip of the island to Key Hole on the south shore.

AKR also hosts the **Roatán Institute for Marine Science** (RIMS), a research center authorized by the Honduran government to work with bottlenose dolphins. RIMS has nine full-time staff members, including three expats. Every year RIMS hosts a conference for Honduran science teachers, providing firsthand fieldwork in the science of marine biology. RIMS also conducts research on the dolphins and undertakes aerial surveys to determine the population of aquatic mammals such as manatees. For kids, RIMS organizes special educational programs about the marine mammals and their aquatic ecosystem. For more details, contact RIMS at 445-1327, fax: 445-1329; or write them at Sandy Bay, Roatán, Honduras.

Visitors to the resort will learn much about the dolphins from daily presentations. Dolphin shows take place at 10:30 a.m. and 4:30 p.m. on weekdays. On weekends, there are three shows: 10:30 a.m. and 1:30 and 4:30 p.m. There are no shows on Wednesdays. From most visitors' point of view, sitting inches above the water on wooden chairs, sipping drinks and snapping photos, the interaction between dolphin and human is mutually beneficial, a form of scientific research combined with public education and entertainment. For closer-up interaction with the dolphins, there are daily (except Wednesday) "Encounters" around 9 a.m., noon, and 3 p.m. (check for current schedule at tel. 445-1327, fax 445-1329, e-mail rimsed@globalnet.hn) in which good swimmers under RIMS staff supervision snorkel and frolic with dolphins next to nearby Bailey's Key, and also Encounters for nonswimmers and kids.

During the summers, students from 12 universities, including Yale, Loyola, and Goucher, converge on RIMS to study marine biology; and there's also a regular "Dolphin Camp" for kids ages 8–14 whose parents are diving, involving education about and interaction with the dolphins as well as horseback riding, hikes, etc.

The dolphins are not kept in swimming pool–like enclosures, as they are at places like Sea World. These animals are linked to the local ecosystem. Their pens are separated from the AKR lagoon by nets with a mesh large enough to let schools of smaller fish pass through, but small enough to keep out predators such as sharks. Of course the nets also keep the dolphins in. But if the beasts can leap a dozen feet in the air to snag a fish from a trainer's hand they could easily leap 6 feet up and over the top of the netting.

In fact, many dolphins are regularly allowed to leave their pens to go frolic on a sandbar a few hundred yards off AKR. Non-AKR guests are allowed to sign up for these dolphin encounters, hanging out on the sandbar and waiting for the magnificent beasts to show up and play catch with conch shells, socialize, or just swim around looking for lunch, depending on their mood. Experienced divers are stunned by these marine mammals' ability to shoot up from the sea bottom, burst through the surface for a breath of air, then fire back down to finish a game of catch without pausing to balance the pressure in their ears or check their depth meters. If you wonder whether the dolphin encounter is for you, hang out at the bar at AKR and watch the videos taken daily by the trainers. The encounter takes place daily (except Wednesday) around 9 a.m., noon, and 3 p.m. (check for current schedule at tel. 445-1327, fax 445-1329, e-mail rimsed@globalnet.hn).

Everything regarding the dolphins, however, is not sunshine and light. According to dolphin-rights activists, keeping any sentient being penned up for our entertainment is degrading. The right thing to do, they say, is to set the animals free. In fact, dolphins kept in captivity for long periods can lose the ability to hunt and fend for themselves in the wild. So, say the activists, they should be retrained and gradually returned to their natural state. Jean-Michel Cousteau, of the Cousteau Society, has become a leading dolphin-rights advocate after observing a captive dolphin commit suicide by ramming its head into the wall of its pen. "The ideals of education do not abide easily in the culture of marine entertainment," says Cousteau.

Other critics of the "circuses of the sea" include the Marine Mammal Conservancy, 305/853-0675, and the Dolphin Freedom Foundation, 954/462-1817. Rick Trout, Director of Husbandry at the Marine Mammal Conservancy, is a bitter foe of the Grassy Key, Florida–based Dolphin Research Center (originally "Flipper's Sea School"), which he accuses of trafficking in the beasts for profit under the guise of science. This trade, he claims, has resulted in the unnecessary deaths of 60 dolphins. Other targets include the U.S. Navy, which has attempted to train dolphins for underwater combat and sabotage, and Anheuser-Busch, owner of Sea World.

In past years, AKR owner Julio Galindo was accused of netting wild dolphins off Punta y Sal in Jeannette Kawas National Park, near Tela. More recently, AKR/RIMS has received dolphins from institutions that can no longer keep them, such as Fort Lauderdale's failed Ocean World. AKR went to great expense to bring the animals to Roatán, chartering a special airplane, placing the animals in slings, covering them with sponges, then transporting them from Roatán's Juan Ramon Galvez International Airport to the pens at AKR in specially adapted trucks. An hour after arriving, the dolphins in question were swimming around happily, leaping up to take fish from the hands of their trainers.

Hurricane Mitch dashed the dolphin enclosures to tatters, and all 14 dolphins headed out to sea to wait out the storm. Only nine returned when things calmed down, and a new set of enclosures was built for them. It is feared that the other five did not survive, as they were raised in captivity, but some may have made the transition back to the wild.

In addition to RIMS, AKR also hosts the adjacent **Roatán Museum,** which shows the intersection of cultures and species that meet in Central America. The artifacts and display interpretations present the history of the Bay Islands in one of Central America's finest small museums. Admission is free to AKR guests; for others, it's $4. To the other side of AKR, behind the dive boat docks, is the **Cornerstone Medical Mission,** a Protestant church–funded clinic that has a fully operational hyperbaric chamber, capable of recompressing divers with the bends. While it was originally thought that the chamber would serve sport divers who stayed down too deep too long, 80 percent of the patients have turned out to be Miskito Indians caught up in the lobster trade. For more on this, see Chapter 10: The Final Frontier.

AKR also sends high-speed boats to Barbareta Island, Cayos Cochinos, and other off-Roatán locations, and has a 36-foot Hatteras and a 25 foot-Mako set up for deep-sea fishing.

Also in Sandy Bay, quite close to AKR, are the **Carambola Botanical Gardens.** The 12-hectare (30-acre) gardens, founded in 1985, showcase exotic plants, flowers, ferns, spices, and fruit trees such as the cashew and, of course, the carambola. The carambola fruit forms a star shape when sliced across the center. The gardens contain a lovely stand of Honduran mahogany and an extensive orchid collection. If, after days of diving, you're in the mood to take a short hike and dry out, take the 20-minute hike up a path leading to the summit of Carambola Mountain, which affords a vista of the island and reefs. A cliff known as Iguana Wall is an iguana and parrot breeding ground, protected from predators by its very steepness. The gardens are open daily from 7 a.m. to 5 p.m. For information, call Bill or Irma Brady at 445-1117.

Nearby is **Tropical Treasures,** with 16 species of birds, including toucans, macaws, and parrots. The $5 entrance fee includes a 30-minute tour and the chance to interact with tame birds. Expats Lloyd Davidson and Janet Matias started taking care of injured and unwanted birds a few years ago and their collection has now grown to about 80. It's open Monday to Saturday from 10 a.m. to 5 p.m.

Details: Located 6 miles west of Coxen Hole, the AKR sign is easily visible on the right side of the road. RIMS is at the far end of the AKR complex, past the boat docks and shops. For more information, contact RIMS at 445-1003, fax: 445-1140; e-mail: akr@globalnet.hn.

West End to West Bay Beach

The West End fits the image of a Caribbean paradise quite well. The white-sand beaches are gorgeous, shaded by palm trees. Small hotels, bars, and laid-back restaurants are cheap and plentiful. If you don't want an all-inclusive dive-resort experience, head 10 kilometers (6.2 miles) west of Coxen Hole to check this place out. In town are plenty of not-too-fancy places to stay for around $10 per person per night. There are also plenty of dive shops, kayak and windsurfing rental shops, and everything you could ask for to satisfy your aquatic needs. You can book your total experience ahead of time through 800 numbers or (except at Christmas or Easter) you can just show up and see what happens.

West End village is a great place to spend some time above the water wandering from bungalow to bar to beach to restaurant. If Paradise starts to get old, well, head down the beach 3 kilometers (1.8 miles) or hop a water taxi down to the very tip of the island, known as West Bay Beach. The white-sand beach is perfect, and the crystalline water is almost always calm and filled with gorgeous coral and schools of multicolored fish. Because the water is shallow quite far out from the shoreline, West End Point is ideal for snorkeling.

Just a few years ago, West Bay Beach was practically deserted. Now there area a few small restaurants and small resorts with a half-dozen bungalows spread out under the palms. But there is also some big-time real-estate development going on. Mayan Princess and Lighthouse Estates are two housing developments oriented toward expatriates buying vacation or retirement homes, Tabyana is a mega-resort open only to day trippers in from the cruise ships, and Henry Morgan is a new all-inclusive Club Med–like resort open only to people who book for an entire week, most of them Italians who arrive and depart on the weekly Milan–Roatán nonstops. The latter two resorts give patrons I.D. bracelets so their security can keep the rest of us out. The best beach on the islands, one of the finest in the Caribbean, is at West End Point, past the town of West End. You can take a water taxi from Foster's Restaurant, a great place for sunsets and Italian food, or walk along the beach.

Details: *It's only 10 kilometers (6.2 miles) from Coxen Hole to West End and there is regular minivan and taxi service. Watch out for the popular scam favored by taxi drivers. If you tell the taxista to take you to West End, he may instead try to drive you all the way to West Bay Beach and then charge you another $10 to $15 for the extra leg. This is a rip-off.*

THE OTHER ISLANDS

Guanaja

On the island of Guanaja there are no roads. Most of the 6,000 or so residents live on the water or, more precisely, over the water in

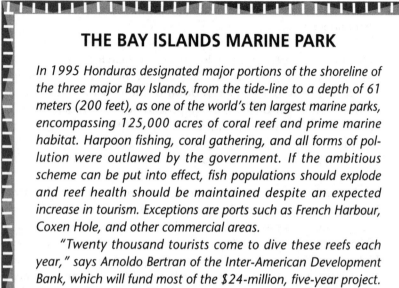

THE BAY ISLANDS MARINE PARK

In 1995 Honduras designated major portions of the shoreline of the three major Bay Islands, from the tide-line to a depth of 61 meters (200 feet), as one of the world's ten largest marine parks, encompassing 125,000 acres of coral reef and prime marine habitat. Harpoon fishing, coral gathering, and all forms of pollution were outlawed by the government. If the ambitious scheme can be put into effect, fish populations should explode and reef health should be maintained despite an expected increase in tourism. Exceptions are ports such as French Harbour, Coxen Hole, and other commercial areas.

"Twenty thousand tourists come to dive these reefs each year," says Arnoldo Bertran of the Inter-American Development Bank, which will fund most of the $24-million, five-year project. "This reef is one of the four best in the world, and key to the development of the Honduran ecotourism industry." Both environmentalists and business circles are quite pleased with the plan. "Protecting natural wonders is a good investment," points out the international financier.

houses built on stilts and linked together by a series of rickety gang-planks. To get from place to place, Guanajans will sometimes walk along the gangplanks. Usually, however, they go by sea, even if it's just down to the corner store. The main town, Bonacca, isn't even on the island of Guanaja—it's built over Hog Cay and Sheen Cay and a mud flat, some 500 yards offshore. Some suggest that the seafaring Cayman Islanders who settled the town couldn't stand the sand flies onshore. In any case, the town looks a bit like a set from *Waterworld*. Forget the image of the Kevin Costner movie, though. This town is not a put-on for tourists. This is the real thing. When Mitch tore up the entire town of Bonacca, tossing planking in the 160-mph wind

Saving a reef is more complicated than one might think, involving sewage treatment plants and sanitary landfills, terrestrial parks to protect the watersheds, and prevention of excessive coastal development. Money has been set aside both to strengthen institutions such as BICA that will be responsible for protecting the marine park and to bring in scientists to monitor the health of the reef system. Construction of housing, hotels, or restaurants on the islands will require permission from one of the four new Environmental Planning Offices to be administered by the Honduran Ministry of Natural Resources and the Bay Island Commission.

Of course, some people are unhappy with the conservation plan, such as owners of polluting industries that might be forced to shut down, and fishermen who will have to leave the reef fish alone and head for deeper water. Nevertheless, the project became operational in April 1996 and, according to the official timetable, should be self-financing within five years. Expanding tourist-oriented income is expected to generate taxes sufficient to maintain infrastructure and repay the low-interest loan over the next 40 years.

like so much straw, killing six people, the Bonaccans just came back to the same place and rebuilt.

Locals like to say that Guanaja is like Roatán used to be: quiet, friendly, slow. The main industry is not tourism but fishing, lobstering, and shrimping. The island has a number of seafood processing plants, all certified by U.S. health and safety inspectors, and most of the catch heads directly up north in refrigerated transport ships.

The diving off of Guanaja is spectacular, comparable to Roatán in most ways but even more attractive for divers who like tunnels, tubes, and arches. Off the eastern shore of the island is an unusual system of

James D. Gollin

Most houses on Guanaja are built over the water.

volcanic caves and tunnels that developed when hot lava met the cool sea. The area is called Black Rock and offers divers a chance to lose themselves in an underwater labyrinth of coral, rock, and sea. For those who like wreck dives, the 79-meter (260-foot) *Jado Trader* lies under 27 meters (90 feet) of water.

Ninety percent of the island and its surrounding reefs are at least theoretically protected by the Guanaja National Marine Park. Texas A&M University, in conjunction with the Posada del Sol resort, has launched a project to analyze coral bleaching on the offshore reefs, locate the causes, and propose mechanisms to reduce and then reverse the damage. U.S. biologists Andre Landry and Thomas Iliffe will join Honduran biologist Gustavo Cruz and graduate students from both countries in the project. Taca Airlines, Scubapro, and several Guanaja resorts are also sponsoring a four-year reef study, and Mayor Terry Zapata plans to install modern sewage treatment and landfills—tricky in a town built on stilts.

In the town of Bonacca are stores, banks, an airline ticket office, and a few small restaurants. There are also simple hotels used by local sailors, where you can sleep for a few dollars. There is even a disco on stilts that gets going late at night, helping to separate ship captains, crew, and even Miskito lobster divers from their pay. If women are friendly to you at the disco, they may well be professionals.

Unlike the rest of the Bay Islands, Guanaja sustained major damage from Hurricane Mitch. Imagine standing on the roof of your car while it's going 80 mph. Then imagine winds twice that speed. It's hardly surprising that most buildings were damaged or obliterated. Further, the salt from the sea coated the pine trees of the island, killing 90 percent of them. Successful reforestation projects are underway, but the fate of the water's-edge mangrove forests is still uncertain. The mangroves, one of nature's toughest plants, were killed off by the storm and efforts to replant mangrove seedlings have been foiled by crabs who think the seedlings are delicious. Without healthy mangroves, coastal erosion and reef sedimentation are a distinct possibility.

Details: Guanaja, 18 kilometers (11 miles) long and 6 kilometers (3.7 miles) wide, is the most mountainous of the Bay Islands, with the hilly interior rising to 427 meters (1,400 feet). There are daily flights from La Ceiba and less-frequent flights from Roatán and Utila.

Utila

Utila is the smallest of the Bay Islands and the closest island to mainland Honduras. In fact, it's just 32 kilometers (18 miles) from the coast. The island lies on the continental shelf with shallow coral gardens, habitat for a great variety of tropical fish.

Utila is home to about 2,000 people, most of whom live along a protected bay at the southeastern end of the island. Utila is famous for its architecture—brightly painted houses with gingerbread trim and wide porches. It is sometimes referred to as the "Rose of Honduras."

Utila is flatter than hilly Roatán and Guanaja. The central portion of the island is a low-lying mangrove swamp. Because of its flatness, researchers believe that Utila may have been a coral atoll. The eastern tip of the island is a dormant volcanic cone called Pumpkin Hill—which, at 91 meters (300 feet), is the highest point on the island. A 4.8-kilometer (3-mile) trail leads to the hill from town. According to legend, pirates hid their treasures in the caves nearby.

Most activity on the island takes place near the small airport. From the airstrip, cross over the Upper Lagoon on a small bridge and you are in town. You will be met by friendly folks offering you a place to stay, a certification course, a private dive boat. Follow the road to the Lower Lagoon, where there is no bridge. Turn around and walk back and you have seen pretty much all there is to see above the waterline on Utila, except for a few newer resorts that you'll need a water taxi to reach. The one land taxi in town can bring you and your bags down the road to the landing strip if your hotel is far away or you are too tired to carry all your gear.

The island has a few beaches nestled in the reef-protected bays of its north shore. One great option for a day off from diving is to rent a boat and visit the nearby cays, mostly clustered off the south-western corner of the island. The nicest is Water Key, popular for camping and snorkeling. Only six people are allowed on the island at a time to prevent overcrowding. Morgan Key and Sandy Key have private homes that can be rented. Ask in town or call George Jackson at 425-3161.

While Roatán has sprouted first-class resorts and is comfortable for doctors and lawyers on vacation, Utila is much more of a casual traveler's hangout. Divers visiting Utila tend to be younger and European (there are always a great number of Germans), and to have more holes pierced in their bodies than visitors to the other islands. Utila is hippie-friendly, largely because it is the cheapest place on the islands—some say in the world—to get certified. While the diving facilities are cut-rate, rental equipment is still well maintained. The cheaper certification price, however, means less personalized attention. A PADI certification course is available from Cross Creek PADI Dive Center and Hotel (425-3134); the four-day course costs $150. Other options include Utila Watersports (425-3134), Utila Dive Center (425-3226), Bay Islands College of Diving (425-3145, 800/282-8932), and Underwater Vision (425-3103). Courses include both book and field tests. Some of the dive centers offer specialty courses: Bay Islands College of Diving, for example, offers a Marine Awareness Course. As you shop around, remember that the cheapest offer is not necessarily the best bargain.

The coral reefs that surround the island include walls of the north coast that plunge into the Cayman Trench. The south coast, in turn, boasts a fantastic variety of fish. Conservation has been assisted by the establishment of the Turtle Harbour Marine

Reserve and Wildlife Refuge. Be aware that, since 1996, all tourists pay a $5 tax to visit Utila. Proceeds fund projects that include Utila Marine Park, coral-reef protection programs, and the creation of the Utila Wildlife Refuge. Visitors purchase the "pass" before their departure from Utila. BICA has a visitors center in front of Mermaid's Restaurant. Donations and profits are funneled into conservation efforts.

Bikes are available for rent at the budget hotel Blue Bayou, at the end of the path heading toward the Lower Lagoon.

Details: *It would be extremely hard to get lost on Utila. The landing strip lies at one end of town, and there is essentially just one road. Actually, it's more of a path than a road.*

Cayos Cochinos

The archipelago of Cayos Cochinos (Hog Islands) is a group of small islands 14 kilometers (9 miles) from the mainland. There are two larger and 13 smaller cays. They are not technically, nor are they generally thought of as being, a part of the Bay Islands, but the sand, sea, and coral quality are quite similar. In other words, they are quite beautiful.

If you are planning on staying at the islands' only hotel, the Plantation Beach Resort, its dive boat can take you from the main pier in La Ceiba in about one hour. It is possible to reach Cayos Cochinos from the mainland in a sea kayak, but this should be attempted only with an experienced guide. Strong currents can carry the unaware off to the Mosquito Coast.

Nearly the entire system of islands and coral, 460 square kilometers (178 square miles) in total, is now a biological reserve, the **Santuario Marino Cayos Cochinos,** under the supervision of the Smithsonian Institution. With financial backing from Swiss industrialist Estefan Schmidheiny, the Smithsonian Tropical Research Institute operates a field station on Cochino Pequeño that carries out basic studies on the ecology of the archipelago's plants and animals. Line fishing is permitted and net fishing by local Garífuna fishermen is permitted two days per month in two specific areas. The restrictions—and reported institutional arrogance—have caused outrage among the small Garífuna community that still lives on the islands, farming and, of course, fishing.

YELLOW PALM

While on the islands, you might notice coconut palms with yellowed leaves. This is the result of a disease known as lethal yellowing. The disease—caused by microbes that are carried from tree to tree by insects called planthoppers—have been reported on Guanaja and in Trujillo on mainland Honduras.

The effects of lethal yellowing can be devastating. It has destroyed 10 million coconut palms (Cocos nucifera) in Jamaica and 1 million in both Florida and Mexico. Consequently, quarantine measures have been imposed by the Ministry of Natural Resources. Susceptible palms include cabada, canary date, Chinese and Fiji fan, footstool, latan, palmyra, and princess varieties. The royal palm is generally considered to be resistant, and cohune and African oil palms have proven resistant in Mexico and Belize.

The theory is that lethal yellowing arrived in Cancún, Mexico, in the late 1970s by means of infected planthoppers (M. crudus) on grass imported from Florida for hotel development. How it migrated to the Bay Islands remains a mystery. But the uncontrolled importation of nonnative species for plantings around new resorts is a prime suspect. Resort owners are scurrying to plant resistant species on their property so their guests can continue to watch the sun set though waving fronds. But there is no telling how many birds, insects, and animals that live in and among the endangered palm species will be able to adapt to a different species.

While on the islands, if you run into Bobby Griffith, the Taipan of Cayos Cochinos, or Billy Kibbet, another local, make sure to ask them for stories about local history.

Details: *To get to the islands, go to the Garífuna town of Nueva Armenia, east of La Ceiba, and negotiate for a motorized dugout known as*

*a dory. You should pay around $10 each way, and make sure to depart
extremely early unless you are planning to spend the night on the islands.
The sea often gets uncomfortably rough in the afternoon.*

LODGING

In Sandy Bay, **Anthony's Key Resort** (445-1003; in the United States
c/o Bahia Tours, 800/227-3483; e-mail: bahia@gate.net; $135) is a
great place for all-inclusive dive packages and more. Nearby, the
Oceanside Inn (445-1552; $44) is a cozy eight-room hotel. **Sunnyside
Bed and Breakfast** (445-0006; $40) is a beachfront home that offers
home-cooked breakfasts with a view.

In the West End, **Lost Paradise Cabins** (445-1306; $68) has
recently remodeled its cabins located at the end of the road, toward
West Bay. **Half Moon Bay Cottages** (445-1075, $74) is a great resort,
with one of the best restaurants in town and various sea-amenities
such as a glass-bottomed boat and a semi-submarine. **Seagrapes
Plantation** (445-1429, $60), a half a mile north of West End village,
has an inclusive hotel/restaurant/dive shop package. Sixteen double
rooms in eight bungalows are spread out over 4.4 hectares (11 acres).
For a complete listing of literally dozens more West End hotels, check
out www.honduras.com/hondurastips/westendhotels.htm.

In West Bay, reasonable resorts include **Banana Rama** (445-1271;
$45) and **Las Rocas** (445-1841; www.lasrocasresort.com, $85). The
Mayan Princess (445-5525, $125) and **Tabyana** (445-1805, $85) bring
up the high end.

In French Harbour, **Coco View** is a lovely diver's resort on a 2.8-
hectare (7-acre) island reachable by boat from French Harbour.
Coco View is dedicated to travelers whose first priority is diving. There
are excellent shore dives from Coco View, including a wall 100 meters
(328 feet) out and a sunken freighter in 20 meters (65 feet) of water
in front of the resort. Coco View is represented in the United States
by Roatán Charter (445-5011, 352/588-4132, 800/282-8932; $725 per
person per week).

El Faro (455-5214; $35), right on the water at the harbor
entrance, above Gio's restaurant, is French Harbour's newest hotel.
All rooms have air conditioning and television, and sea kayaks are

WANT TO OWN A BIT OF PARADISE?

According to Article 107 of the Honduran Constitution, foreigners can't own land within 40 kilometers of the coastline, for national security reasons, with the exception of urban areas. Always ready to work an angle, the Bay Islands declared themselves an urban area, opening up a boom in real-estate investment and speculation by foreigners, mostly North Americans. To purchase a piece of land larger than a half-acre, which is the official limit, foreigners simply need to set up a Honduran corporation and have that corporation purchase the land. Developments range from Parrot Tree Plantation, east of Fantasy Island on Roatán, where condos, homes, and commercial space are available in a gated community that is a ZOLT, or tax-free zone, to people paying $6,000 to $10,000 for an individual plot of land and to restaurateurs paying up to $450,000 for 100 feet of waterfront in West Bay Beach. In general, a $50,000 investment is enough to establish legal residency in Honduras. For more information, contact Gayle Hood at J. Edwards Real Estate, 455-5917, e-mail: jedwards@globalnet.hn.

available for rental. El Faro is often booked up with marine biologists from the Cousteau Society, so phone ahead to be sure of a room. El Faro is owned by Giovanni Silvestri, while his brother Romeo owns the **Casa Romeo** (455-5518) nearby, above Romeo's restaurant. Their father was the founder of Ricardo's restaurant in La Ceiba; clearly good things run in this family.

Fantasy Island (455-5119; in the United states 800/676-2826; $120), a resort on a 6-hectare (15-acre) cay 2 kilometers (1.2 miles) east of French Harbour is the best place or the worst place on Roatán, depending on your attitude. If you want air conditioning, carpeting, satellite TV, and a good bar scene, come here. Original owner Albert Jackson also owns the nearby Agua Azul seafood processing plant and the mall and movie theater near Coxen Hole. When a competitor began to pay higher wages and treat his workers better than Jackson's, the Taipan sent his thugs to deliver a coffin to the upstart as an ominous warning. Jackson also destroyed a reef to build Fantasy Island. New management took over the hotel in 2000.

Up Island, **Reef House Resort** (435-2297) in Oak Ridge has rooms with three meals and diving for $120, while **Paya Bay Resort** (435-2139) has similar offerings. **Barbareta Beach Resort** (445-1062) has rooms at $35.

On Utila, there are plenty of cheap hotels with rooms for around $10 per night, such as **Sonny's Villa** and **Captain Spencer's.** You get what you pay for, but that may well be enough. You should also be aware that, except at the higher-priced resorts, there is usually no electricity on Utila between midnight and 5 a.m., so don't get too used to that ceiling fan. For higher-end places, try **Laguna Beach Resort** (425-3239, 800/66-UTILA) on the far side of the Lower Lagoon, accessible by boat. **Utila Lodge** (425-3143, 800/282-8932) is near the Hondutel office, on the water, in the western part of town and offers $650 week-long all-inclusive dive packages. Dedicated sport fishermen and those looking for something a little more upscale should head here. Two boats and trained staff are ready to head out in search of marlin, tarpon, snook, and bonefish. All rooms are air-conditioned with attached screened-in porches. **Sharkey's Resort** (425-3212; $20) is a mid-range hotel located near the landing strip. Harry Jackson (alias Sharkey) can arrange for scuba diving, fishing, boat trips, or anything else you might desire. You can hire a local fisherman to take you around the island (a full day) for $20. Sharkey's actively supports coral-reef research on the island and has participated in sea turtle–rearing projects in the past.

Hurricane Mitch caused tremendous damage to Guanaja, shutting down every resort and hotel for a time. They are all up and running again, but be aware that some damage to trees and mangroves will still be evident for years to come. **Bayman Bay Club** (453-4191; in the United states 800/524-1823) is one of the island's top resorts. On the northwest corner of the main island, it runs $270 per person per day, including meals and diving. The club is more like a rain-forest lodge, with 16 hardwood cottages, each with balconies, breezes, and views of the sea. The cottages are set amid dense foliage on a steep hill that runs down to a beach and a 91-meter (300-foot) dock built out over the coral. The hotel is represented in the United States by Terra Firma Adventures. **Nautilus** (453-4389, 800/535-7063) is another good resort; it runs $130 for a double, with meals, and $180 for a double with unlimited diving. **Posada del Sol** (668-3348, 800/642-DIVE; e-mail: posada@hondutel.hn), east of Nautilus, runs $130 for a double for nondivers and around $1,000 for a week, all-inclusive, including unlimited diving. The resort is built in the Spanish style, with tile floors and high-beamed ceilings, with 72 acres of grounds rising back into the hills from 457 meters (1,500 feet) of beach front. This luxury resort has a deep commitment to reef protection and is highly recommended.

For those who want a hotel instead of a resort, **Hotel Alexander** (453-4326; $30), in town overlooking Pond Cay, has clean rooms and three-bed apartments. **Hotel Miller** (453-4327) in Bonacca town has simple rooms for $30.

On Cayos Cochinos, the only place to stay is the **Plantation Beach Resort** (442-0974, 800/628-3723; e-mail: hkinett@hondutel.hn) where weekly all-inclusive packages start at $750. On privately owned Cayo Grande, the largest island, the resort has room for 20 people in ten hardwood-and-stone cabins. There's very little to do besides dive, snorkel, read, eat, and sleep. The resort owners and divers carefully follow the Smithsonian guidelines for preserving the area.

FOOD

In Roatán's West End, try **Half Moon Bay** (445-1075) on the north edge of town. For an upscale meal, the seafood here is phenomenal. Owner Rene Seron has been turning out great meals for decades. Keep an eye out for newcomer **Gio's Paradise,** a branch of the original Gio's in French Harbour, a great place for King Crab. The **Coconut Tree,** on the corner at the entrance to town, is a sports bar and restaurant, where passers by shout up to patrons ask the latest score. The **Bite on the Beach** is a great place for fresh seafood and sunset views. Also on the beach, **Papagayos** is a good place, as is Pinnochio's. Sea Ray, over Sueño del Mar dive shop, sits on stilts over the water, as does Fosters, a bit further down. Both are great places to have a beer and watch the sun set. If you want to fix your own meal, head to **Eldon's** grocery, just off the beach.

In French Harbour, be sure to visit the famous **Gio's Restaurant,** on the water by the harbor, famous for oversize Caribbean king crab dinners, as well as lobster, grilled fish with cilantro jalapeño, and a variety of other dishes. Gio is on hand every night attending to his guests. You can eat in air conditioning inside, or out by the water. See how many Honduran presidents or U.S. senators you can recognize from the photos on the wall, all famous folks who stopped in for the famous crabs. If you're inspired, pick up an "I Got Crabs at Gio's" T-shirt. Nearby, **Romeo's** restaurant serves excellent food in a quiet environment, also with indoor and outdoor dining areas.

On Utila, most of the hotels have their own restaurants, but for something different, head to the **Bucket of Blood Bar,** 1 block inland from Bancahsa on the inland road, famous for its drinks as well as novelty T-shirts. The bar is just a few meters from a private Victorian-style house, where fruit trees and bushes attract almost a dozen varieties of hummingbirds. **Mermaid's Corner Restaurant,** at the Point, specializes in pasta. Marjorie Fleming provides a wealth of local information, not to mention good food. **Thompson's Bakery,** on the inland road, has the best breakfasts in town and is open only in the mornings from 6 a.m. to noon. **Bundu Café** has a full cappuccino bar and light meals. The **Jade Seahorse,** up the Cola de Mico road from the municipal dock, is an eclectic place famous for seafood and odd décor, set in a lovely tropical garden.

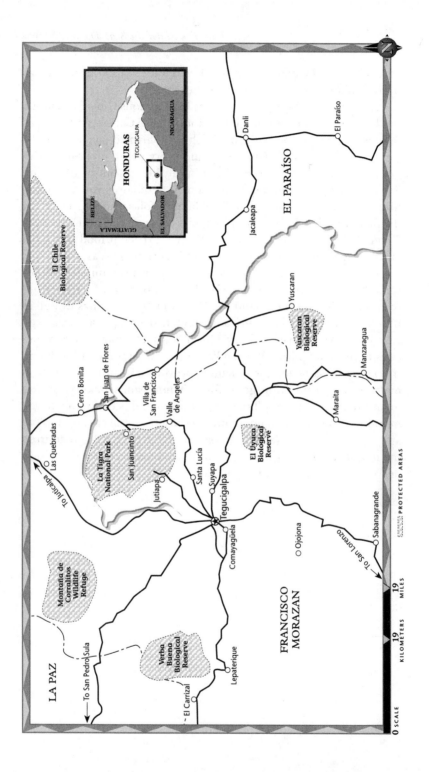

CHAPTER 7

Tegucigalpa and the Mining Towns

Tegucigalpa, the capital of Honduras, is not a colonial gem, but it does have a beauty of its own. Built upon the fortunes of silver, it has raced into the 21st century and now sports a buffet of fast-food joints from Wendy's to McDonald's to Pizza Kitchen and their Central American imitators. The once-grand colonial architecture now houses mini-malls. Parts of Teguz (pronounced "tay-GOOSE" by the locals) have a certain *Blade Runner*–esque charm. While there's little reason to spend a great deal of time in the metropolis, surrounding mountain towns such as Santa Lucía, Valle de Angeles, and San Juancito are worth a visit, as is the local national park, La Tigra (The Tiger), close enough for an easy day trip. A bit farther afield, Zamorano, Yuscaran, and Danlí all have their distinct attractions.

Tegucigalpa, with a population of more than a million, is the seat of the government, and the buzz in this town is definitely political. With budgets tight and many jobs filled by political appointees, resources to get anything done are as short as interest in achieving the lofty goals put forth by politicians at election time. Many bureaucrats hide behind their desks, inactive, but others are taking a chance, stepping out, and helping Honduras step forward.

As the nation's capital, Tegucigalpa is the headquarters of many of the country's environmental groups as well as of government offices, the Ministry of Natural Resources and COHDEFOR,

James D. Gollin

Tegucigalpa

the forestry agency charged with overseeing the protected areas system. Unlike the regional environmental groups, the Tegucigalpa-based groups do not act as tour providers, but if you're looking for in-depth information or would like to volunteer time or services, it's best to contact them directly. Important groups based in Tegucigalpa include Proyecto Aldea Global (PAG), AMITIGRA, and MOPAWI.

HISTORY AND CULTURE

In the Indian language Nahuatl Tegucigalpa means "silver mountain," and, indeed, the city's history is inextricably linked to the mining of precious metals. The city was founded in 1578 as the Real de Minas de San Miguel de Tegucigalpa in honor of the mother lode of silver that was discovered on St. Michael's Day. Although no one seems to have kept records, it is estimated that $160 million in gold was taken out of the mountain beneath La Tigra, as well as enormous amounts of silver and other minerals. While mining is no longer a major industry today, most towns in the Tegucigalpa region owe their existence to the pursuit of silver and gold.

Tegucigalpa's location in a valley 914 meters (3,000 feet) above sea level, surrounded by mountains much higher still, made it an inauspicious choice as a seat of government. Tegucigalpa was a simple mining town while Comayagua served as the capital during much of the colonial era. In 1880 Tegucigalpa took on the role of national capital when, according to the commonly accepted story, the wife of President Marco Aurelio Soto pressured her husband to move the capital away from the Comayaguan society that had snubbed her. A more practical explanation for the shift in the location of the capital is that President Soto was a partner in the Rosario Mining Company, centered in San Juancito near Tegucigalpa.

The mineral wealth triggered a major construction boom. Indeed, many of the buildings in central Tegucigalpa date from the 19th century. Similarly, it was the immense mineral wealth that, in the early 1800s, brought the first U.S. embassy in Honduras not to Comayagua or even downtown Tegucigalpa, but to El Rosario, the mining camp near San Juancito.

The city is bisected by the rather polluted Choluteca River. Technically, what lies south and west of the river is Comayagüela (not to be confused with Comayagua) and to the north of the river is Tegucigalpa proper, but since 1938 the entire metropolitan area has been referred to as Tegucigalpa, or Teguz. With the exception of the airport, Comayagüela offers little to the visitor and is reputed to be significantly more dangerous than the neighborhoods across the river. You might notice that Tegucigalpa area addresses are often followed by D.C., which stands for Distrito Central (Central District).

Teguz's population is growing steadily as landless peasants abandon exhausted soil and head for the city, hoping for a better life. Slums and shantytowns dot the outskirts of the city. The urban population is estimated at 800,000, far more than city services can handle. The airport is inadequate, requiring approaching planes to bank heavily to avoid the surrounding mountains. There is no railroad, and the Pan-American Highway passes through Honduras well to the south, along the Pacific coast. Buses are crowded, traffic chokes the streets, and the distinctly irrational maze of streets is confusing.

But despite all that Teguz exudes a certain charm. Indian women roast corn and hawk tortillas by the roadside under sooty, crumbling walls built in colonial times. Hookers strut their stuff, young lovers wander through small parks, fast-food joints sell fried pigskin wrapped in tortillas, Chinese immigrants stand in the front doors of their small groceries, all in a benign, friendly way. The city is decaying, yes, but gently. Many streets are still cobblestone or too narrow and steep for cars. So people walk. If this is the way the world will look after the apocalypse, things won't be so bad.

ORIENTATION

While San Pedro, La Ceiba, and Choluteca are built on easy-to-understand grid patterns, Tegucigalpa seems to have been laid out by a drunken miner leading a recalcitrant mule. Roads twist up and down hills, curve back onto themselves, and angle oddly, a situation further complicated by a vain attempt to introduce vehicular order through a series of one-way streets. To further confuse things, many streets have been renamed with numbers, with Calles heading east–west and Avenidas north–south, but the locals still use the old names. The center of Tegucigalpa, around the Parque Central, is referred to as El Centro.

When in doubt, grab a cab, which should take you to any destination in Tegucigalpa for around $2. If the driver sizes you up as a newcomer he might attempt to charge much more, so negotiate before setting off. If the driver is unreasonable, simply look for another cab. If he picks up another passenger heading in the same direction, relax and smile. It's normal in Tegucigalpa. If you like the driver, consider hiring him and his car for longer excursions, up to El Picacho or out to Santa Lucía and Valle de Angeles. The typical half-day rate is $25, depending on how much gasoline will be needed.

Tegucigalpa's Toncontín International Airport is just 5 kilometers (3.1 miles) south of the Parque Central, making entry and egress easy for some 1.5 million passengers who use the terminal each year. The best news is that after years of public outcry and numerous accidents, the airport will receive a $20-million renovation that will include extending the runway 300 meters (984 feet), leveling surrounding hills, and demolishing a nearby neighborhood. The departure lounge was recently rebuilt, and you can even get a cappuccino as you wait to check in.

Cabs into town cost $7 or, if you take your bag and walk 100 meters (about 200 yards) down to the street, $3. There is a bank at the airport, open irregular hours, but money changers just outside the rather shoddy terminal will offer good rates for U.S. dollars. Street urchins will run and find you a money changer or attempt to carry your bag to a taxi in exchange for a tip. You'll have to hold onto your bags tightly if you don't want to play their game. While it's no fun driving around downtown Teguz, the airport is a good place to rent a car.

Tegucigalpa was hit rather severely by Hurricane Mitch, with 40 inches of rain falling in six hours. The resultant flooding brought the river up 65 to 95 meters (about 20 to 30 feet) and destroyed the homes of 10,000 families. When the rains stopped there was fear that the heat, filthy water, and un-retrieved bodies would create a plague-like atmosphere, but the people of Tegucigalpa and the foreign aid crews teamed up to avert a secondary wave of disease-related deaths. Indeed, the World Food Program brought 70,000 metric tons of corn in to Honduras to avoid starvation. Since the total annual consumption of Honduras is only about 50,000 tons, according to the FAO (the Food and Agriculture Organization of the United Nations), the surplus made it hard for farmers to sell their first post-Mitch crops.

THINGS TO SEE AND DO IN DOWNTOWN TEGUCIGALPA

Tegucigalpa's **Parque Central,** also referred to as the Plaza Morazán, is a good landmark to locate early in your stay. In the center of the park is a statue of Francisco Morazán, the national hero of Honduras, astride a powerful stallion. Looming over the east side of the Parque are the twin towers of the Cathedral of San Miguel, built in the late 18th century. It is noted for pillars in the form of mermaids, for pleated columns, and for ornate gold and silver altarpieces. You can also visit the cathedral's museum of colonial religious art, open weekday afternoons and Sunday mornings. South of the cathedral, at 3a Calle, are the municipal government offices where, in September 1821, the Declaration of Independence of Central America was ratified.

West of the Parque, around 4a Calle, are various streets lined with all the fast-food joints from home as well as a few local variants, a Radio Shack, banks, street vendors, and higher-end clothing shops. A bit further west, follow 5a Avenida north toward the **Iglesia de los Dolores,** which was established in 1732. Its golden altars testify to the mineral-related riches that rolled through Tegucigalpa a century ago. On 7a Avenida is the 17th-century **Plaza de Merced,** built by Mercedian monks, presently the site of the Museo del Hombre Hondureño, the Museum of the Honduran Man, which we have never been tempted to visit.

For a break visit the Parque La Concordia on 2a Avenida, a small park containing replicas of stelae from Copán, a botanical garden, and a tiny lake. The **Museo Nacional,** a bit further north and east, was the home of former President Lozano and now has displays on pre-colonial Honduras, the encounter with Spain, and the colonial era. The most interesting displays are on Honduras's ethnic and indigenous groups including the Lenca, Chorti, Miskito, Pech, Tawahka, Jicaque, Isleña, and Garífuna.

In addition, Tegucigalpa is the base for the Instituto Hondureño de Antroplogía y Historia (**Honduran Institute of Anthropology and History**), a good stop for those interested in archaeological findings. Archaeologists, biologists, and other academics are generally associated with the most important Honduran university, the Universidad Nacional Autonoma de Honduras, known as UNAH. The biology department is first-rate, with faculty such as Gustavo Cruz and Sherry "Pilar" Thorne. So few foreigners come to places like this asking questions that, as long as you are polite and patient, you may well be rewarded with fascinating conversations and an invitation to lunch.

Tegucigalpa is, of course, a good place to get Honduran or onward visas. A list of embassies and consulates appears in Appendix B.

If you are in Teguz for more than a day, take the time to follow El Hatillo, a corkscrew twister of a road, north toward the 1,270-meter (4,167-foot) summit of **El Picacho.** The view from the higher elevations is magnificent, and you will find yourself in what appears to be a different city, with a different climate. Up on the hill the air is clean, houses are well kept up, and there are spacious parks, including the Parque de Las Nacionas Unidas, the United Nations Park, created to honor the 40th anniversary establishment of the United Nations. Honduras's National Zoo is within the park; admission is 10L. A German-Honduran family has operated the zoo single-handedly for years, and is just now receiving national and international support. Many of the animals adopted from private collections had been neglected prior to their arrival at the zoo. You'll find a good collection of Central American birds and monkeys, along with the American grizzly bear and African lion.

It is no surprise that many embassies and much embassy and expatriate housing is located uphill from the toiling heat of downtown Teguz. Once up the hill, you can continue on to Jutiapa and one of the two entrances to La Tigra National Park. Near the Jutiapa entrance are a couple of B&Bs, La Estancia and Quinta Linda, in the town of Corralito.

Biologist Olvin Andino has developed an iguana farm, La Granja de Iguanas, on the south side of Teguz on Calle Principal 28-25 in Colonia La Joya. Once in the area, ask for La Granja de Iguanas, or call 230-6346. You're welcome to photograph, videotape, or touch the green beasts. The iguana population is kept at around 300. Each year, 10 percent of the population is released into national parks by COHDE-FOR and the rest is sold to the pet market, satisfying a traditional local demand and relieving pressure on the iguanas still in the wild.

Tom Taylor runs **Shakespeare and Company Bookstore** near the Granada hotels, a book exchange where used books often sell at half-price or trade at quarter-price. The store functions as a café where you can meet other travelers and Hondurophiles. Check out the bulletin board; browse the books in English, Spanish, German, French, and Dutch. Tom also offers trips to La Tigra ($20) and overnight excursions to La Muralla, and his Tobacco Road Cavern behind the main Cathedral is a great place for a beer.

The **Honduran Institute of Interamerican Culture** is located on Calle Real in Comayagüela. Plans are to move to a new headquarters on Boulevard Centroamerica in Tegucigalpa. The center has a large library and an art gallery.

Librería Guayamuras, downtown on Avenida Cervantes (232-4140), offers the best selection of Honduran books. It also publishes a variety of interesting titles on such subjects as politics, sociology, and women's issues. There are not many books on environmental issues, but this may change in the near future.

Metromedia, on Avenida San Carlos (421-0770), has Honduras's largest stock of English-language books, magazines, and videos. Owner Michael Midence moved the former Book Village from Los Castaños shopping center to a new residence (with a new name) 2 blocks away, 2 blocks behind the American Embassy. The new store has a large collection of children's books as well a video collection and coffee shop.

On weekends, handicraft bargains can be found at the **Artesanias** market at Parque El Soldado in Comayagüela. Hide your wallet and hold onto your camera in this neighborhood.

The **San Isidro** market, just across the river from the Parque Central, is the main utilitarian market for Tegucigalpa and a fun place to browse. Again, take precautions with your valuables.

The Associacion Nacional de Artesanos de Honduras has a shop, the **Tienda de Artesano,** on the south side of Parque Valle. **Candu,** on Avenida República de Chile across from the Hotel Honduras Maya, is where visiting diplomats shop for souvenirs. There are also many shops near the Iglesia Dolores

THINGS TO SEE AND DO OUTSIDE TEGUCIGALPA

Eight kilometers (5 miles) southeast of downtown Tegucigalpa, the suburb of **Suyapa** is the site of a 6-inch statue of the Virgin Mary that, according to the faithful, materialized miraculously in a cornfield in 1743. The statue is said to have effected various cures and other miracles and is now housed in a large basilica, replete with giant stained-glass windows. Pilgrims visit Suyapa throughout the year, but for the nonfaithful it is best to visit on a religious holiday, especially during the early February Feast of the Virgin and the following two weeks. Also in Suyapa is the Ciudad Universitaria, the main campus of UNAH, the Universidad Nacional Autonoma de Honduras.

Heading East, **Santa Lucía** is a lovely former mining town just 16 kilometers (10 miles) from downtown Teguz. At an altitude of 1,524 meters (about 5,000 feet), the air is significantly cooler and flowers grow abundantly. White homes with neat black grills and red-tiled roofs line cobbled roads, while lush green trees surround colonial churches. Santa Lucía is an altogether pleasant place. Stroll the cobbled lanes or take a hike in the countryside. In the town's main church, be sure to notice the crucifix with the black Christ, donated in 1574 by King Philip II of Spain in thanks for the mineral wealth that Santa Lucía produced.

Many long-term expatriate residents live in Santa Lucía, including Chet Thomas, director of PAG, and writer and painter Guillermo Yuscarán (a.k.a. Bill Lewis). Guillermo is the world's greatest expert on the noted primitive painter José Antonio Velazquez, who lived in the nearby mining town of San Antonio de Oriente. Santa Lucía is also the main training center in Honduras for the U.S. Peace Corps, so you may well come across a group of young Americans learning about water sanitation or tilapia ponds. Santa Lucía is also probably the only place in Honduras, if not in all of Central America, where you can get a good Czech meal, at the Marushka restaurant.

Artisan's shop in Valle de Angeles

211

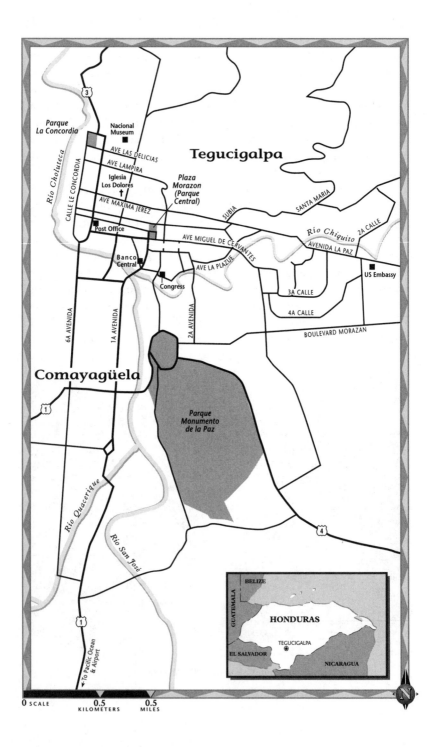

While many Santa Lucíans now commute to and from Tegucigalpa every day, a significant local business is the cultivation of flowers destined for both domestic and export markets.

Just 30 kilometers (19 miles) from Tegucigalpa, past Santa Lucía, is another charming former mining town, this one appropriately named **Valley of the Angels** (Valle de Angeles). As in Santa Lucía, the adobe houses here are plastered with white lime and covered with red tile. The town has been called the Chichicastenango (a city in Guatemala) of Honduras (as has La Esperanza) due to the extensive handicraft production in the town. Local woodcarvers, leather workers, weavers, painters, and ceramic artists show their wares in countless small shops, and handicrafts from other parts of Honduras are also available. One of the most famous local shops is Lessandra Leather.

Valle de Angeles has many pleasant restaurants, most with terraced gardens. Outside of town is the appealing Restaurante Turistico Valle de Angeles, set in a pine forest.

Flowers are always in bloom in Valle de Angeles, a town of eternal springtime. Unfortunately, the town church has been modernized and has lost much of its charm. Valle de Angeles has been officially declared a tourist zone, which means no further modernization is likely. Most of the center of town has been restored to look as it did in the 16th century. Santa Lucía is cool and Valle de Angeles cooler still, so bring something to keep you warm.

From Valle de Angeles it is a 20-minute drive to San Juancito. After Valle de Angeles the paved road ends, but an excellent dirt road continues on to San Juancito, a little mountain town that clings to the side of the cliff, more reminiscent of Nepal than Central America. Most people in this area walk or ride horses. Cars are not terribly useful on the steep terrain, and 56 houses were lost during the rains of Hurricane Mitch. Unlike its picturesque neighbors, San Juancito did not cease mining at the end of the colonial period. The business of pulling silver and gold from the earth persisted here until the late 1950s. Once home to the richest silver mine in Central America, San Juancito was the site of the first electric light bulb and the first Pepsi-Cola bottling plant in the region. San Juancito has been declared a national historic site, and one day there will be a history museum, hotels, and perhaps even a cable car up to El

James D. Gollin

San Juancito

Rosario. For now, the town is slow and friendly, a stopping point on the way up to La Tigra.

From San Juancito you'll need a four-wheel-drive vehicle to make it up the last 4 kilometers (2.5 miles) to **El Rosario,** the old head-quarters of the Rosario Mining Company. Otherwise, you can walk or hitch a ride. Be aware that the road rises about 396 meters (1,300 feet) over that short distance. Rosario is at 1,580 meters (5,184 feet).

During the boom, which started in 1879 and persisted until 1954, El Rosario was home to 4,000 men and many families; workers hailed from every corner of the globe. Now the old wooden houses are quiet, except for the occasional park guard or tourist on their way into or out of the park.

La Tigra National Park

La Tigra, a wonderful cloud forest filled with dense vegetation and rich animal life, is remarkable in that its closest entrance is only 11 kilometers from Tegucigalpa. One of the best-developed national parks in Honduras, it was first declared a protected area in 1959 and received national park status in 1980. The park is supervised by the nonprofit ecological foundation AMITIGRA.

Many visitors choose to approach the park through San Juancito. It is possible to enter through that town, hike through the park, and return to Tegucigalpa from the Jutiapa entrance. On the San Juancito side, just before the entrance sign that welcomes you to La Tigra, there's a white house belonging to Doña Amalia, who will offer you a *plato típico* for about $1.50 as well as beer or soft drinks. It's a good idea to head into the park with some food in your stomach and a full water bottle. Also, elevations in the park are as high as 2,290 meters (7,513 feet), so remember to bring something warm and, preferably, waterproof.

A few hundred yards beyond Doña Amalia's is the ghost town of El Rosario, a once-booming town built into the cliffside. Due to the steepness of the terrain, houses are built on long stilts. The place has outrageous views, clean air, and a quiet charm. The old hospital building has been converted into a dormitory for visitors. There's room for 30 people in the old hospital, but for the moment you'll have to bring your own sleeping bag.

Guide Franklin Amendares is in charge of the visitors center that stocks maps and information on flora, fauna, and geology. There is a cafeteria serving full meals and an Eco-Albergo with ten rooms and two adjoining houses, some with private bath, for $10 per night. Guides are available, including trained biologists such as Ivo Alvarado, but the trails are well marked and a simple map can guide your cloud-forest wandering. It's possible to walk across to the park's other entrance, which has a similar visitors center, in about 2.5 hours along an old, overgrown mining road. Although it would be a great mountain-biking route, no bikes are allowed on the old road. A favorite walk is the Rosario Road, which leads to a 30-meter (100-foot) waterfall about 90 minutes in. From there, head back to Rosario or take the Cascade Lane west to the San Juancito Road and Mist Forest Lane, which leads to the Jutiapa visitors center. Other trails include Hope and Plancitos Lanes and the Jucuara Road.

La Tigra's high elevation and the local weather system ensure that the park receives regular rain throughout the year, which sustains a thriving abundance of cloud-forest vegetation including thick mosses, bromeliads, orchids, and ferns. Lower ranges of the

ENERGY GROUPS

National capitals always attract environmental groups, and two in Teguz deserve special credit for their nationwide efforts to conceive and promote sustainable energy policy.

Honduras, like other countries in Central America, enjoys sunshine almost every day of the year, so solar energy is a natural. Promoting this technology is ENERSOL, a nonprofit international development organization working to improve the quality of life in rural areas of developing countries by fostering the use of solar energy for rural electrification. The Honduran affiliate, Solar Energy Development Association (ADESOL), was founded in January 1997.

ENERSOL pioneered the Solar-Based Rural Electrification Concept (SO-BASEC) in the Dominican Republic, beginning in 1984. The organization has had an office in Tegucigalpa since 1992. To date, nearly 1,300 solar-electric (photovoltaic, or PV) systems have been installed by a network of local ENERSOL-trained technicians in Honduras.

Your visits to rural parks in Honduras may be assisted by these efforts. ENERSOL trained a staff member of the Fundación Ecologista HRPF, which subsequently installed a solar-electric system for radio communication in the visitors center of Cusuco National Park. ENERSOL also trained a technician from MOPAWI, who installed three solar-electric systems in communities bordering the Río Plátano Biosphere Reserve.

park, where it is drier, include pine forests. The quetzal, one of the showiest birds in the tropics, is regularly seen in La Tigra, as are dozens of other bird species, butterflies, and giant winged insects. The cloud forest is also home to tapirs, ocelots, jaguarundis, pumas, and the occasional monkey, though many of these beasts will see you long before you see them and will make themselves scarce. The area is also famous for its snakes. Most of the snakes

In addition, the organization uses an innovative finance scheme to promote rural investments. Capitalized with outside grants, a U.S. guarantee fund is used as collateral at local banks, which then lend funds to NGOs, which then lend directly to families interested in solar energy systems. ADESOL has granted credits for more than $60,000 in Honduras.

"Before ADESOL existed, all funds used to come from abroad, but now it is possible to seek and obtain local supporters," says ADESOL Executive Director Diana Solis.

For example, ENERSOL also brought solar energy systems to a coffee cooperative in Marcala, a small town in the mountains near El Salvador. Marcala now leads the rest of the nation in this alternative form of rural electrification, and users have paid off most of the loan ahead of schedule. For more information, contact ADESOL-Honduras or ENERSOL Associates at 239-0383.

Eighty percent of the wood consumed in Honduras is used for fuel, and traditional woodstoves use only 10 percent of the wood's energy content and contribute to respiratory infections. Proleña, the Association for Wood, Energy and Development, was created in Honduras in 1993 to address the problems relating to unsustainable and inefficient use of firewood (leña means "firewood" in Spanish). The group promotes laws and policies as well as technical innovations. Proleña began operations in 1996 in Nicaragua as well. For more information, contact the group in Tegucigalpa at 32-0639.

are not dangerous, but be careful where you step. Coral snakes are present throughout most of Honduras, but they are as slow as they are colorful. However, their venom is said to be ten times stronger than any other snake's.

Take care around any mine shafts you see. Overgrown and mysterious, they might seem fun to poke into, but they are often quite deep and dangerous. Do not venture in or near any without a local guide.

As with nearly all parks in Honduras, La Tigra is threatened by encroachment. In the buffer zone, approximately 10,000 people grow corn, beans, and coffee; efforts are underway to end farming in the park's nuclear zone. Of course, the park was the backyard of the Rosario Mining Company for a century, a legacy evident in the scattered piles of rusting mining equipment. Perhaps not so apparent, the miners used a lot of timber to build their houses and shore up their tunnels, so much of what seems to be pristine forest in La Tigra is in fact secondary growth.

It is possible to enter through San Juancito, hike through the park, and return to Tegucigalpa from the Jutiapa entrance. At the Jutiapa side is another visitors center with photos, maps, guides, a cafeteria, and a souvenir shop.

Details: While the shortest route from Tegucigalpa is to drive toward El Picacho, then through El Hatillo to Jutiapa, 11 kilometers (6.8 miles), many choose to make the trip around through San Juancito. Each year 100,000 visitors come to this 238-square-kilometer (92-square-mile) park. Admission is $10 for foreigners; 10L for Hondurans. La Tigra has one of the best and most comprehensive websites of any park, anywhere: www.nps.gov/centralamerica/honduras/home.shtml.

Excursions to the East

Along with Santa Rosa de Copán, **Danlí** is a major center for the production of premium cigars, many of which are exported to the United States and Europe. Whereas production of many brands is centered around one large factory in Santa Rosa, the artisan-based Danlí system supports many small cigar-making firms, most of which produce just one brand. Danlí cigars are so good—among the best in the world—partly because many of the factories belong to Cuban expatriate families such as the Placensias. Although importers are flocking to Honduras, few tourists come to this pleasant town, and most of the small factories will offer an informal tour if you ask politely. Like Santa Rosa, this is a great place to purchase a box of factory seconds. They may give you lip cancer, but the smoke helps keep the mosquitoes away.

Yuscaran has been the capital of the El Paraíso department since 1779. It is a charming colonial city that boomed with the mining industry in the 18th and 19th centuries. Nearby, the **Yuscaran**

Biological Reserve offers plenty of options for hiking and camping. Under the looming Montserat, Yuscaran is also the center of production of an excellent *guaro,* a cane-based *aguardiente* that can take the paint off your car or sterilize wounds. It goes for around $2 a bottle.

Zamorano is a small town, just 40 kilometers (25 miles) from Tegucigalpa on a lovely mountain road that winds up and down through a 1,550-meter (5,085-foot) pass. Zamorano has been home to the Pan American Agricultural School since it was founded in 1942 by Samuel Zemurray, Thomas Cabot, and Wilson Popenoe, the founder of Lancetilla Botanical Gardens near Tela. Instrumental in the school's founding was Doris Zemurray Stone, daughter of banana king Samuel Zemurray, who persuaded her father to purchase the land that became Zamorano.

The school's red-tiled buildings are home to students from all over Latin America in one of the hemisphere's most innovative and respected agricultural programs. Students learn by doing and spend at least four hours a day in field laboratories. The focus here is on farming techniques, not conservation, but increasingly the two are becoming interrelated. While male students outnumber female, there has been a dramatic increase in enrollment and now women represent almost 30 percent of incoming students.

Many foreign professors, from North America and Europe as well as Latin America, are in residence. Tourists are also welcomed. In Zamorano, you can buy homemade ice cream, yogurt, mango jam, and even fresh cheddar cheese (a rarity in Central America).

The campus now covers more than 6,500 hectares, ranging from the valley to the cloud forest. During the 1994 drought, crop losses exceeded 30 percent in much of Honduras. Zamorano was also affected, but losses were minimal due to diversified production and the location of rain-fed crops in areas that could receive emergency supplemental irrigation. These practical lessons— taught in a Latin American country—will undoubtedly have a positive influence on future Latin American agricultural leaders.

You don't have to be an agriculture student to study here. Zamorano now offers short-term summer courses. For more information, check out http://www.zamorano.edu.hn or call 776-6240 in Tegucigalpa or 202/785-5540 in the United States.

The Pan American Agricultural School has taken on the responsibility to protect the adjacent Uyuca Biological Reserve, critical watershed for the school's 5,000 hectares and for the local community. When small fires break out, students and professors drop their books and head for the hills with shovels to put out the flames before they spread. Although this is private property, it is often hiked. Even novice trekkers can enjoy views of both valleys from the summit.

Ojojona, 30 kilometers (19 miles) from Tegucigalpa on the road heading to the Pacific, is a pleasant little hill town with whitewashed houses topped by red tiles, three colonial churches, and a thriving handicraft industry centered on ceramic water jars shaped like roosters. Visitors interested in Central American art will want to see the town museum, just opposite the main church, which contains the works of the painter Pablo Zelaya Sierra. The town is also home to Honduras's most famous living painter, Carlos Garay, an impressionist who specializes in landscapes. Ojojona was also the home of Hon-duran hero Francisco Morazán.

Sabanagrande, located one hour south of Tegucigalpa on the main highway to Choluteca and the south is a typical old colonial town with cobblestone streets, colonial architecture, and an old colonial church dating from 1809. There several vistas where you can view the Pacific Ocean and Gulf of Fonseca. The town is famous for its "Rosquillas" biscuits.

Details: Zamorano is 40 kilometers (25 miles) east of Teguz, and Ojojona is 30 kilometers south.

GUIDES AND OUTFITTERS

The Honduran Institute of Tourism, in Spanish the Instituto Hondureña de Turismo, or **IHT,** is located at the intersection of Avenida Ramón Ernesto Cruz and Calle República de Mexico, two floors up in the Europa building. The office is east of the Barrio El Central in Colonia San Carlos, near the Hospital San Felipe. IHT has reinvented itself in recent years, offering help to tourists throughout Honduras via a toll-free domestic number, 800/220-8687. Give them a call and ask for advice on hotels, guides, or parks. They have simple maps and other information. For detailed and topographical maps, go to the Instituto Geográfico Nacional in Barrio La Bolsa; it's open weekdays from 7:30 a.m. to 3:30 p.m.

Local tour operators include **Adventure Expeditions** (237-4793; e-mail: cyberplace@hotmail.com), **Destinos de Exito** (232-9651; e-mail: dexito@hondutel.hn), **Explore Honduras** (236-7694; e-mail: info-@explorehonduras.com), **Go Honduras** (235-7464; e-mail: gohon @hondurastur.com), **Mayan and Caribbean Tours** (239-4045; e-mail: info@mayacaribbean.hn), and **Trek de Honduras** (239-9828).

LODGING

The **MacArthur** (8a Calle between 4a and 5a Avenidas, 237-5906; $40) offers simple but clean air-conditioned rooms, and is well located a few blocks from the Parque, with secure parking. You're likely to run into visiting academics and environmentalists here. **Hotel Granada** (Avenida Gutemberg 1401 with two nearby annexes, 222-2654; $15), located just northeast of the Parque, is a good deal if you're on a strict budget. The staff is friendly, though the lighting is dim. There are public spaces, but unfortunately no bulletin boards for messages. At the Granada you're likely to run into friendly Peace Corps volunteers who are in town after spending a few months in the rural country-side. Another cheap choice is the **Cristal** (237-8804, $30).

If you have a larger budget, try the *Hotel Honduras Maya* (3a Calle and Avenida República de Chile, Colonia Palmira, 32-3191; e-mail: hondurasmaya@globalnet.hn; $165/double). A 12-story modern building on a hill just east of the Parque, the hotel has Mayan carvings as a theme and is decorated with Honduran marble and hardwoods. This is where visiting U.N. consultants and World Bank employees often stay. The hotel gift shop has a terrific selection of international newspapers and magazines.

Nearby, there has been a tremendous high-end hotel building boom, with the Del Libertador, the General, the St. Martin, the Camino Real, and the Crown Plaza all coming on line, with very little increase in demand. "Perhaps they see something we don't see," says Ricardo Vinelli of the Honduras Maya.

Be forewarned that the streets around the Hotel Honduras Maya are filled with prostitutes at night. If folks outside are being friendly, they are probably interested in a business transaction. And that pretty woman with the large Adam's apple? Many of the prostitutes are transvestites. And many are infected with HIV.

In Santa Lucia, the **Hummingbird Haven Bed & Breakfast** (221-0071; $50/night) is nestled in a private *colonia,* surrounded by pine forests just five minutes from town. Hummingbird Haven is operated by a Canadian and has all the amenities of a North American home. Contact Susan Hasse Tompkins, Apartado Postal 1293, Tegucigalpa.

Valle de Angeles has a few nice hotels, including the **Posada del Angel** (236-2233, double rooms for around $15). At the Rosario entrance to La Tigra, the old hospital has been converted into an **Eco-Albergo** with ten rooms and two adjoining houses, some with private baths, for $10 per night. On the Jutiapa side, the **Hotel Gloriales Inn** is located in the park's buffer zone, 19 kilometers (12 miles) from Teguz in the middle of a pine forest.

FOOD

Simply put, Tegucigalpa has plenty of good food, both Honduran and international specialties. For a cheap meal based on rice and beans, follow your nose into any *comedor,* simple restaurants that serve grilled chicken, stew, and other local specialties.

Don Pepe's offers typical Teguz-style dishes on Avenida Cristobal Colon, 2 blocks west of the park. **El Patio,** in the Morazon area, is another local favorite. **Los Gauchos,** Boulevard Juan Pablo 11, is rapidly becoming a chain with expansion in Comayagüela and Copán. This restaurant is known for its fine Uruguayan-style parrillada. For cheap Chinese food, try **Nan Kin** on Avenida Gutemberg. The restaurant also has accommodations for travelers on a budget. For vegetarian and natural food in a garden setting, try **Restaurante Al Natural,** Calle Hipolito Matute and Avenida Miguel Cervantes, just behind the main Cathedral off the Parque Central. Adjacent is the **Tobacco Road Cavern,** a great place to meet up with other travelers or Peace Corps volunteers, or to listen to Garífuna or Andean music. From 4 to 7 p.m. Monday through Friday, beers are only 10L.

For a treat, try **Restaurant Alondra,** Avenida República de Chile, next to the Hotel Honduras Maya. In a colonial house with terraces outdoors, this is one of Tegucigalpa's better restaurants. Or head up the mountain to Hatillo to watch the sun set from **La Cumbre** and enjoy their European cuisine. Make reservations in advance at 211-9000.

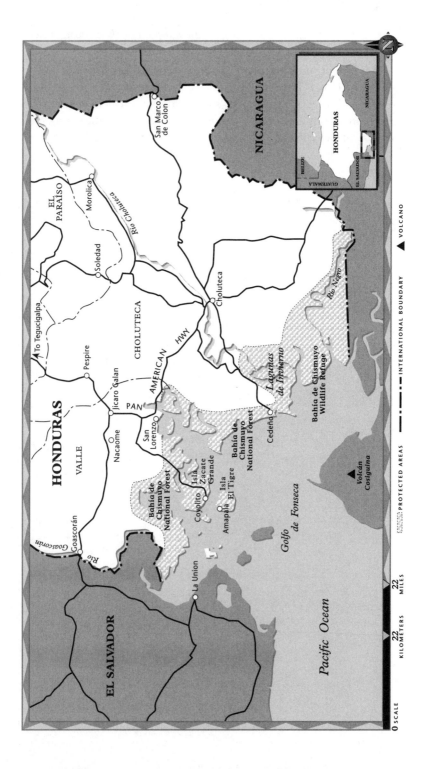

CHAPTER 8

From Mangrove to Volcano: The Pacific Coast

A friend from the Caribbean coast, a Norteño, once told us that when the Devil visits Honduras, he avoids the southern coast because it's too hot for his taste. Indeed, during the November-to-April "brown season," heat and dust can limit rational thought and unnecessary movement in southern Honduras. But, on the positive side, the Gulf of Fonseca is blue and it never rains. From May through October, during the "green season," warm, sunny days end in torrential showers that cool the air, clean the streets, and feed fresh water into a network of estuaries, lagoons, and mangrove swamps that host an incredible variety of bird and animal life. Just a few hours south of Tegucigalpa, the coast near Coyolito is lined with the weekend mansions of Honduran millionaires, while the 30-kilometer (19-mile) beach stretching from Cedeño to Punta Ratón hosts thousands of middle-class Hondurans during weekends and holidays. Very few foreigners visit this land of mangroves and volcanoes, an important Mesoamerican biological corridor that stretches 312 kilometers across the entire Pacific coast of Honduras. You can be among the first.

In the early 1980s, aquaculture boomed in the Gulf of Fonseca. Southern Honduras became the second-largest producer of farm-raised shrimp in the Western Hemisphere. This boom is spreading to

Nicaragua. Shrimp is now Honduras's third-largest export, after coffee and bananas. In a review of the development, U.S. researchers Billie DeWalt, Philippe Vergne, and Mark Hardin have documented that the price of development has been the destruction of the mangrove forests, depletion of fishing stocks, the disappearance of seasonal lagoons, and the deterioration of water quality. This nontraditional export industry was stimulated in part by USAID loans channeled through the Federation of Agriculture and Agro-Industrial Producers and Exporters. DeWalt's report traces the destruction of one-third of the mangroves to the expansion of the shrimp industry. CODDEFFAGOLF, Honduras's home-grown organization, has allied with international groups such as the Industrial Shrimp Action Network that have formed to fight this aquaculture boom that threatens to destroy important environmental resources. The industry has organized its own Global Aquaculture Alliance, which is said to "speak green" but is not walking its talk.

Meanwhile, a declining number of fish plus a growing number of fishermen equals increased pressure on natural resources and a

James D. Gollin

Shrimp farm near San Lorenzo

notable impact on the environment. Environmental damage must be stopped, but how? Local tourism offers one alternative.

VISITOR INFORMATION

The small coastal town of San Lorenzo lies just 90 minutes from Tegucigalpa and makes a great base for exploring southern Honduras. The well-maintained road from downtown Teguz to the airport continues on through high mountain passes with stunning views, then descends to the town of Pespire (which bills itself as "land of the mango") before meeting the Pan-American Highway on its short Honduran leg that connects El Salvador and Nicaragua.

San Lorenzo is a bustling town with acacia-lined streets and red-tiled adobe and brick houses. Its status as Honduras's only port on the Pacific has brought it some relative prosperity over the past decade, while its proximity to 41,000 hectares (98,400 acres) of mangrove forest, dozens of islands, and miles of beach give it great nature tourism potential.

There's not too much to do or see in San Lorenzo, but it is a good place to make contact with the most important environmental group in the region. CODDEFFAGOLF is the rather ungainly acronym for the Committee for the Defense and Development of the Flora and Fauna of the Gulf of Fonseca, a network of 75,000 artesanal fishermen and others concerned with sustainable economic development and mangrove ecosystem preservation. They receive support from overseas groups such as the World Wildlife Fund, the Angelica Foundation, and from Dutch and Swiss groups, and have formed a strategic partnership with Greenpeace. The San Lorenzo office of CODDEFFAGOLF (881-2016) is on the west side of the main street, coming in from the Pan-American Highway. Ask for Justo Garcia. Their Tegucigalpa office (238-0415) is near the Parque Central and led by Jorge Varela.

NATURE AND ADVENTURE SIGHTS

Bahia de Chismuyo Wildlife Refuge
From Coyolito west to the border with El Salvador is a riverine maze of 27,000 hectares (66,700 acres) of mangrove forest designated in

1992 as the Bahía de Chismuyo Wildlife Refuge and jointly adminis-
trated by CODDEFFAGOLF, COHDEFOR, and the Honduran Navy.
While many paper parks in Honduras lack enforcement of conservation decrees, locals joke that the Bahía de Chismuyo lacks even the
paper, as its official boundaries and status have never been deter-
mined and COHDEFOR lacks both the budget and the institutional
will to combat encroaching shrimp farmers, cattle ranchers, and
Salvadoran woodcutters. Justo Garcia, a self-educated artesanal fisherman and guide, told me that CODDEFFAGOLF acts like a child
throwing stones at the rear of a donkey in order to get it to move a
heavy load up the hill. COHDEFOR, of course, is the donkey.

After passing by huge estates of Honduran millionaires and ex-
Presidents as well as the shacks of artesanal fishermen living without
power or running water, the coastline shifts from rock and sand to
mangrove. Rounding the well-preserved national marine park comprised of the Isla de Exposición and its surrounding waters, boats
enter the snaking estuaries and brackish creeks of the Bahía de
Chismuyo. Make sure you bring enough drinking water and gasoline
to explore this area, and do travel with a local—it's easy to get lost in
the mangroves.

The word "mangrove" is often followed by the word "swamp," but
the Bahía de Chismuyo is more of a mangrove forest. Six species of
mangrove soar up to 27 meters (90 feet) in the air, their roots sunk
firmly into the muck that lies a meter or so beneath the water. The
interlaced roots keep out larger fish and other predators, creating a
natural nursery for all forms of marine life. In addition to the mangroves, 73 other plant species have been inventoried here by COD-
DEFFAGOLF. The forests teem with birdlife, hosting more than 100
species, including eagles, hawks, jabiru storks, and doves. Two dozen
species of mammal and reptile stalk the forest, including lagartos,
land turtles, garobos, iguanas, cusucos, and tree cats known as ardil-
las. The water below is alive with minnows and fish larvae.

The forests of Chismuyo seem impenetrable at first, but sturdy
mangrove roots form an above-water network so dense that people
with a good sense of balance can climb out of the boat and walk for
miles, stepping from root to root without ever touching the water. A
good place for the less nimble to get off the boat is the sandy island of
Puerto Nuevo, where CODDEFFAGOLF and COHDEFOR have plans

to build an educational center. At present, however, the area is still used as an occasional camp for Salvadoran woodcutters, who cross the border with impunity. Mangrove wood burns at a hot, even temperature and is much sought-after by bakeries, while a natural red dye used in shoe polish can be extracted from certain of the species.

Details: *West of Coyolito to the border with El Salvador, the main refuge consists of 31,616 hectares (about 75,900 acres).*

Choluteca

Thirty minutes east of San Lorenzo and just two hours away from Tegucigalpa, Choluteca is Honduras's fourth-largest city. It is the only principal Honduran city on the Pan-American Highway and offers easy access to El Salvador and Nicaragua.

To reach the old part of town, featuring some of the most intact colonial architecture in all Central America, take the second right after crossing the bridge over the Choluteca River and look for the church of La Merced, built in 1643. At the Casa de Cura (882-0132), ask for Padre Jesus Valladares, a Cuban-born, Montreal-educated priest who speaks English and is the region's Chief of Culture and the Arts. Padre Jesus delights in showing off the best of his adopted home. He works with Padre Alejandro, also Cuban-born, in promoting the Associación Surena para la Conservación de la Naturaleza (ASCONA), which organizes reforestation and environmental education projects and watches over the tropical dry forests of **Cerro Guanacaure National Park,** 25 kilometers (15.5 miles) out of town, protecting the watershed for Choluteca. This area of Honduras has the highest population density and the lowest rate of forest cover in the land, making it seem more like El Salvador than the land of the Catrachos. The deforestation has actually transformed the climate, raising the ambient temperature and drying out freshwater wells. One unintended positive consequence of this creeping desertification is that malaria, once a problem in the zone, has all but disappeared. The Pacific coast, it seems, is too hot for the anopheles mosquito.

Padre Alejandro runs an impressive grassroots organization called the **San José Obrero Mission,** which organizes integrated rural and urban development projects such as vocational training, housing for the poor, clinics, and a glove factory that supplies work gloves throughout Central America. San José Obrero also imports broken kitchen appliances from the United States, has their technicians repair them, then sells them at discount prices to poor Hondurans. Surrounding the town are Chorotega Indian ruins and mounds, still unexplored. The European community is considering funding a major study of these mysterious Maya- and Inca-influenced cultures and their trade routes under the rubric of La Ruta del Golfo.

Back toward El Salvador at Jicaro Galan, where the Pan-American crosses the highway to Tegucigalpa, is the Oasis Colonial Hotel, which almost went out of business during the bad old days when fighting in nearby El Salvador and Nicaragua wiped out the tourist trade. But when the FMLN began to attack U.S. military advisors in San Salvador, U.S. armed forces rented out the entire hotel for a few years. In those days, Huey helicopters were always parked out back and the bar was always busy. Peacetime has returned tranquility to the Oasis, and the staff are very helpful in helping travelers plan their onward trips. Drop by for a meal and a dip in the pool. If you are heading toward Nicaragua, stop in the cool, friendly mountain town of San Marcos de Colon, which has two simple hotels.

Details: From San Lorenzo head east for 34 kilometers (21 miles) on the Pan-American highway. The road is good and buses are fairly frequent. For more information, contact ASCONA at 882-0132, or Choluteca's CODDEFFAGOLF office, 882-5433.

Coyolito

An early morning departure from San Lorenzo is essential to appreciate the birdlife in the gulf. While hotel restaurants will surely be closed, the main market in San Lorenzo opens at 4 a.m. daily selling sweet, cardamom-flavored coffee and cakes for 1L each. The main departure point for excursions into the gulf is Coyolito, a small town on the island of Zacate Grande, which is connected by a bridge to the mainland. The road to Coyolito, 30 minutes by bus or private car, passes vast shrimp farms that once were mangrove forests. On the more positive side, it also passes abandoned salt factories where locals used to boil sea water to make salt, using mangrove wood for fuel. While all salt production was wood-fueled just a decade ago, 98 percent is now solar-powered due to innovations promoted by CODDEFFAGOLF, protecting the mangroves while preserving local jobs.

James D. Gollin

All manner of boats are available for rent in Coyolito.

After passing to the east of the 655-meter (2,149-foot) peak of Zacate Grande, an expansive vista of the Gulf of Fonseca opens up. The ocean—clear blue during the dry season and tan with sediment from May to November—is dotted with dozens of small islands. The seascape is dominated by the volcanic cone of El Tigre Island, rising 783 meters (2,421 feet) out of the ocean. To the west lies the Chonchagua Volcano in El Salvador. To the east is Nicaragua's Cosiguina Volcano. Below, a strip of giant boulders heads out into the ocean. A jetty? No. Just an optimistic beginning to a bridge linking the port of Amapala on El Tigre to the mainland, a project that was dropped when the Italian government declined to pay for the construction.

Coyolito itself is a small town with a few small restaurants and a place for the boatmen to gas up. Condo developments litter the hills above town, while the locals live in shacks on stilts next to the water. From Coyolito, collective taxis take the 15-minute trip across to Amapala for 50 cents. A private boat will make the trip for $5, and boats can be hired for expeditions to sites throughout the gulf. Boats

THE SHRIMP INDUSTRY

About half of the 1 million people living in southern Honduras make their living directly or indirectly from the sea. For hundreds of years, small-scale artesanal fishermen have cast their fine-meshed nets into the myriad waterways that drain into the Gulf of Fonseca, pulling out kicking, wriggling Pennaus vannamei. In 1973, entrepreneurs first cleared mangrove forests to open up wide flats of brackish water, ideal for farm-raising shrimp. In 1984, foreign capital from the United States and South America arrived and the boom began. By 1993, 9,000 hectares (21,600 acres) of lagoon and mangrove had been ripped out or burned to make way for shrimp farming on an industrial scale. That same year the annual harvest peaked at 17 million pounds, nearly all of it heading to the United States, Europe, and Japan.

The shrimp industry relies upon wild-caught shrimp larvae, regularly spreading 37-meter (120-foot)-wide nets across entire tidal estuaries, trapping larvae and minnows from all species of fish, crab, and shrimp. The catch is poured into large vats infused with specialized poisons that kill all living things except the hardy shrimp larvae. The poisoned water and dead non-shrimp species are dumped into the gulf. For the 4 billion larvae harvested by the shrimp industry each year, an estimated 36 billion larvae of other species are killed.

As the demand for larvae grew and the local supply began to dwindle, cheap larvae were imported from Ecuador. Along with the larvae, however, came a disease called taura that infected shrimp in farm after farm.

Theoretically, the tiny shrimp spend their short lives in the hot, shallow water gorging on pellets of corn, sorghum, and calcium until, approximately 90 days later, they are harvested at a weight of 12 to 20 grams each and sold at $9 per pound, making the shrimp ponds virtual money machines. But disease *has cut seriously into profits. Despite the fact that shrimp farmers clear more mangroves each year to expand their production, harvests have dropped each year from 1993. Export sales dropped from $95 million in 1994 to just $62 million in 1995. Production increased again through 1998, when Mitch tore apart the farms, depressing production by 30 percent. In 1999 a new disease, called "white spot," appeared in the crowded shrimp ponds. To contain the spread of profit-eroding disease in these crowded conditions, thousands of pounds of insecticides, hormones, and antibiotics are now poured into the shrimp ponds, chemicals which soon wash out into the estuaries and eventually to the gulf.*

Most of the hard-currency profits are immediately expatriated to the United States and Asia, and only a third of the promised 15,000 local jobs ever materialized. As seafood catches in the gulf decreased year after year, desperate fishermen began crossing the shrimp ponds to gain access to fish in estuaries—and, according to the industry, to poach shrimp from the ponds. By 1999, shrimp farm guards, instructed to shoot any interlopers, had killed nine fishermen.

Starting in 1988, though, many local fishermen realized that the shrimp boom was leaving them behind and destroying the ecosystem upon which they depend. Grouping themselves as the Committee for the Defense and Development of the Flora and Fauna of the Gulf of Fonseca (CODDEFFAGOLF), members now have offices in San Lorenzo, Choluteca, and Tegucigalpa. They organize protests whenever a fisherman is shot and pressure the government to protect the 60 percent of the mangrove ecosystem that remains intact. At the same time, they are promoting an upsurge in ecotourism and bird-watching in the area, offering customized tours to the mangrove forests of the Bahía de Chismuyo and to the islands and beaches of the Gulf of Fonseca.

make the crossing when they fill up the eight seats. Prices are fixed, so if you don't want to wait for the extra passengers you can pay a little extra. Per-person costs can be significantly reduced by forming a group, as boats can hold ten or more people.

Details: *Just 30 minutes from San Lorenzo, Coyolito is the main point of departure for exploring Amapala and the Bahía de Chismuyo. CODDEFFAGOLF's two boats can be rented by prearrangement for around 300L ($25) per hour per boat or 1,200L ($100) for the whole day, including a driver and guide.*

El Tigre and the Islands

More than a dozen Honduran islands dot the waters of the Gulf of Fonseca, most filled with extravagant birdlife. Some, such as San Carlos, have small fishing villages. One unpopulated island, Inglesera, has a small lagoon on the back side that can be entered through a cave, an excellent spot for a picnic. The queen of the gulf, however, is the volcanic island of El Tigre, named for a solitary tiger (jaguar) that is said to have stalked the Spaniards who first occupied the island. El Tigre is ringed by a dirt road that connects several small fishing villages and a dozen beaches of black, volcanic sand.

James D. Gollin

Amapala

The town of Amapala was once the only Honduran port on the Pacific, but it was bypassed in 1985 by the new port near San Lorenzo. With the collapse of the maritime trade, the once-prosperous town has been all but abandoned. The casino is shuttered and the giant customs house is empty. England occupied Amapala in the mid-19th century, and during the Central American revolution in the 1980s the North Americans came close to doing the same. Sandinistas smuggling arms across the Gulf of Fonseca to the Salvadoran FMLN caused the

United States to build a radar and helicopter base in the crater at the peak of the volcano and to fully equip a Honduran naval base next to Amapala. But peace has brought an end to the industry of war, and there's nothing left in Amapala but fishermen and a few tourists.

Offering beautiful beaches and tranquility, Amapala is off the tourist path. The island lacks major hotel facilities, but if you ask you'll be able to find a room or a house ($10/night) for rent. Ask for Doña Mariana, 3 blocks up from the pier and 4 blocks to the right in a restaurant/bar on the corner. Amapala has a bank, but you may have trouble cashing traveler's checks, so bring Honduran currency.

It takes about three hot hours to climb the volcano, but the intrepid will be rewarded with a splendid view of the bay and half a dozen volcanoes in three countries. Bring plenty of water and sunblock, and don't be surprised if the summit is buzzed by a U.S. helicopter on a training flight out from Palmerola. Horses can be rented at Playa Negra, and from time to time a horse-drawn carriage circumambulates the island. Taxis also make the round-island trip every few hours.

Details: *From Coyolito, collective water taxis make the 15-minute trip across to Amapala for 50 cents. A private boat will make the trip for $5.*

Lagunas de Invierno and Punta Raton

South of Choluteca is a vast, shallow lagoon system that teems with birdlife in the winter months of the green season, from May through October. Best times to visit are before 7 a.m. or after 4 p.m. Seasonal lagoons such as the **Lagunas de Invierno** are dry most of the year, though when filled with rainwater they become nurseries for fish and crustaceans. Migratory birds, many from the United States, benefit greatly from these areas, some of which have been declared wildlife reserves. During the dry season the birds move on as the brackish water dries to leave a 5-inch-thick cake of sea salt which is harvested by campesinos who use it to preserve fish and shrimp and to feed to their cattle. Nearby, the shrimp farm of Aquacultura Fonseca offers tours of their operations, but you might not want to go there with a COD-DEFFAGOLF guide as the relationship between this environmental group and their shrimp-industry adversaries is sometimes quite tense.

The beach at **Cedeño** is famous for its coffee-colored sand. Small restaurants and houses on stilts are scattered across the beachfront. There are no public toilets, so the area can get rather filthy during weekends and holidays. There was one decent motel just out of town, the Punta del Sol (882-0920), but it was destroyed by high tides during Mitch and may not yet be rebuilt. The beach stretches for 30 kilometers toward **Punta Ratón,** just across the bay from Zacate Grande and Coyolito. Punta Ratón is much cleaner than Cedeño but lacks formal overnight facilities. Punta Ratón is closed each year during September, at the peak of the turtle season, when endangered Golfino and Carey turtles *(Lepidochelys olivacea olivacea* and *Erethmochelys imbricata)* arrive to clamber up the beach and lay their eggs. Those interested can contact the Ministry of Natural Resources Fisheries Department (DIGEPESCA) to volunteer to protect the turtles and dig up their eggs, which are then allowed to hatch in predator-free enclosures. The area is also rich with parrots, doves, pelicans, and other birdlife. This region was once famous for the hunting of white-winged doves, a practice that is now prohibited. Hunting of quail, pigeons, and wild turkey continues on a seasonal basis.

Details: Lagunas de Invierno is about an hour from San Lorenzo, half that from Choluteca. Cedeño is 40 minutes south of Choluteca. Punta Ratón is another 30 kilometers (19 miles) beyond Cedeño.

GUIDES AND OUTFITTERS

Like many environmental groups in Honduras, CODDEFFAGOLF (881-2016) doubles as an ecotour agency and arranges expeditions around the gulf. An alternative is San Lorenzo Tours (881-2392), which offers estuary, beach, and mangrove tours. But a trip with CODDEFFAGOLF will provide the additional benefit, for those who speak some Spanish, of a thorough education in the politics and ecological consequences of the south's major industry, shrimp farming.

LODGING

In San Lorenzo, the **Miramar** (881-2138; $27) is the town's best hotel and is built on stilts over the water of a major estuary. Just follow the main road down to the water, past a shrimp-packing plant. Rooms have air conditioning, cable television, a balcony overlooking the water, and there's even a pool. On weekends, live music booms out from the crowded dance floor attached to the restaurant. On weekdays, the place is deserted. **La Perla del Pacífico,** in town, is a lower-priced and recommended alternative to The Miramar. **Hotel Morazon** (north of the Pan-American Highway, 881-2400; $17) has air conditioning and TV.

In Choluteca, the **Hacienda Gualiqueme Hotel and Club** (on the Pan-American Highway next to the Choluteca bridge, 882-312, fax: 882-3620; $60) is newly built with beautiful surroundings and gardens. Restaurant, bar, hot water, TV, horseback riding, tennis, and racquetball are all available. **Hotel La Fuente** (in Barrio Los Mangos on the main road in town, 882-0253, 882-0263; $10–$15) is a clean hotel for budget travelers. **Oasis Colonial Hotel,** where the Pan-American Highway crosses the highway to Tegucigalpa (895-4007/8; $20–$70), is colossal, with 40 rooms, six cabañas, and five suites. **Pierre Hotel** is downtown near main market (882-0676; $10–$15).

In Amapala, on the south side of the island, the **Hotel Villas Playa Negra** (232-0632, $45) has 18 rooms and will send a launch to pick up guests at Amapala's main dock. (The place may now have been taken over by new management and renamed Las Lomas Hotel Club.) Closer to town are the **Casa del Colonel** guest house and smaller hotels catering to middle-class Hondurans.

FOOD

In San Lorenzo the local specialty, *sopa marinera,* is a giant bowl of soup made of fish, shrimp, and crab with a coconut-milk base. It tastes more Southeast Asian than Central American and is almost worth a trip to the Pacific coast in itself. The food is good at the **Miramar Hotel** or you might try **Maravilla 2,** in La Cabaña *(zona viva).* Locals swear that this is the best place to try the *marinera,* but there is an almost unbroken chain of restaurants stretching along San Lorenzo's short coastline, each offering fresh fish.

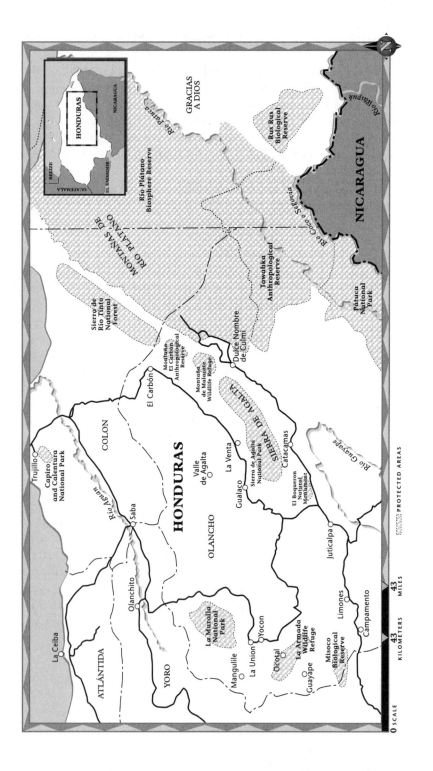

CHAPTER 9

The Wild East: Olancho

People who live in big cities love to refer to less-sophisticated areas as "wild." In Honduras, it is Olancho that holds this position in the national psyche. Olancho is often referred to as "the Wild West" of Honduras, even though it's in the east. True, this *is* cattle country, and men do carry pistols, and you won't find yuppies with cellular telephones here. But the wildness we refer to in this chapter is the region's natural wilderness. The parks here encompass greater expanses of undisturbed forest than those closer to urban areas, such as Cusuco or La Tigra. If you want to get to know all of Honduras, Olancho is a must-see. If you're a birder, the state's largest parks—La Muralla, Sierra de Agalta, and El Carbón—are pieces of heaven on earth.

The only trouble, now that we mention it, is that most of Olancho is well off the tourist track. Your choices will be to contact a travel agency in Tegucigalpa or make your own way. This is a little more difficult than in other areas of the country. When you read the phrase "tourist infrastructure is limited," believe it. But if you do visit, your efforts will be well rewarded.

Olancho enthusiast and geographer Mark Bonta suggests that anyone traveling in these rural areas contact the *municipalidad* in the town. "They often have environmental subcommittees, or know of any local groups working on environmental questions," he writes. In this section of the book, we draw upon his work and observations. Having worked in the Sierra de Agalta for the U.S. Peace Corps, Bonta continues to promote the region and will likely return to live there.

Olancho is the largest department in Honduras. In fact, it's bigger than the nation of El Salvador. Environmentally, the region is the meeting ground of North and South. Bonta writes, "The montane habitats and species (pines, bluebirds, jays) representative of Mexico and northern Central America meet the rain forest that over several million years migrated northward from South America along the Caribbean coast. Hence, the area of Central Olancho is where rain forest becomes dry forest, where pine forest borders lowland rain forest." Many mini-ecosystems here, such as the Honduran thorn forests and Honduran elfin forests, are unique in the world. These habitats are stacked on top of each other due to the terrain that rises and falls 2,000 vertical meters (6,562 feet), resulting in tremendously high biodiversity.

Politically and economically, Olancho has been "frontier" territory and, until recently, has been left alone. Bradford Brooks, who lived in the area during the Contra wars, recalls a road sign at the entrance to Olancho that read: *"Bienvenidos a Olancho. Entre si Quieres. Sale si Puedes"* ("Welcome to Olancho. Enter if you'd like. Leave if you are able to.") These gun-toting tough guys weren't afraid of the CIA-armed Contras living in camps lining the Nicaraguan border to the east.

Olancho was originally blanketed with thick rain forests, but the tough guys have deforested large areas for agriculture and cattle ranching. The deforestation is blamed for the diminishing rainfall in the region. Whether this will lead to reforestation projects remains to be seen. Meanwhile, the fact that travelers are arriving on a regular basis to encounter the virgin wilderness provides a clear economic incentive for maintaining the remaining expanse of forest cover.

Even though the original stewards of the forests and valleys, the Pech and Tawahkas, have been pushed to the remotest edge of the department, there is still time to preserve some of the richest habitats in Central America, found within the Cordillera de Agalta and within La Muralla National Park.

NATURE AND ADVENTURE SIGHTS

La Muralla National Park

An exceptionally beautiful and under-visited wildlife reserve, La Muralla is a cloud forest painted in vibrant shades of Technicolor green. Located 14 kilometers (8.7 miles) north of La Unión, the park is roughly halfway between Tegucigalpa and La Ceiba (roughly 200 kilometers [124 miles] or three hours from either city). With an area of 21,885 hectares (54, 056 acres), it is reminiscent of Costa Rica's Monteverde reserve, except with less development and more wildlife. The best time to visit the park is between March, the driest month, and May, before the summer rains. This is also the period when the quetzals often nest next to the visitors center and are easy to observe. Without a doubt, if you're looking for wildlife instead of a mere respite from city life, La Muralla is the best developed national park in Honduras. Locals call this "the Pride of Olancho." The park has one of the best visitors centers in all of Honduras, with exhibits on the local flora and fauna, particularly the insects and mammals found at La Muralla. You'll also find someone who can answer your questions and provide advice if you want to hike on your own. The visitors center is just a 15-minute drive from the center of town. Take the road toward El Dictamo and La Muralla National Park. Stay to the right when the road splits. If you walk, it's a four-hour, uphill climb. You can hitch a ride or see if someone at the COHDEFOR office can help you.

The park boasts knowledgeable guides who can lead you through the forest and explain the interrelationships within it. There is no restaurant in the park, but there are several places to pitch a tent.

Tourism has only recently arrived at La Muralla. The park was designated a *refugio silvestre* (forest refuge) in 1987, when 37 cloud forests in Honduras received status as protected areas. The declaration was a boon for conservationists and at the same time was problematic: There were and are few funds for implementing actual conservation measures. Major improvements toward conservation and ecotourism were launched by COHDEFOR and USAID in 1990, when La Muralla was chosen as a priority area for conservation. In 1993, the park was expanded and its status changed to *parque nacional.*

The number of visitors has slowly increased over the past few years. According to the official registry, 749 people visited the park in 1992 and 2,093 in 1995. The park is busiest from Thursday to Sunday, but even then the numbers are quite low. It is a favorite destination for international forestry groups and hikers alike.

One of the first major buildings you'll come to in La Unión is the COHDEFOR office, which is in charge of the park. This is an excellent place to check on the status of the park and to hire a guide. When you arrive in town, arrange for transportation and a guide for the following day. You can travel to the park on your own, but a local service has been set up that helps the community as it provides invaluable assistance to the traveler. Guide service starts at 30L, though that may change. Prices are negotiable.

The U.S. Peace Corps has a long relationship with the park, so it is a good idea to seek out a local volunteer as well. There is also an information booth across from the Parque Central, though it's often closed.

La Muralla is a virgin cloud forest, home to three-toed sloths, white-faced monkeys, jaguars, white-crowned parrots, and porcupines. The magnificent quetzals live here year-round and nest in dead snags from late March to June. The birds feast on the fruits of the *aguacatillo* tree (a species of wild avocado) and supplement their diet with insects and frogs. The park boasts at least 200 different species of birds, including great curassows, crested guans, emerald toucans, king vultures, and hawk-eagles. This number will likely increase as more scientists and bird-watchers visit the park.

The easiest mammals to spot in the park include the variegated and Deppe's squirrels, howler and squirrel monkeys, and *tepezcuintles* (pacas) and *guatuzas* (agoutis, rather like a cross between a large rabbit and a rat). It's best to be the first person to hike the trails in the early morning if you want to see wildlife.

The park comprises the territory surrounding three mountains: La Muralla, Los Higuerales, and Las Parras. The park protects areas from 900 to 2,064 meters (2,953 to 6,772 feet) high and contains three separate ecosystems (subtropical humid forest or pine/oak forest; subtropical wet forest, or mid-level rain forest; and lower montane wet forest, or cloud forest). The nuclear zone of the park begins at 1,410 meters (4,626 feet) elevation and comprises 13,135 hectares

(32,443 acres). An additional 8,750 hectares (21,613 acres) surrounds the park in the managed-use or buffer zone used by the tourists.

Like other mountains in Honduras, La Muralla provides water for the *municipios* of La Unión, Yocon, and Mangulile, serving more than 20,000 people. The community of La Unión depends on coffee production and agriculture. The coffee *fincas* can be found in the buffer zone of the park. Coffee is mostly grown in shaded areas and has minimal impact on the park ecosystem.

The park is experimenting with a *microtarifa* as a form of entrance fee for the park. The cost is 5L (about 40 cents). Your receipt is a Parque Nacional La Muralla peel-off bumper sticker.

There are three different, well-marked trails in the park, offering more than 25 kilometers (15.5 miles) of varying terrain. You'll find discarded bromeliads lying on the *senderos* (paths). Our guides told us this is a sign that monkeys have been drinking water from the plants and discarding them when empty. You'll also come across one of the common flowers here, the red-hued and aptly named *beso de novia* (A Girlfriend's Kiss).

El Pizote (3.7 kilometers/2.3 miles) leads to two incredible vistas, Mirador El Tucanillo and Mirador Quetzales, as well as two camping sites. The 4-kilometer (2.4-mile) Jaguar Trail branches off into the forest. The Monte Escondido Trail goes further up the mountain. Peace Corps volunteer Craig Perham reports the construction of a brand-new circular hiking trail in the park, which connects two of the existing trails. It's perfect for the visitor looking for a day hike; the average duration should be a comfortable four to five hours. And if all you're looking for is a taste of the cloud forest, the 1-kilometer Liquidambar Trail circles around the visitors center and offers a great introduction to the forest.

In the area surrounding La Muralla, ex–Peace Corps volunteer Mark Bonta suggests a visit to a beautiful area is called **Mucupina** (the Indian name for La Muralla), where waterfalls cascade off the eastern rim of the park. Mucupina is easily accessible from the La Unión–Mame highway, about one hour from La Unión. The hike up to the falls passes through pine forest and a logging concession.

The road from La Unión to Mangulile continues to Yoro, from which the traveler can reach San Pedro Sula. There are buses along this entire route, and it is quite spectacular.

Another reserve (a more remote one) under the jurisdiction of COHDEFOR is **El Armado,** known for its vast caves. The reserve itself is a remnant of cloud forest, accessible from the town of El Rosario. El Dictamo is a good village to find guides; the hiker can circumnavigate the park through the rain forests on the back side in several days, coming out on the road to Olanchito.

Midway between Los Limones and Catacamas is **Juticalpa,** the capital of Olancho. Compared to the nearby sleepy towns, it is a bustling city. Juticalpa was an Indian town, perhaps an Aztec colony, when the Spaniards arrived in the 1520s. The town honors the Virgen de Concepción with an annual festival every December 8. The city is 50 kilometers (31 miles) from Los Limones and is the jumping-off point for El Boqueron and Sierra de Agalta.

Details: To get to the park from Tegucigalpa, take the highway to Olancho. After two hours of travel you'll come to the small town of Limones. Head north for approximately 90 minutes. The first part of this gravel road is the worst. If you are traveling from La Ceiba or Trujillo, take the road from Olanchito-Tocoa (at the desvio de Mame, or detour) and then travel to La Unión over one of the most mountainous routes in the country.

The long-distance buses from Teguz (Comayagüela) to Trujillo and Olanchito run every day past La Unión, and some go into the town; others just stop at the desvio a short walk out of town. They are much faster than taking the Olancho bus and waiting at Limones. A daily bus travels between La Unión and Juticalpa. Note that buses between Limones and Mame have recently been stopped and robbed by bandits.

The bus station in Juticalpa is on 1a Avenida NE, southeast of the Parque Central. From Juticalpa there are daily buses that go directly to La Unión (about three hours) as well as transportation to Catacamas and Gualaco for trips into Sierra de Agalta. You can catch a ride in a passing truck or walk to the park.

Las Montañas del Carbón National Forest

Santa María del Carbón is a small town inhabited by the 1,200 Pech Indians at the base of the El Carbón mountains, part of the Sierra de Agalta range. While surrounding territory is being deforested for cattle ranching, this area has been fairly undisturbed and is a vital link in a biological corridor between the southern portion of the Sierra de Agalta and La Mosquitia.

Until the last century, the Pech tribe was the major ethnic group in northern and eastern Olancho, extending as far as the north coast. According to their mythology, they once lived in a large *ciudad blanca* (white city). Today their culture is endangered and they have been reduced to two small nuclei, in Carbón and near Dulce Nombre de Culmi. Because the Pech do not keep cattle, 90 percent of their 7,000 hectares is forest. The Pech maintain their language, legends, and myths, which mix with Catholicism to give them a unique outlook on the world. Although their food doesn't differ much from Ladino cooking, it depends heavily on yucca, from which they make everything from a wet gummy tortilla called *cha ah* to a customary alcoholic beverage called *munyah*. Their traditional crafts are unique and worth taking home. They make hammocks and woven tote bags from the bark of *chumeco* and *baboso,* two trees that grow in the tropical rain forest surrounding the village.

An environmental group formed by the Pech tribe, WATA, promotes environmental awareness and responsible tourism. It is also working toward the official designation of the area as a Pech anthropological reserve. Future plans are to construct a visitors center, and two *hospedajes* are under construction in El Carbón. In addition, a trail has been cleared to the La Cascada waterfall, the headwater of the Ojo de Agua River. This spectacular waterfall is at least 80 meters (262 feet) high and 35 meters (115 feet) wide, dropping out of the cloud forests that rise behind the village of El Carbón. WATA leader Linton Escobar and Peace Corps volunteers Kevin Postma and Kate Thompson have cleared a large ruin site within the dense jungle. This takes a day to visit. Be sure to bring insect repellent.

Connected to the Pech territory are Las Montañas del Carbón, an area covering approximately 40,000 hectares (98,800 acres). It is currently designated as national forest but is awaiting declaration as an anthropological reserve. The mix of tropical forest habitats contained within will be an attraction to the ecotourist. El Carbón is located in a frontier zone where pine savanna changes to rain forest. As you ascend the mountains, the rain forest changes to cloud forest and eventually to dwarf cloud forest. This mosaic of forest habitats makes El Carbón a unique site for those interested in birding and observing other wildlife. The forests are home to jaguars, macaws, tapir, monkeys, curassow, parrots, and white-tailed deer. A 1995 U.S.

Peace Corps survey by Richard Albers recorded 231 different species of birds in these forests.

Local expert Kevin Postma writes: "From personal experience I can account that the mountains contain jaguars; ocelots; pumas; tapir; *quequeos* (white-collared peccaries); river otters; kinkajous; howler, white-faced, and spider monkeys; *pizotes* (coatimundi); deer; and iguanas." A number of trails that to the forest habitats used by the Pech for hunting, crossing the mountains, and collecting resources. Trips from one day to a week can be arranged depending on your interests and schedule.

Details: *El Carbón is on the road that connects Trujillo to Juticalpa, about 90 minutes south of the Pueblo Bonito Oriental and about 90 minutes north of San Esteban. From Trujillo it's a three-hour bus trip to El Carbón. It is a much longer trip from Tegucigalpa, but to the traveler already headed to the north coast, El Carbón is on the way. The forest comprises 40,000 hectares (98,800 acres).*

Sierra de Agalta National Park

The Sierra de Agalta mountain range includes the highest peak in eastern Honduras, 2,354-meter (7,723-foot) La Picucha Peak in the Montañas de Babilonia. The name "Agalta" is of indigenous origin and one hypothesis suggests it combines *actl*, meaning "carrizo," the indigenous bamboo of the cloud forest, and *tla*, meaning "abundant." In the region, Agalta refers not only to the Sierra but to the Valle de Agalta as well.

The mountain range includes a large expanse of accessible dwarf (or elfin) forest and numerous caves. The varieties of forest are home to rare species including jaguars, ocelots, two-toed sloths, and howler monkeys. Nearly 500 bird species and more than 230 butterfly species have been recorded here. Morpho butterflies dart through the forest like fluorescent blue angels.

The park is just west of the Río Plátano Biosphere Reserve. Environmentalists are targeting the region, which also includes the Malacate Mountains and the El Carbón Reserve, as a protected biological corridor for animals that use both the mountain and lowland ecosystems.

The Grupo Ecologico de Olancho (GEO) environmental group works in the Sierra. GEO has two chapters, one in Gualaco, active on the north side of the Sierra, and one in Catacamas, active on the south side. In Gualaco, GEO contacts are Francisco Urbina, Ramón ("Monchito") Veliz, or Benjamin Bellis. Francisco manages the park and is knowledgeable about birds and wildlife; Benjamin and Monchito offer the tours. All guides should be paid, no matter how short the trip is. Establish prices beforehand. The group organizes trips to La Picucha (see below) and works with schools and local communities. Gualaco has minimal accommodations, but one, the Hotel Calle Real, is between the highway and the Parque

View of La Picucha

Mark Bonta

Central. From Gualaco, a day hike takes you to La Chorrera waterfall, on the trail to La Picucha.

GEO's Catacamas chapter, like the town, is larger; contact Conrado Martinez at the COHDEFOR office in town. This is one of the most active environmental groups in the country. Here GEO works with farmers to develop sustainable agriculture.

The hike to **La Picucha** is one of the most spectacular backpacking hikes anywhere, taking you through pine forest, rain forest, cloud forest, and elfin forest. It takes at least four days round trip, and guides are essential. The turnoff is marked on the road from Gualaco to San Esteban (which continues to Carbón and Trujillo); it's about 30 minutes from Gualaco. Buy provisions for group and guide in Juticalpa or Gualaco. Pack mules to as far as La Chorrera (base camp) can be arranged from nearby villages. The base camp, located in pristine sweet-gum (liquidambar) rain forest, is at 1,100 meters (3,609 feet) above sea level; jaguar and tapir tracks are often found here along the Río del Sol.

La Chorrera waterfall is a pretty twin falls, with a white-collared swift colony that is quite interesting to observe. From La Chorrera, the trail heads steeply up toward La Picucha; the cloud forest camp, El Filo, can be reached in six hours. Please, camp only in Chorrera or El Filo, and do not camp on top of the peak; the ecosystems are very fragile. Base camp has a tin-roofed shelter and latrine; El Filo is primitive, though there is running water nearby.

From El Filo you can reach the peak in a couple of hours; early morning is best, but it does rain every day. Don't visit in September or June if there has been a lot of rain; storms approach hurricane conditions. On clear days, views from La Picucha take in most of Olancho; you can see as far as Pico Bonito and La Mosquitia. The elfin forest is in part a windswept heath dominated by terrestrial bromeliads and dwarf pines; an endemic species of frog lives in the cups of the bromeliads. Other areas of elfin forest sheltered from the incessant winds have a mossy aspect that is quite beautiful. Some mosses here are extraordinary Ice Age relics that are found only in this spot and in South America.

Three-wattled bellbirds are also common and vocal here during certain seasons. The most common animals are monkeys, which you will hear if not see. Over the past six years GEO members and Peace Corps volunteers have observed or tracked almost every possible large mammal, including rarities such as tayra, grison, and white-lipped peccary. Five of Honduras's wild feline species make their home in this park. In fact, in honor of a jaguarundi that walked right past two bathing Peace Corps volunteers, the base camp is named El Motete (actually campesino slang for a huge bush or agglomeration of plants).

A good area for bird-watching is the **Bosque el Nacional,** right outside of Gualaco; early morning hikes here yield jacamars, parrots, doves, and hummingbirds (more than 68 species were spotted in two hours). Contact GEO member and schoolteacher Eliezer Meza.

The **Valle de Agalta,** between Gualaco and El Carbón, is also recommended by Mark Bonta. GEO member Francisco Urbina is the best contact here; he has a farm in La Venta (45 minutes from Gualaco) where ecotourists can find lodging. From his farm you can access the Sabana La Lima to find the Honduran emerald, a small hummingbird that is globally threatened and is found only in a couple of valleys in Honduras. It lives only in the attractive thorn forests, which are characterized by giant agaves, thorny acacias, and, especially, columnar tree cacti and prickly pears. There is no protected area here yet, so the birds are found only on large haciendas, easily spotted in all seasons. Always request permission to enter the properties. The emerald is the only bird endemic to Honduras; the thorn forest, along with the elfin forest, is one of Honduras's truly unique habitats.

From the village of La Venta there are multiple possibilities for hikes into the Sierra de Agalta, including day hikes that take you as far as the rain forest, or longer trips that cross the Sierra in two places (San Agustin–El Cerro and Los Dos Ríos–Vallecito). Mark Bonta recommends a hike that loops past some of the nicest waterfalls in Honduras, such as the Chorros de Babilonia, which is visible from the main road. The Río Babilonia plunges down an escarpment from the rain forest to the valley, dropping over 2,000 feet in 2 kilometers and forming at least eight waterfalls, some higher than 150 feet. The lower falls can be visited in one day, but a better idea is to take a few days, spending the night in the town of Planes de Babilonia, a remote coffee village ensconced in the towering rain forest. The Planes can be reached by foot or mule in half a day from the village of El Ocotal, near La Venta. There is excellent hiking deeper into the rain forest, where monkeys leap about in trees that often reach a diameter of over 10 feet.

The waterfalls are accessible from the main trail up the escarpment between Ocotal and Planes, but to see them up close you have to follow a rugged, circuitous route that only local people know. Francisco Urbina, again, is an excellent guide for this trip. La Picucha, Pico Bonito, and Lago Yojoa excepted, this is the most aesthetically pleasing place we know in Honduras; it easily compares to major parks in the States.

Another place that is well known are the **Cuevas de Susmay,** in the Gualaco Valley, accessible on foot (about 45 minutes) from the town of Gualaco. GEO member Monchito loves to take tours here. This is a series of three caves stacked one on top of the other. The top two are dry, but the bottom cave is the exit route for the Río Susmay. Take along a waterproof flashlight, the kind that scuba divers use, and swim about a kilometer into the cave. There, the narrow passage opens up into a cathedral-like space, 45 meters (150 feet) high and 30 meters (100 feet) wide. Clearly, you should not try this alone. So far the cave's end has not been reached. Another recommended spot around Gualaco is the Cueva del Espino.

Details: 50 kilometers (31 miles) northeast of Juticalpa and 20 kilometers (12.4) north of Catacamas, this park spreads across 92,500 hectares (223,475 acres).

Talgua Caves Archaeological and Ecological Park

This is where the famous "glowing skulls" were discovered by amateur spelunkers in the mid-1990s. Archaeologists explored the 3.2-kilometer-long (2-mile) caves and found ritual offerings and painted skeletons of almost 200 people that dated to 2,500 years ago. Calcite deposits dripped endlessly over the centuries, making the cave and the ochre-painted skeletons sparkle or "glow" when light is shined on them.

The site will be eastern Honduras's first national archaeological site. No date has been set for the opening of the Talgua Caves Archaeological and Ecological Park, but officials promise the construction of 4 kilometers (2.5 miles) of new highway leading from Catacamas to the site, plus various walking paths, a footbridge, a visitors center, and a network of ladders and platforms to help visitors navigate the caves. The project is sponsored by the Honduran Social Development Fund (FHIS), the Honduran Institute of History and Anthropology, and the Ministry of Culture. President Reina took part in the groundbreaking ceremony in May 1997.

Investigations began only in 1994, when the treasures inside the caves were discovered. The discovery offers new evidence of the development of Mesoamerican civilization. Human use of the caves dates back to 900 b.c.

Nearby are ruins in the middle of a cattle pasture. More than 100 mounds, remnants of a settlement, may provide clues to solving the various mysteries of this civilization. The burial site is

Mark Bonta

El Boqueron

off-limits without special permission, but you can visit the upper caves without a permit.

Between Juticalpa and Catacamas, **El Boqueron National Monument** is an excellent area for bird-watching and hiking. The main path winds through the canyon and up to the top of Cerro Agua Buena. Nearby, **Catacamas** is a humble town, far from the tourist trail yet the best jumping off point for the Sierra de Agalta, the Talgua Caves, and El Boqueron. A good day trip from Catacamas is a visit to the coffee villages of El Murmullo and Las Delicias, where you can put together a pack train to penetrate the heart of the Sierra.

Details: A good base for exploring the Talgua Caves and El Boqueron is the city of Catacamas, located in the Río Guayape valley (known as the Valle de Olancho), at the foot of the Sierra de Agalta. You will need a guide to explore the park, which is only 6 kilometers (3.7 miles) outside Catacamas. Ask for the GEO office, a local environmental group. Until the current road is paved, note that during the rainy season it easily metamorphoses into a muddy river.

GUIDES AND OUTFITTERS

Tegucigalpa-based and La Ceiba–based tourism operators such as La Mosquitia Ecoaventuras offer tours. In **La Union,** guides can be contracted from the COHDEFOR office. The building is a prominent landmark on the edge of town. Guide service starts at $5, though this will likely increase in the future. Prices are negotiable. If you travel on your own, the best access points are from Catacamas and Gualaco, and you may be able to find a local man to act as guide by asking at the GEO office.

LODGING

In La Union, **Hotel Karol** is close to the Parque Central. Clean rooms with shared bathroom and showers cost $5. Nearby, **Hotel La Muralla** is similar. **La Carta** is a dormitory 10 kilometers (6.2 miles) out of town. Bring food, as there is no kitchen or nearby restaurant.

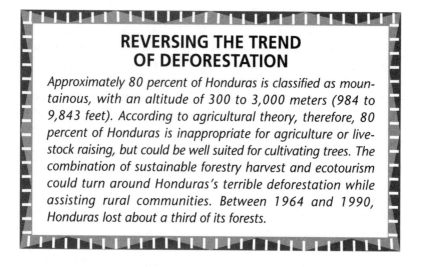

REVERSING THE TREND
OF DEFORESTATION

Approximately 80 percent of Honduras is classified as mountainous, with an altitude of 300 to 3,000 meters (984 to 9,843 feet). According to agricultural theory, therefore, 80 percent of Honduras is inappropriate for agriculture or livestock raising, but could be well suited for cultivating trees. The combination of sustainable forestry harvest and ecotourism could turn around Honduras's terrible deforestation while assisting rural communities. Between 1964 and 1990, Honduras lost about a third of its forests.

Researchers frequent this place, and arrange accommodations with COHDEFOR in La Unión.

Juticalpa has several hotels, none of them exceptional but most are clean and friendly. At **Boarding House Alemán** (a half-block west of Parque Central toward the Cine Maya; $5), owner Marcy Alemán offers a friendly dose of information and is known to pamper travelers. **Hotel Antunez** (1a Calle NO y 1a Avenida NO, 1 block west of Parque Central toward the Cine Maya) has rooms for $5. **Hotel El Paso** (1a Avenida NE y 6a Calle; $8) is between the bus station and the Parque Central. **Hotel La Muralla** (3 blocks from the Parque Central; $10) is relatively new hotel, with hot water.

In Catacamas, accommodations are simple, but the owners are friendly and proud of their beautiful town in the heart of Olancho. **Hotel Central,** Barrio El Centro, has clean, $7 rooms in a simple hotel that boasts a courtyard with a mango tree. **Hotel Colina** (off the Parque Central in Barrio San Sebastian) is reputed to be the best hotel in town, with hot water and televisions. **Hotel Rapalo,** Barrio San Sebastian, is a simple hotel with a restaurant, a parking garage, and $4 rates.

The *hospedajes* and visitors center in El Carbón are located north of the central pueblo along the road, not difficult to find. Just tell the bus driver to drop you off at the *colegio* (a large cement block building; all others are little mud huts) that sits along the east side of the road. The *hospedajes* are located right behind the *colegio;* just ask people for the *hospedajes del comite ambiental WATA*.

FOOD

La Union is a rural town, so you will not find fancy restaurants there. Several *comedores* provide typical Honduran fare. Check out **Cafetería La Muralla, Comedor Cindy,** and **Cafetería El Oasis**. Peace Corps volunteer Craig Perham recommends the Repostería Ruth bakery, where Salvador, the owner, bakes tasty treats that are even better after a day of hiking.

In Juticalpa, cattle country, beef dishes reign. The best cheap food is inside the main market (across from Cine Maya), where you can get good food at simple *comedores*. Choose one where a lot of local people are eating. **El Rancho,** 2a Avenida NE, serves mouth-watering *anafres* (simmering bean and cheese fondue) and *pinchos* (shish kebabs). **La Fonda** is one of several restaurants located along the highway. **Tropical Juices** serves just that. There are two locations, one on the park and one on the boulevard. The *licuados* (blended fruit shakes) here are as good as those on the coast.

In Catacamas, the best cheap eateries are said to be inside the market. At **As de Oro** (Ace of Gold), 10 blocks from the town center, bull testicles get their own sub-category on the menu: in soup, fried, or grilled. How hungry are you? **The Rodeo,** on the highway in town, offers traditional fare in a clean setting.

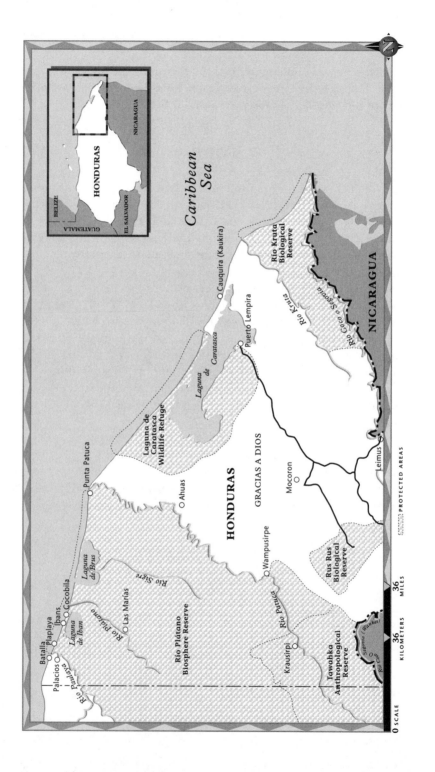

CHAPTER 10

The Final Frontier:
The Mosquito Coast

The very name "the Mosquito Coast" brings to mind the mystery of an unexplored wilderness, where the benefits and perils of modern civilization are still unknown and where the land seems threatening to the outsider yet offers shelter and protection to the Indians still living there. Paul Theroux's novel *The Mosquito Coast* (made into a 1986 movie starring Harrison Ford) is the story of a North American man who flees modernity, takes his family deep into a remote jungle, and then slowly goes mad. While the movie gave the region a bit of Hollywood exposure, it was not actually filmed in the Honduran Mosquitia, but in nearby Belize. The true Mosquito Coast is still too rough and not yet ready to support an international film crew.

In many ways, of course, the romantic image of the region is simply a romance. On the other hand, the Mosquito Coast is still one of those wild places where magic lurks, mixed with danger, laced with opportunity. The remote area is becoming increasingly more popular with adventurous travelers. For the wild at heart, the Mosquito Coast is the ultimate destination. Don't expect to find air conditioning or fluffy white towels. If you don't like what's for dinner, don't think about hailing a cab and going somewhere else. There are no roads and there are no real restaurants. Don't forget bug repellent, a mosquito net, and a water purification system. Bring your camera and lots of extra film along with a waterproof storage bag.

LAY OF THE LAND

The Mosquito Coast is a remote area of mangrove swamps, beaches, tiny islands (cays), lagoons, rivers, thick jungle, low mountains, and pine savannas. Located in northeastern Honduras and across the Coco River into northeastern Nicaragua, the region contains what is probably the greatest stretch of intact complex ecosystems in Central America. The terms "Mosquito Coast" and "La Mosquitia," the Spanish equivalent, are used interchangeably in this book. The word "Miskito" refers to a specific tribe of indigenous people who make their homes in the Mosquito Coast region.

Nearly the size of El Salvador yet with a population of only around 50,000, the Mosquito Coast is the most sparsely populated region in Central America. With a density of fewer than three people per square kilometer, traditional peoples still live by subsistence hunting, fishing, and agriculture, their small numbers ensuring the capacity of the land to survive into the future. La Mosquitia has the largest area of virgin rain forest in Honduras and one of the largest in Central America. Species of wood include balsa, ceiba, guayacan, mahogany, rosewood, sapodilla, Santa María, cedar, and pine. Fauna of the region, many of them endangered species, include the very rare black jaguar, ocelot, tapir, white-lipped peccary, white-faced and mantled howler monkeys, giant anteater, and deer. Birds include scarlet macaws, toucans, motmots, harpy eagles, the aplomado falcon, toucans, and tanagers. West Indian manatees, various species of sea turtle, caimans, and American crocodiles occupy the lower river and the lagoons, but the upper river is good to swim in and quite safe.

HISTORY AND CULTURE

We have little information about the earliest inhabitants of the Mosquito Coast region. But hundreds of small archaeological sites, thousands of artifacts, and dozens of petroglyphs suggest habitation

James D. Gollin

A typical home in La Mosquitia

by a non-Mayan, pre-Columbian civilization. The chief ethnic group living in the region at the time of the first European incursion was the Miskito Indians, who still dominate the area today.

Christopher Columbus sailed along the Mosquito Coast in the late 15th century. Upon his first sighting of the land, after a particularly stormy passage across from Guanaja, he named the region Gracias a Dios (Thanks to God). After Columbus' arrival, waves of Spanish conquistadors, settlers, and missionaries came to Central America. With few exceptions, these new explorers completely ignored the Mosquito Coast. The Spanish set up colonies in more profitable areas where their Indian slaves could grow export crops or dig silver and gold from primitive mines. While the Indians suffered, the Spanish prospered. The British and French were jealous of the wealth pouring out of the Spanish New World, but could do little about it. Quietly at first, and then increasingly brazenly, they encouraged buccaneers to raid Spanish ships and even seize port towns such as Trujillo.

Famous pirates from the region include Sir Henry Morgan, whose base was on Roatán, and the "freebooters," or politically

257

unconnected pirates, such as Edward Teach, who was known as Blackbeard. Whenever pursued, the small and maneuverable pirate ships headed for the Mosquito Coast. There they could hide out behind tiny cays or deep inside complex lagoon systems, slipping past uncharted coral reefs that would rip the bottom off any warship that dared give chase. The pirate era gave the coast many of the names still currently in use. Brus Lagoon, for example, was originally "Brewer's Lagoon," named after a pirate named "Bloody Brewer" who based himself there. Similarly, Cannon Cay was fortified with cannon, first by pirates and then by Captain Robert Hodgson, the first British Superintendent of the region.

The buccaneers and their allies in the British government eventually established dominance in much of the Caribbean and remote parts of Central America, including the Mosquito Coast. The dominant tribe of the coastal region, the Miskito, were known to the buccaneers as "Mosquitos" and the region became known as the "Mosquito Shore." The shore was upgraded to "the Kingdom of the Mosquitos" in 1687 when the English governor in Jamaica crowned a Miskito as king and used this as a pretext to set up a series of trading posts that the Spanish would never have allowed. From Black River, near present-day Palacios, British aristocrat William Pitt built a major outpost based on the export of mahogany, and other woods, bananas, sugar, cattle, and pitch. To this day, British influence in the area is evidenced by place names, surnames, and the relatively frequent use of English words in the Miskito language.

Spanish attempts to kick the British out of what had become their de facto protectorate, were uneven. In one bloody battle, Spanish troops on Cannon Cay were massacred by Miskitos and their British allies. Similarly, a Franciscan missionary crusade to convert the "heathen" Miskito along with the Jicaque, Paya, and Sumu met with violent resistance from the indigenous peoples and ended in complete failure. Victories won by the Miskito in the field, however, were lost at the negotiating table. The British agreed to abandon all claims to La Mosquitia in exchange for mahogany-logging rights in "British Honduras," present-day Belize. The Spanish, having won the prize of the Mosquito Coast in the late 18th century, proceeded to ignore the region completely for another two centuries.

In the 19th century, the United States kept the British from moving in and reestablishing their protectorate. The Americans wanted to keep the British from building a canal across the isthmus to the Pacific. During the early 1980s, another superpower rivalry played itself out along the Honduran–Nicaraguan border. The revolutionary Sandinista government, motivated by a desire to firm up control of their deepwater port at Bluefields (source of all their Cuban and Soviet aid), attempted to pacify and collectivize the Miskito and Sumu inhabitants of the never-tamed region of the Nicaraguan Mosquitia. Their rough-handed tactics fed right into the plans of the CIA. When the Sandinistas attacked, approximately 10,000 Miskito refugees crossed the Coco River to Honduras. While the United Nations High Commission on Refugees took care of many of their physical needs, many were recruited into MISURA, a CIA-backed, Honduran-based counterrevolutionary force. With overt and then covert U.S. support, MISURA operatives regularly crossed the Coco from Honduras to plant mines, blow up bridges and power lines, and generally make the Sandinistas regret their attempt to pacify the region. With the end of the Sandinista regime, most Nicaraguan Miskito have returned across the border to their former homes. The Río Coco region itself, however, is still laced with thousands of land mines that are only slowly being dug up and destroyed.

Who exactly are the Miskito and what distinguishes them from other indigenous peoples of the area? The question is not easy to answer. The first Miskito were probably a mixture of Sumu, Rama, and Paya peoples who mixed freely in the Caribbean lowlands, forming a syncretic culture. Friendly and open, these Miskito intermarried with British and other European visitors and settlers, escaped African slaves, Ladinos, and Chinese. The Miskito have their own language, which includes various subdialects such as Kabo, Mam, and Wangki. Miskito language and culture are very much alive in the region, and MOPAWI is developing a bilingual school curriculum so that Miskito children can learn in their own language as well as Spanish.

For the most part the Miskito people live in the Caribbean coastal area, from Palacios all the way to the Río San Juan in the southeastern Nicaraguan department of Zelaya. Another ethnic group still living along the Río Plátano and at Baltiltuk are the Paya, or Pech, who speak Chibcha, the language of the Chibcha Indians of South

America. The Pech live well inland with their main villages located at least two days on foot from Las Marías and at El Carbón; near San Esteban in Olancho; at Silin in Colón; and in Nueva Subirana near Culmi in Olancho. Most Pech still practice subsistence agriculture, eating a yucca-based dish called sasal and fishing or hunting with lances for peccary for protein to supplement their diets. Some Pech farmers also raise chickens and ducks. According to Pech legend, they once lived in a great lost city known as La Ciudad Blanca (The White City). In fact, Pech territory once extended much further than the half-dozen remote villages they still occupy in the Río Plátano region. Over the last centuries, however, the dominant Miskito, armed with muskets received from their British allies, have forced the Pech inland, deep into the rain forests. Currently, approximately 1,500 people claim to be of Pech descent, many of whom live in the increasingly touristed region around Las Marías in the heart of the Río Plátano Biosphere Reserve. It remains to be seen whether the influx of tourism will save or destroy this ethnic group.

Members of the Tawahka tribe, a subgroup of the larger Sumu tribe, live primarily between the Patuca and Wampu Rivers and in the area around Culmi in Olancho. Their territory stretches up to the Cerros de Pimienta, Cerros Krautara, the Río Wampu region, and the Río Aner. Important Tawahka villages include Krautara, Krausirpe, Kamakasna, and Yapuwas. Unfortunately, the Tawahkas' territory lies directly in the path of Ladino colonization, which increasingly threatens traditional Tawahka lands. Furthermore, many Tawahka from Nicaragua crossed the border into Honduras during the 1980s and some remain to this day, stressing the carrying capacity of the delicate ecosystems of the area.

Finally, many Garífuna peoples, descendants of African slaves and Carib Indians (described elsewhere in this book), live in the coastal areas of western La Mosquitia, specifically in the villages of Batalla and Plaplaya.

Many of the indigenous peoples of the Mosquito Coast retain traditional religious beliefs, going to medicine men known as *sukya* for healing and for ceremonies to mark births and deaths. While most of these ceremonies are private, the ceremony for death, the *seekrow*, is public and involves the drinking of fermented cassava mash known as *mishla*. Nearly all of the indigenous peoples of the area rely on the forest for food, medicines, and building materials, and they still practice ancient traditions in sacred sites in their homelands.

Unlike the majority of the Honduras population and of Central America, not all the indigenous peoples of the coast are Catholics. The Ladino culture of Honduras and Nicaragua never penetrated far into the Mosquito Coast. Most Miskito consider themselves to be devout Moravians, a group somewhat similar to the Amish that originally hailed from the German–Czech border region and also have a major presence in Pennsylvania. Moravian missionaries arrived in La Mosquitia in the 1930s, evangelizing and developing community programs. Now Moravians from around the world support much of the health and human services infrastructure of the region, a responsibility historically abdicated by the distant government of Tegucigalpa. The Moravian Church funds school programs, clinics, cooperative bakeries, and a host of other social services throughout the region. It is also a major supporter of the nondenominational NGO known as MOPAWI.

The economy of the Mosquito Coast, still largely based on subsistence fishing, hunting, gathering, and small-scale agriculture, has been transformed by the modern economic forces at work outside the riverine systems, pristine rain forest, and pine savannas that the Miskito call home. The traditional agricultural system of the Miskito itself is now under threat by forces far upstream. The Miskito generally live in small villages located on navigable rivers, and usually plant their crops of rice, beans, and yucca in thin swatches of land along the rivers, an area naturally irrigated, annually replenished with fresh mud from upstream, and easy to clear and access.

Deep inland, mountainous regions are becoming increasingly deforested by cattle-ranchers, timber barons, and migratory agricultural practices of the campesinos. With less forest to absorb and slowly release rainfall, the rivers that flow through the Mosquito Coast become significantly narrower during dry periods and rage over the riverbanks during rainy seasons. In an industrialized or modern agricultural society, such turbulent river activity can take out bridges, complicate irrigation, and negatively affect the rural economy. In the delicately balanced Mosquito Coast environment, however, crops began to dry out during dry periods and be washed away in the floods. Without their subsistence crops, Miskito were forced to look to outside help to avoid starvation.

The advent of geopolitics began in the 1980s, when the Soviet-supported, Cuban-trained Sandinista army attempted to collectivize Nicaraguan Miskito villages. Thousands of Miskito crossed the unmarked border and found refuge with their Honduran Miskito cousins. The munificently anti-Communist forces of Ollie North, backed by a budget swollen by arms sales to Iran and perhaps even cocaine sales in East Los Angeles, handed out free food and other support to these "anti-Communist" refugees. In what amounted to something of a late 20th–century cargo cult, some Miskito came to believe that the easiest path to economic growth was to petition the Honduran government and their American patrons for aid. The aid, of course, dried up with the waning of the perceived Communist threat and the embarrassing revelations of the Iran-Contra scandal in Washington.

The Miskito, however, still need to raise cash to buy clothing, medicine, and, when the crops fail, enough food to survive. In the late 1980s, soon after the AK-47–toting Sandinistas and the M-16–armed Contras withdrew from the area, the modern world again arrived on the Mosquito Coast. This time, the outsiders weren't military advisers. They were skippers from the Bay Islands in fishing boats outfitted with air compressors. Boat captains first came to the coast in the late 1970s in search of quick riches through the harvest of the "white gold" of the Caribbean: spiny-tailed–lobster meat. By the early 1990s, lobster diving had come to dominate the Miskito economy.

The Miskito Indians, renowned for their free-diving ability, have long supplemented their incomes and diets by harvesting lobster and conch. Over the last decade, however, the introduction of primitive diving equipment has transformed lobster diving into a major export industry. Each year, hundreds of boats set out from Roatán, sail to the Mosquito Coast to pick up a diving crew, and then fan out across the Caribbean in search of lobster-rich waters. After two to three weeks, they drop the Indians back on the coast and sail to the Bay Islands with holds full of iced lobster tails. They stock up on supplies, sail back to the Mosquito Coast, and repeat the process again and again.

On a two-week trip, divers can make about $500—about as much as the average Honduran would make in six months. But the bounty has not always brought prosperity to the divers and their families.

Many Indians head home to their villages between dive trips and, in more cases than not, blow their income on alcohol, prostitutes, and cheap cocaine. Osvaldo Munguia, Executive Director of the Miskito Indian organization MOPAWI, is saddened by the fact that alcoholism and drug abuse soak up the lion's share of many divers' pay, but points out that the divers' income still manages to support about half of La Mosquitia's population. Over the last decade, lobster diving has become by far the largest contributor to the cash economy of the Mosquito Coast.

In the long term, though, the reduction in population of the lobsters will force Miskito to look to other marine resources. MOPAWI is attempting to develop a sustainable harvest program for sea urchin, sea cucumber, shark fin, and various seaweeds that have a market in Japan. "It would be a mistake to develop another industry without any sense of control or stewardship," says Munguia. MOPAWI also hopes to develop other economic activities in La Mosquitia, including the cultivation of organic cacao and, of course, ecotourism.

PROTECTED AREAS AND THREATENED AREAS

In 1980, an immense portion of the Mosquito Coast surrounding the Plátano River was proclaimed as Central America's first biosphere reserve. The Río Plátano Biosphere Reserve was also declared a World Heritage Site by UNESCO. The biosphere reserve lies in the western section of La Mosquitia, bordered roughly by the Río Paulaya to the west and the Río Patuca to the east. In the center of this reserve lies the Río Plátano, a pristine river running from perfect virgin rain forest down toward the lagoons and white-sand beaches of the coast. The 800,000-square-hectare (almost 2-million-acre) Río Plátano Biosphere Reserve is now appearing on maps, its border stretching from the Río Patuca to the Río Wampu.

The Río Plátano, while immense in itself, is a part of a network of parks, biosphere reserves, and indigenous reserves that, in theory, will protect the wonders of the Mosquito Coast into the next millennia. Directly to the south and contiguous to the World Heritage Site is the Tawahka Anthropological Reserve. Further south is the proposed Patuca National Park, forming a steady band of protected

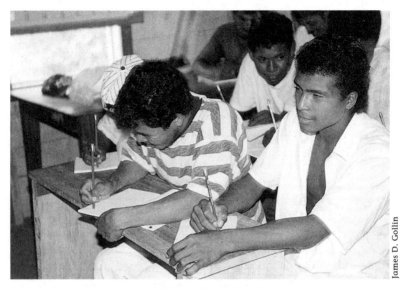

James D. Gollin

A MOPAWI-run lobster diving school in Cocobila

areas that will cut off the migration of landless campesinos from the south and west. Theoretically, at least, this system is buttressed by a companion system across the border in Nicaraguan Mosquitia, and by the Rus Rus and Río Kruta Biosphere Reserves and the Caratasca Lagoon Wildlife Preserve in Honduran Mosquitia. Together they protect the entire region for the benefit of local indigenous peoples and, as the United Nations has pointed out, for the future generations of the world.

In 1994 President Reina inaugurated a new plan for the region known as Plapawans, a system of reserves whose protection would be backed by the state. According to the plan, colonists in the Sico-Paulaya valleys would be relocated further away from the Río Plátano Biosphere, but, in fact, very few people have been relocated and the system of reserves exists primarily on paper.

Another ambitious program is Paseo Pantera, an effort to create a mega-biocorridor linking protected areas across national boundaries throughout Central America, from Panama to Guatemala.

In 1992, 500 years after the encounter between Europeans and the indigenous peoples of America, MOPAWI organized an

Indigenous Indian Congress and called for the merging of the Río Plátano Biosphere Reserve with adjacent reserves to form a unified corridor from the western coastal areas all the way down to the Nicaraguan border. In July 1993, however, the Honduran press reported that campesinos were clearing thousands of acres of land in the neighboring Sico-Paulaya district, the area between the Río Sico and the Río Paulaya. Recently there has been a tremendous incursion of landless campesinos who, according to the official story, were given the right to farm in the flat areas near the river banks by a beneficent and compassionate government. The truth of the matter is somewhat more complex. It seems that cattle interests, some in partnership with military officers, are the actual beneficiaries of the Sico-Paulaya land-grab. Campesinos enter an area and claim land simply by erecting wooden posts or slashing the trunks of existing trees. Next, timber companies, often connected to unscrupulous politicians or soldiers, take the valuable trees, then often pass the ruined forest on to cattle ranchers. The campesinos, many of whom were lured to the area with promises of a better life, have no power to claim this cleared land. They are forced up into the tropical mountainsides, still using agricultural techniques suitable for fertile plains.

The subsistence farmers who came to the region over the last two decades are also being forced off the arable lands of the valleys by more profitable and politically connected cattle-farmers. Heading up into the mountains of the Sierra de Río Tinto National Forest and the Montaña El Carbón Anthropological Reserve, these campesinos are tilling soil so poor that they must burn new land and move nearly every year.

Officially, there has been a moratorium on the cutting of mahogany in the Sico Paulaya region for three years, but *Honduras This Week* newspaper reports that tens of thousands of board feet of mahogany logs, cut from the nuclear zone of the biosphere reserve, regularly make their way to Palacios, where they are sold to the international market. COHDEFOR, the national forestry agency, is generally looked down upon by local inhabitants familiar with accusations that it gives permission for outside timber companies to log extensively while locals are denied permission to clear bush for subsistence farming. A blatant example of this was COHDEFOR's closing small resin- and timber-extraction cooperatives in the buffer zone of the

Río Plátano Biosphere Reserve while ignoring the operation of a larger commercial sawmill in the nuclear zone. While COHDEFOR has the authority to stop such cutting, it is the people of the area who are organizing to protect the forest.

The Miskito Indian group MOPAWI has conducted aerial surveys of La Mosquitia with the aid of the North American "Environmental Air Force" Lighthawk in an attempt to press traditional land claims. MOPAWI combined the high-tech aerial surveys with old-fashioned legwork, visiting residents of over 200 communities in 22 regions of La Mosquitia. Indigenous and nonindigenous residents were asked where they farm, hunt, fish, pan for gold, gather construction materials, and collect medicinal plants. The results of the survey were then collated into a general land-use map by Dr. Herlihy, a "cultural" geographer from Southeastern Louisiana University. The rough draft was then taken back to the communities and corrected, and then the composite land-use map of La Mosquitia was presented to the Honduran government. While progress has been slow, there have been measurable victories. The North Carolina–based timber company Wellington Hall, for example, was recently refused permission to log in traditionally used La Mosquitia lands.

Currently, the Honduran government still has land-tenure laws based on 19th-century U.S. homestead regulations. "Undeveloped" land belongs to the state but anyone who can improve the land by cutting trees, growing crops or cattle, and living on it for a number of years has a right to claim ownership. The Miskito claim that they have been living on the land of the entire region for many centuries and have the right to formal ownership but that their traditional uses of the land (religious ceremonies in one area, cutting of large trees to build dugout canoes in another, hunting for small game in a third) were carried out in such an environmentally responsible way that there is little physical trace of their economic activity. The Miskito feel that they are being penalized for their environmental consciousness and that land-tenancy rules should be written to favor those who can live off the land without destroying it. The government has, at least in principal, indicated its intention to protect Miskito and other native's land rights within the Río Plátano Biosphere Reserve and other protected areas of La Mosquitia, but the details are dangerously vague.

VISITOR INFORMATION

Almost everyone has heard of the Mosquito Coast, but very few know where it is and fewer still have actually been there. Modern air transport, however, has made the region superficially accessible. Hop on a plane in La Ceiba, and you'll land in Palacios before you know it. Regular flights are also available to Puerto Lempira, close to the Nicaraguan border; to Ahuas, home to the Moravian Mission Hospital; or to Wampu Sirpi, a lovely little town on the Patuca River. Take a motorized dugout canoe along the coastal waterway and enjoy the lagoons and beaches of the nearby coastal towns, or inland up the Río Plátano to Las Marías and beyond. But don't be fooled by this ease of access. Most of the Mosquito Coast is still a very primitive place, with no roads, no electricity, no telephones, and no system of transportation more advanced than the dugout canoe. If weather or mechanical problems ground your plane, you will soon realize how far away you are from everything you take for granted.

Despite its wildness, La Mosquitia is an extremely friendly place. Travelers will come across simple villages with tidy wood-and-thatch homes, populated by welcoming men and women and an army of half-naked children who will dance in glee at the appearance of a stranger. Here, more than anywhere in Honduras, you will need to be conscious of the effects of your travels and of preserving the paradise-like quality of the area. For example, don't hand out candy or pens to the kids, as it could lead to a pattern of begging, and don't snap pictures without permission. If you want to offer the kids a gift, teach them how to count in your native language and ask them how to count in Miskito. If you take photographs, get an address and send copies back to the coast, probably in care of the local MOPAWI office. Especially here, be patient, be kind, be considerate. You will be rewarded with a profound and unforgettable adventure.

In general, there are three ways to get to and around in the Mosquito Coast. Regularly scheduled planes fly in and out of the region, generally from La Ceiba. In addition, tiny four-seaters run by Sami Air Taxi work their way around a network of dirt runways. Based in Ahuas, the missionary-funded air ambulances of Alas de Socorro

INDIGENOUS ORGANIZATIONS IN LA MOSQUITIA

You might meet up with representatives of some of the following organizations while traveling in the Mosquito Coast, all of whom deserve your cooperation and respect. With the exception of MOPAWI, which has offices in La Ceiba and Tegucigalpa, none are easily reached from outside the region.

MOPAWI, active throughout La Mosquitia, promotes ecotourism and is attempting to create systems that will maximize the benefits and minimize the damages inherent to the industry.

The **Consejo del Turismo de Las Marías** was recently formed to help supervise the guides and packaged trips available in Las Marías.

RAYAKA, formerly the Commite Vigilante de la Tierra, or CVT, is an organization comprised mostly of Miskito and Pech that, from their head office in Cocobila, is attempting to develop a network of guards to protect the Río Plátano Biosphere Reserve and the Patuca National Park.

Organización Para Consego Tribo Pech (OPCPT), a Pech Indian group, works with RAYAKA in supervising the development of appropriate infrastructure for sustainable ecotourism in the area around Las Marías. **CCTM** is a Garífuna group out of Plaplaya. Other smaller groups work on specific issue areas, such as the preservation of the sea turtle.

(Wings of Help) also crisscross the region, picking up patients and ferrying them to the Moravian clinics or out of the region to larger hospitals. When there are no planes, the next-fastest mode of transport is boat, usually a motorized canoe, or *cayuco*. Or, in shallow waterways, you can take a light, hand-paddled *pipante*. Finally, the sturdy of limb can walk, either along the white-sand beaches, up shallow watercourses, or down faint jungle paths. Ideally, a trip to the coast will involve all three forms of transportation.

Costs of travel in the region are quite reasonable, but planes do not necessarily fly every day. Airfares from La Ceiba to Brus Lagoon on Sosa Airlines are $51 one-way, flying in and out on Monday and Friday only. Isleña Air flies from La Ceiba to Palacios for $36 one-way, every day except Sunday. Isleña also flies from Tegucigalpa to Palacios for $70 and from San Pedro Sula to Palacios for $61. It recently resumed service to Puerto Lempira. Check with other airlines, such as Sami Air Taxi and Caribbean Air, who may be flying where you want to go when you'd like to go. You can estimate that a nonscheduled trip will cost around $100 per person, more for a charter. In many cases, the best bet is to ask around at La Ceiba Airport. There may well be a charter or a nonscheduled cargo flight about to take off with room for you and your bags.

The best time to visit is February through May, when rainfall is infrequent.

James D. Gollin

Río Plátano Biosphere Reserve

NATURE AND ADVENTURE SIGHTS

The Río Plátano Biosphere Reserve

The Río Plátano Biosphere Reserve is one of the largest protected areas in Central America. Established as a World Heritage Site in 1980, the biosphere reserve has long been populated by indigenous peoples, including Miskito, Pech, and Garífuna, most of whom live in small villages on the coast and along navigable rivers. On the western edge of La Mosquitia, near Palacios, this 5,200-square-kilometer (2,008-square-mile) area of lowland tropical rain forest, lagoon systems, sandy beaches, mangrove swamps, and extensive pine savanna is the most easily accessible part of the remote Mosquito Coast, ideal for "soft adventure" travel.

The coastal and inland sections of the Río Plátano are pristine. The southern zone of the biosphere reserve, however, is imperiled by Ladino colonization, with over 25 percent of the area deforested or badly degraded in the years since its founding. Six army officers have established cattle ranches in the nuclear zone. Commercial loggers have been at work in the area since the 1950s, cutting through log extraction roads to the headwaters of the Paulaya and Plátano Rivers. Laborers in the sawmills and on logging crews, once in the region, filed land claims and cleared land with chainsaws to grow corn. An estimated 3,700 people live in the zone of the Río Plátano Biosphere Reserve, the vast majority of whom have entered illegally since 1980. Most of them were originally from the Pacific Coast region, pushed out to the frontier by soil degradation and overpopulation in that area. As in southern Honduras, deforestation in the southern part of the biosphere reserve is already affecting the local climate. In the past, rain used to fall throughout the year, but now the dry season has become more pronounced, increasing the risk of forest fires.

Palacios is a small town at the western edge of the Río Plátano Biosphere Reserve, home to a small fishing camp, a small hotel, and a long, thin central park that doubles as the airport. Since the runway is cleared of major vegetation, grass grows. And because there is grass, horses and cows graze in the park and kids play soccer. Do not be surprised when the pilot of your small plane buzzes the runway a few times before landing. He's chasing the livestock off the runway. A small shack at the edge of the runway, right next to the wreckage of an

Hand-carved cayuco *canoes used by divers*

Isleña flight that botched its landing, serves as the local terminal. If you spend any time in Palacios, you can't help but run into Felix Marmol, proprietor of the local Isleña airline ticket office, the hotel, and a small restaurant. Felix is also planning on getting more involved in the ecotourist dollar by organizing trips upriver from his hotel.

You can find simple supplies in Palacios such as drinking water, batteries, and toilet paper. Stock up on whatever you need. Simple as it is, Palacios is a modern metropolis compared to the small towns of the coast and the interior.

From Palacios, a network of rivers, waterways, and lagoons linked by motorized dugout canoes form a slow but efficient system of public transportation. Regular water-taxi service links Palacios to coastal villages in the reserve such as **Cocobila, Raista,** and **Belen.** The pleasant trip passes dozens of stilted, thatch-roofed family compounds of Miskito Indians interspersed throughout the area. The boat ride is a great introduction to the flora and fauna of the region as it passes through the habitat of a variety of bird species. The direct trip to Cocobila takes about two hours and costs around $2.50. If you have

271

SAVING MISKITO LIVES

*"If they outlaw diving, 50,000 of my people will face starvation,"
says Celestino Rivas, a 20-year diving veteran and member of
HOMIBAT, a Miskito divers group. Similarly, MOPAWI's strategy
is to educate divers in safe diving techniques while asking the
government to strictly enforce a diver certification program.*

*In 1993, MOPAWI and the Moravian Church brought for-
mer U.S. military intelligence operative Robert Armington to the
remote Mosquito Coast town of Cocobila to set up a diver training school. When he heard about the plight of the Miskito,
Armington gave up a lucrative career as an underwater demoli-
tion and salvage expert. He moved to a one-room shack in
Cocobila, built a school with his own hands, and started teaching basic concepts of safe diving. For example, opening a bottle
of warm beer.*

*Armington would simulate the formation of nitrogen bub-
bles in the bloodstream. Soon he was taking semiliterate divers
through the U.S. Navy dive tables, training them in basic equipment maintenance, and developing strategies for minimizing
bottom time.*

*Armington's best students, such as the partially paralyzed
former diver Roberto Hernandez, were trained as dive instructors*

the time, pay a bit more for a private boat and ask the driver to take a
less-direct route, through the smaller waterways where there is more
birdlife and the overhanging branches on either side form a green
tunnel. Typically, planes arrive in Palacios at around 11 a.m. and
boats depart shortly thereafter.

Along the coast east of Palacios, a narrow spit of land separates
the Caribbean from the inland waterway and the **Ibans Lagoon.** The
spit is dotted with small villages, including Plaplaya, Ibans, Cocobila,
Raista, Belen, Nueva Jerusalem, and Kuri. It is easy to walk from

and later opened their own schools. As of 1999, a dozen Miskito diving instructors have been certified. They in turn have certified approximately 2,000 divers out of a total diving population of around 5,000. Dive-boat owners, eager to preserve their future income, are now helping to fund diver training and are providing their divers with some rudimentary safety equipment. Dive-related injuries, while still far too numerous, have decreased significantly since the inception of the diver training program.

The story of lobster diving off the Mosquito Coast is indicative of an all too familiar pattern which has emerged wherever indigenous peoples are impacted by the modern economy. Their traditional cultures dissolve in a flood of new diseases, alcohol, and the exigencies of living in a cash economy. In the case of Honduras, landless peasants and cattle barons gradually extend roads into La Mosquitia, logging and burning the forests, and "colonizing" the lands that the Indians used to hunt, trap, and fish. It is impossible to convince a diver making $500 in two weeks to go back to subsistence farming, especially when he feels powerless in defending his traditional land and livelihood. By and large the diver training program has been a success, but with lobsters becoming scarcer, divers are heading ever deeper into dangerous waters.

village to village along the beach, an inland trail, or along the inland waterway. There is also an old pickup truck that sometimes lumbers along the palm frond–shaded path that links the coastal villages, acting as a sort of bus. Each town has developed small *hospedajes*, often rooms in the homes of relatively well-to-do families who have managed to hold onto some of their lobster-diving earnings. The freshwater inland waterway runs parallel to the coast and crosses the Ibans and Brus Lagoons. The water in the coastal lagoons is beautiful and almost always calm. The shallow water is home to tremendous marine life including the manatee and crocodiles; ask a local before you decide to swim.

Don't be surprised if, in a remote town with neither telephones nor electricity, families congregate in the house of a relatively wealthy resident to watch Mexican soap operas and MTV on a battery-powered television. Barefoot teenagers who have never seen pavement have learned to wear their baseball caps backwards and their shorts extra-baggy, in hip-hop style.

At Raista, be sure to drop in on the **butterfly farm,** a sustainable-development project that is helping to diversify income sources from lobster diving. With aid from the Peace Corps and several U.S. foundations, butterflies are raised and their pupae are shipped off to the San Diego Zoo and other live butterfly exhibition houses, providing an environmentally friendly export income to the people of Raista as well as ecotourism income. Take a guided tour of the butterfly farm, donating around $1.50 per person.

Further down the beach, near **Plaplaya,** MOPAWI is struggling to keep a program alive that protects leatherback and loggerhead sea turtles. When the turtles come up to the beaches at night from March to June to dig out nests and lay their eggs, villagers patrol the area to ward off poachers and predators, then gather up the eggs and rebury them in a hatchery where they will be guarded until they hatch.

Plaplaya is home to a Garífuna population and, if you're lucky, you may witness their traditional dances. If the Garífuna are dancing, watch politely and join in only if you are invited.

Guided boat trips across the Ibans Lagoon or up the Río Tinto Negro are wonderful ways to watch wildlife.

While the coast is pleasant, the true Río Plátano experience must include a trip upriver to **Las Marías** and possibly beyond. Las Marías is a small Miskito and Pech village that is rapidly becoming a center for adventurous ecotourists. Ask around on the coast for a boat that can take you up the Río Plátano, a six-to-eight-hour journey. Small boats known as *pipantes* are cheaper but less comfortable than larger *cayuco* dugouts. A typical round-trip fare including a day up, a day in Las Marías, and a day return costs $100 to $125, which you can share with up to four other people. One-way trips, if you can find them, are less expensive. Make sure that your boat is in good shape and tell the driver that you are not in a hurry. Part of the fun is taking regular stops to swim, sunbathe on sandbars, and take short hikes.

The territory on the banks of this part of the Río Plátano, while wild, is not uninhabited. Rather, small Miskito and Pech communities live off the land, planting their crops alongside the river and hunting and gathering in the forest. With low population density, the rain forest can support such activity. The impact of ecotourism, however, can threaten the balance. Don't contribute to the decay of this delicate balance by thoughtlessly offering money or gifts from the modern world to children, and of course don't purchase bird feathers or animal skins.

In Las Marías, basic accommodations are available for about $2.50 per night, with meals an additional $1.50 each. The people of Las Marías are attempting to negotiate a difficult transition as they move from a neolithic existence to playing host to adventurers from North America and Europe. We encourage you to be considerate and, when things get confusing, be forgiving. In order to preserve their culture from the impact of drugs and alcohol, Las Marías has been declared alcohol-free, so don't ask for beer or rum *(guaro)*. Other rules include a prohibition on removing archaeological relics, live animals, or animal products. Do not eat native wildlife, and do catch-and-release if you want to fish. Ask permission before taking photographs of people and, if you do, send copies to them c/o MOPAWI Las Marías, A.P 2175, Tegucigalpa.

Early visitors to Las Marías were regularly set upon by competing teams of boatmen and guides and two rival town governments which competed for the right to collect income from the tourists, but the situation is now relatively well-organized. When you arrive in town, a representative of the guides association will let you know what services are available at what price. To simplify matters, they ask that you elect a leader in your group to act as spokesperson and that you agree on a total price with the head guide before you leave on your trip. Also, follow instructions about proper behavior in the canoes. Stay near your guides when you are in the forest, and respect the guides when they say they cannot travel more that day. You can custom-design any type of trip that you want. If possible, meet with your actual guides (as opposed to the head guide) and talk about potential trips and activities, but don't try and bargain one guide against

STONE CONTAINER

In 1991, the Honduran government under President Callejas signed an agreement with Stone Container Corporation, a giant multinational paper and packaging company, giving Stone exclusive rights to cut over a million hectares of forest in La Mosquitia—essentially, to pulp the Mosquito Coast and make cardboard boxes out of it. While Stone claimed that it would replant in a responsible manner, environmental NGOs did some research and, with the help of American activist Pam Wellner, exposed Stone's ugly record of abusing the environment, making quick profits, paying fines, then moving on. MOPAWI vowed to fight the Stone-Callejas plan and enlisted the support of religious leaders, the press, businesses, and even labor unions. The fight against Stone Container was formative for the Honduran environmental movement, with middle-class Hondurans expressing their national pride by rejecting the backroom deals made between big gringo corporations and leaders of the Honduran government. In televised debates, Hondurans declared, "We are no longer a banana republic." Faced with overwhelming public pressure, the government reversed course and canceled Stone's permission to pulp La Mosquitia. Like the refinery proposal for Trujillo, though, bad ideas never seem to die. The battle to preserve the wilderness must be re-fought and re-won time and time again.

another. The 30 or so guides in Las Marías have formed a cooperative and pool their set-price income, sharing the benefits of ecotourism with other guides and the overall community.

While walking around Las Marías, you will probably be offered miniature wood carvings of *pipantes* or dugout canoes (complete with miniature paddles), bags of locally produced cocoa, and other hand-icrafts. Spend some time shopping around and learn to bargain for a fair price. Think of purchasing something to help support the local economy.

There is a small medical clinic in town, staffed by Carlos Adelmo Hernandez and equipped with snake-bite serum and other life-saving necessities.

From Las Marías you can take pleasant day hikes around the village or head up to Pico Dama on a very strenuous three-day hike. **Pico Dama** adventurers need to have good boots, water bottles, light backpacks, and enough food for the boat trip, the two-day hike in, and the one-day hike back. There is an open-air shelter for sleeping on the second night that offers no protection from insects; bring a tent and/or mosquito netting. The current fixed cost for the trip is 650L for two people, 225L more for each additional person. The price includes the canoes and canoe guides (to take you to the trail-head) and the trail guides to take you to the summit. In the rainy season the trip takes an additional two days and is not recommended. I have not been to this rain forest–clad mountain peak, but have been told that the scenery is spectacular.

An easier expedition is to **Pico Baltimore.** Two guides are manda-tory for any hike of over two days. Each guide charges 100L per day (125L on Sunday), so a two-day trip to and from Pico Baltimore would cost 400L and could be split among four trekkers. An extra day would be an additional 200L. At the summit, there is a *champa* (an open-air, thatched-roofed structure) for shelter. Be prepared to cross rivers several times during your trek.

Heading upriver, you can day trip by *pipante* to the mysterious **petroglyphs** at Walpulbansirpi, inscribed in the rock by an unknown pre-Columbian civilization. Or take a multiday trip visiting other petroglyph sites and keeping an eye out for wildlife in the heart of the biosphere reserve. Whatever you do, don't do it alone. Even close to the village, it is easy to get lost on the jungle trails. Hire a guide for about $6 per day (a bit more on Sunday), splitting the cost among up to five people. Guides can also provide food and equipment for an overnight hike.

Upriver from Las Marías, the river is often too shallow or too choked with vegetation to use a motor, so the *pipantes* are pushed along by a wooden pole. Depending on the flow of the river, as many as three guides per boat will be needed to push upstream through small rapids and wield machetes to chop vines and fallen tree that may block the passage. One small boat with three guides will generally have room for two tourists and their gear. Don't demand to take three tourists in a boat if the guides say no. Whatever you bring with you should be packed in waterproof bags, preferably the kind used by rafters.

While a day trip up to the petroglyphs is more economical, you will spend most of your time in the boat. On an overnight trip, you'll have time to hike up the Sulawala or Wahawala Creeks. Floods during the rainy season wash away streamside vegetation, providing a natural path up these magical waterways. Walk carefully and quietly and, especially early in the morning, you'll have an excellent opportunity to see birds and other wildlife. Make sure to wear footwear suitable for the water, as you'll be wading back and forth.

Overnight trips cost about $22 per boat per day, including the cost of the three guides and their food. Bring your own camping gear and, if possible, bring your own food in from the coast. You can purchase simple things such as rice, beans, yucca, and plantains in Las Marías, but be aware that the local people will be tempted to sell you food they should really hold onto to feed their families. In any case, the guides will prepare a fire and cook your food for you. The guide will want to see the food that you brought with you before you depart. If they offer to hunt wild game for you, refuse politely.

Very little camping gear is available in Las Marías. Think about offering any extra camping gear to the guides as a tip if you won't be needing it for the rest of your trip. They will surely put it to good use. Most of the guides speak Spanish as a second language and have limited English, but with a little patience, you can exchange stories around the campfire and learn of the creatures and spirits that inhabit the forest around you.

Some travelers who have made it upstream from the coast want to try their hands at returning to the Caribbean without a guide. This is not advisable unless you've traveled the river many times and have an "Instituto Geográfico" topographic map. For expert kayakers with modern gear, the trip to the coast can take seven hours—but it could also take two days, depending upon how rapidly the water is running and how often you get lost.

Details: *All roads may lead to Rome, but none lead to the Río Plátano. The easiest way in is to book a trip with an outfitter or just hop a regular flight on Isleña Airlines, Sosa, or Rollins Air from La Ceiba to Palacios (daily except Sunday) and make arrangements there. Adventurers and those on a tighter budget can take a bus from La Ceiba or Trujillo to Límon, then walk in 60 kilometers (37 miles) along the beach to Palacios. But this is wild country and the wildness is both exhilarating and dangerous. Anyone planning such rough travel on their own should purchase a copy of Derek Parent's book* La Mosquitia: A Guide to the Land of Savannas, Rain Forests and Turtle Hunters, *which provides detailed information that can save travelers serious discomfort and even their lives.*

Farther along the Coast

From Cocobila, it is a 12-kilometer (7.5-mile) beach walk to **Brus Lagoon,** crossing the mouth of the Río Plátano by dugout. Head into this area with the understanding that tourism is quite new. Think of it as civilized camping, plan on using pit toilets, and don't even think about washing with hot water. Though the coastal area is relatively mosquito-free due to the constant offshore breezes, always bring a portable mosquito net and plenty of repellent.

The village of **La Barra,** at the confluence of Brus Laguna and the Caribbean, is so infested with no-see-ums from May to September that you have to wear a completely enclosed "bug jacket" with built-in hood, or generously apply 40 percent DEET to all exposed areas of your body. Without repellent, you'll literally be "eaten alive." Also, make sure to have water purification pills or a Katadyn-type water filter on hand, as bottled water is nonexistent.

Derek Parent, author of *La Mosquitia: A Guide to the Land of Savannas, Rain Forests and Turtle Hunters,* strongly recommends bombing your water with a purification tablet after filtering. Derek also suggests that anyone who is not allergic to antibiotics and who is traveling into remote regions carry 500-mg doses of Ciprofloxacin antibiotic as insurance.

The Río Plátano enters the Caribbean between Ibans and Brus Lagoons. In Brus Lagoon, look for Cecilio Colindres, owner/operator of COVITUDENA, which in his words is "a grass-roots non-lucrative organization exclusively formed by the Native Indians of the Reserve of

MOPAWI

MOPAWI is the acronym for Mosquitia Pawisa which means "the development of La Mosquitia." Founded in 1985, MOPAWI works in the areas of agriculture, forestry, women's issues, fisheries and diving, bilingual education, sustainable development, and environmental protection.

With a staff of around 30, MOPAWI maintains offices in Tegucigalpa, Puerto Lempira, and La Ceiba and "bases" in Belen, Cocobila, Sico, Batalla, Las Marías, Ahuas, and Wampu Sirpi. MOPAWI maintains a two-way radio system at its bases throughout the region for use in medical emergencies and in spreading important news and human rights issues through offices in Tegucigalpa and La Ceiba. While the radios don't always work, they are the best means of communication in the region. MOPAWI is mainly a Miskito organization, but it represents all of the people of the region, and its Executive Director, Osvaldo Munguia, is of Jicaque Indian descent. Other local NGOs, such as the diver organization HOMIBAT, RAYAKA (formerly, the Comite Vigilancia de Tierra), and COVITUDENA, also operate in the region, but MOPAWI is the largest and most effective NGO operating in the Mosquito Coast.

Contact MOPAWI in Puerto Lempira at 98-7460 or in Tegucigalpa at 237-7210, fax 239-9234, 2a Calle #1336 Apartado Postal 2175, e-mail: mopawi@optinet.hn.

the Río Plátano, whose purpose is to defend their ancestral rights and the natural beauty of the biosphere against ambition and greed from outsiders." He uses an old fishing lodge in Palacios as his base of operations. Colindres recommends an expedition to the Río Sikre, another river in the biosphere reserve, sometimes referred to as the Sigre.

Cannon Island, located in the Brus Lagoon, is named after the massive iron cannons abandoned by the British in the 1700s. Traditionally a source of food, fresh water, and then a hideout and fort for pirates, explorers, and then the British Navy, the island is still lush and filled with fruit trees such as breadfruit, orange, grapefruit, papaya, three species of coconuts, guavas, limes, and cashews. The appeal of the cay, though, is not its beauty or its fruit, but its location in a lagoon that may have the largest population of tarpon in Central America.

Referred to as "royal tarpon" or "pig tarpon," the fish grow to over 200 pounds, feeding on the schools of mullet, pilchard, sardine, snook, and shrimp that spawn in Brus Lagoon and connected estuaries. Five rivers flow into Brus Lagoon, and the locus of fishing shifts from one to another during different seasons. Four species of snook are abundant in the area, as are cubera snapper, black and yellowfin tuna, barracuda, Jack Crevalle, kingfish, and wahoo. Most people who come to Cannon Island stay at the Cannon Cay fishing lodge.

To head up the **Río Sikre,** make your way to Brus and from there walk for a half-hour through the savannas to a motorized dugout that will zigzag up the Río Sikre past huge trees in the river. In dry spots passengers disembark and push the dugout, but most of the time is spent following the S curves of the river, often through overhanging vegetation so dense that it forms a green tunnel. Spend the night at the Campamento de Auka Benk, the old camp of former "oil collectors." On the second day, head out on foot through the bamboo forest. The six-hour round-trip hike winds through low-altitude jungle terrain—the territory of tapir, jaguar, jaguarundi, and *tepezquintle,* just to name a few—and then back through savanna. The third day involves a hike through mahogany forests to a small lagoon that is home to many alligators, then setting up a camp. On the fourth day, trek over a small range of mountains, the territory of spider monkeys, back to Auka Benk, then back down the river to Brus Lagoon, pausing to view roseate spoonbills and pelicans.

Heading inland, located just off the Río Patuca at the border of the Río Plátano Biosphere Reserve and between the Brus and Caratasca Lagoons, **Ahuas** is home to the Moravian Mission's clinic. This is where the lobster divers with decompression sickness go for treatment and rehabilitation. While it's not an especially beautiful town, should you run into trouble, it is the seat of the volunteer air-ambulance corps, Alas de Socorro. In late 1996, when airfares to Ahuas increased, enraged locals attempted to burn a commercial

DIVING DANGERS

According to Dr. Fermin Lopez, who operates the hyperbaric chamber at the Cornerstone Emergency Medical Mission on Roatán, most Miskito have never heard of nitrogen and can't read dive tables if they can read at all. A lobster diver straps on a tank, drops to the bottom, spears lobsters until his air runs out, then ascends rapidly to a waiting canoe, paddled by his cayucero *partner. He exchanges his empty tank for a new one and heads back down to the bottom again, while the* cayucero *follows him on the surface. The Indians dive all day, every day, typically going through eight to 12 tanks. Their joints begin to ache and their extremities go numb. Some blame the pain on rheumatism, and others believe that they are the victims of a "mermaid's curse."*

When a diver stays down too long or ascends too rapidly, the pain and numbness typical of stage I decompression sickness blossoms into full-blown, paralytic stage II sickness. These paralyzed Indians are dropped off on the Mosquito Coast at the end of the dive trip, where they seek the help of traditional curandero *medicine men or attempt to make their way to a clinic such as the one operated by the Moravian Church in the Miskito village of Ahuas.*

plane. As a result, Isleña suspended air service to Ahuas and now the only air service available is via Sosa Airlines. If you are in Ahuas overnight, ask at the hospital if there is a bed available in the housing used for visiting doctors. If they don't ask you to pay, offer a donation.

Further up the Patuca River, **Wampu Sirpi** saw its population swell as a result of the migration caused by the Contra war. With this larger population in the area, hunters began to return with less game, causing concern about the future. Biologist Gustavo Cruz has been working with the locals in experimenting with iguana protec-

Approximately two-thirds of the ill divers respond well to the treatment in a primitive recompression chamber, while the other third are partially or completely crippled. In the moist heat of the Mosquito Coast, paralyzed Indians frequently develop skin infections and, since they must self-insert a catheter every time they need to urinate, they frequently develop bladder and kidney infections. Most die within three years. Others die more suddenly from embolisms, ruptured lungs, and asphyxiation. Each year, the Cornerstone Emergency Medical Mission at Anthony's Key Resort in Roatán treats over 100 divers, 80 percent of whom are Miskito Indians.

Divers are also creating an environmental catastrophe. Despite regulations, many use Clorox bleach to flush their increasingly scarce prey out from tiny crevices in the coral, killing a wide variety of reef organisms. A few years ago, lobster divers could work in 12 to 18 meters (40 to 60 feet) of water, but over-harvesting in shallow waters has forced them to have to dive deeper and deeper each season, causing a corresponding increase in the incidence of decompression sickness. Decreasing lobster harvests have prompted business interests to support a government-enforced, four-month diving moratorium, generally from around March 15 to July 15 each year since 1994.

tion, and there is hope that ecotourism will create a stream of sustainable income in the future. There is a dirt airstrip ten minutes' walk from the town and another larger one, capable of handling DC-3s, 30 minutes away. Wampu Sirpi is a pleasant town, and its inhabitants are looking forward to an influx of ecotourism. Already, locals are making souvenirs out of pounded bark called tunnu and arranging for boat trips and hikes both down and upriver from town. Well upriver from Wampu Sirpi is the still relatively inaccessible Tawahka Reserve.

Children in Wampu Sirpi

Up the Río Ibantara from the Tansin Lagoon is the town of **Mocoron,** the site of much activity during the Contra war. Recently, the Texas-based Norma I. Love Foundation initiated a volunteer program to refurbish the Red Cross hospital adjacent to the old "Quinto Batallion" military base. Potential health-care, teaching, and carpentry volunteers may contact Norma at San Pedro Sula number 504-533-0262or, in the United States, call Elizabeth Merrell at 972-335-5256. Alternatively, check out http://www.hondurasaid.org/ and e-mail Elizabeth@saltworth .com. Inland from Mocoron is the proposed Rus Rus Biological Reserve, where the Rus Rus Hospital is run by a group called Friends of America. There is a landing strip and dirt paths crossing the rolling hills that one day will make ideal terrain for mountain biking.

Puerto Lempira is the largest town in the Mosquito Coast. As you might imagine, it's a frontier town with little sophistication. From the Río Plátano Biosphere Reserve, the best way to reach Puerto Lempira is by making your way back to Brus Lagoon, inland to Ahuas, or to the strip at Belen and catching a quick flight for around $30. If there is no regularly scheduled flight, ask about Sami Air Taxi. Cargo boats sometimes go down the coast, but you'd have to be lucky to find one when you are ready to leave. Alternatively, walk down the beach for 125 kilometers (78 miles), but only after carefully reading Derek Parent's warnings about scarce drinking water, alligators, and falling coconuts. The six-day trip could be wonderful or fatal, depending upon your preparation.

Puerto Lempira has the dubious honor of having the only true road in La Mosquitia, and you'll be able to make basic purchases and phone calls, and even take a hot shower or spend a few hours in air conditioning.

The **Caratasca Lagoon Wildlife Refuge** and the interlinked **Warunta and Tansin Lagoons** form one of the richest wetland ecosystems on the entire Caribbean coast. Hundreds of kilometers of inland waterways wind through mangrove swamps and thousands of tiny islands filled with local and migratory birds.

Cauquira, across the Caratasca Lagoon on a spit of land separating the lagoon from the Caribbean, is a much more pleasant town than Puerto Lempira, an obvious site for a first class ecotourist lodge. Right now, though, you can rent a simple room in a private house and dream about the future.

To the east of Cauquira along the coast, where the Río Kruta meets the sea, is the undeveloped Río Kruta Biological Reserve. Beyond the reserve and the Cabo Gracias a Dios is Nicaragua.

The **Río Coco** forms the border between the Honduran Mosquitia and that of Nicaragua. While Miskito cross the border freely, it is officially closed. Recall that this area was hotly contested during the Sandinista period. Quite a few outlaws who have held on to their AK-47s live in the Nicaraguan Department of Zelaya del Norte.

If you are thinking of heading on to Nicaragua, ask around before you make the attempt. Unless the border is closed, a truck leaves from the Aracelly cafeteria in Puerto Lempira each morning for a 3.5-hour trip down to the Río Coco and the Nicaraguan border, crossing at the Honduran town of Leimus. The border was closed for a time in 1997–98, but reopened in 1999. We hear reports that the border there is now firmly closed. Confirm that it is still open before you make your way from Leimus up to Waspam in Nicaragua, then take a half-day passenger truck trip down to **Puerto Cabezas** in the Nicaraguan Mosquitia.

Details: Beyond the Río Plátano Biosphere Reserve, La Mosquitia has almost no facilities for tourists. Those interested in exploring this vast zone are advised to sign up with an expedition led by outfitters such as those listed below. That being said, I have traveled throughout the area a number of times researching articles or investigating environmental crises, and has never been without a meal or a place to sleep. Travelers should be aware that this is one of last truly wild places left in the region, and plan accordingly. Remember that tiny Sami Air Taxi flies to many dirt strips in La Mosquitia, including Ahuas, Brus, Puerto Lempira, Belen, Wampu Sirpi, Raya, and Auka.

A SAFE ADVENTURE

Anyone considering a serious trip to the Mosquito Coast should purchase a copy of Derek A. Parent's La Mosquitia: A Guide to the Land of Savannas, Rain Forests and Turtle Hunters *(Intrepid Traveler Publications, 1995), available from the author (514/698-2288 or e-mail derekp@generation.net). The book contains an in-depth discussion of the history and ecology of the region and provides incredibly detailed information for the rough-and-ready, budget-minded traveler. Derek also posts regular updates to the information in his book on his web page,* Walkabout in the Honduran Mosquitia *(www.generation.net/~derekp/), and he also leads groups into the region.*

Unless you have researched the area well and are confident of your survival skills, it would be wise to stick to regularly traveled routes, such as the Palacios–Las Marías route into the Río Plátano Biosphere Reserve, or follow the lagoon system along

GUIDES AND OUTFITTERS

Typically, full tour packages including domestic airfare cost from $300 to $1,700 for trips lasting from a few days to two weeks. Most visitors to the Río Plátano come with commercial groups organized by agencies. Responsible operators will bring in food and supplies from the outside, paying locals a fee for services and sundries, avoiding excessive impact on the scarce food resources of the area.

La Moskitia EcoAventuras, with offices on Ave. 14 de Julio, across from the Parque Bonilla in La Ceiba (442-0104, 441-1248; e-mail: mosquitia@laceiba.com), may be your best bet for touring the area. La Mosquitia native Jorge Salaverri knows his way around the coast and runs highly professional tours throughout the region. **Go Native Tours,** at El Tunkal Bar in Copán Ruinas (651-4432; e-mail: ixbalan@hn2.com), is another good choice. Rene Hernandez has been leading tours for more than 20 years.

the coast. A visit to the Las Marías area, while not to be underestimated, should go quite smoothly. Because a canal links Palacios with the Laguna de Ibans and the Río Plátano, enterprising boatmen can pick up passengers right at the airstrip and take them all the way into the heart of the reserve. By contrast, visits to the Tawahka Anthropological Reserve are extremely complicated. There are no regularly scheduled flights to the area, boat trips are long and arduous, and even gasoline for motorized canoes is hard to find. If you wish to penetrate into the lightly inhabited interior of La Mosquitia, the best idea is to go with a group.

In early 1996, four German travelers headed east in a chartered motorboat, which sank in front of Río Miel. They made it to shore safely despite the 16-foot tiger sharks prevalent in that area but lost all their gear and had to walk partially naked to Punta de Piedra, where they procured a four-wheel-drive vehicle back to Trujillo.

Ríos Honduras, which books through Caribbean Travel Agency on San Isidro in La Ceiba (443-0780), can be contacted directly at 441-1985, or in the United States at 800/255-5784 (e-mail: rios@hondurashn.com), is the leader in rafting and kayaking tours. The pioneering white-water company runs completely catered trips through La Mosquitia. Emphasis is placed on minimizing the impact on nature (as in trips to U.S. wilderness areas, no garbage or even human waste is left in the reserve).

Adventure Expeditions (232-4793) in Tegucigalpa is led by New Orleans–born Ricardo Madrid. Before becoming a guide Ricardo was a food industry expert, so all the food you eat will be vacuum-packed, clean, and tasty. Ricardo has a passion for La Mosquitia history and will show you graveyards and old forts from an abandoned British colony, and might even take you hunting for the fabled "White City."

LODGING

There are no full-service hotels in the region, and outside of Palacios and Puerto Lempira lodgings are extremely simple, but most villages have at least one large home that has a few clean rooms available for an overnight stay and a home-cooked evening meal. There are no addresses or phone numbers and reservations are not taken, but if you are stuck in a strange town with no place to stay, ask for a *hospedaje* and you will most likely find a place to sleep. Ask the *hospedaje* owner, usually a Miskito woman, the price for a bed and a meal, which might vary depending on her mood but will usually run from $2 to $10.

Felix Marmol charges $10 per night in his small hotel in Palacios located next to the airstrip. In Cocobila, stay and take meals at the home next to the lobster-diving school, or stay at a bunk in the school itself. Near the butterfly farm in Raista is the **Bodden Hospedaje** with clean rooms for $3. Elma Bodden will cook meals for a dollar or two more. **Hospedaje Carter** is located in the village of Ibans. Miskito writer **Jacinto Molina** takes lodgers for 50L per person in Ibans. Great seafood meals are available at 35L per meal at **Hospedaje Yosira,** located in the village of Nueva Jerusalem. In Las Marías, **Eliseo Tinglas Smith** charges around 30L to 40L for four beds (less to sleep on the floor), and offers rice, beans, and yucca for 20L. **Mariano Davis,** a short ride by boat from the center of town, houses up to eight people for 20L per person. Meals are available at 12L. **Ovideo Martinez** has 11 beds in two houses with a separate, clean outhouse, for 25L per person.

The fishing lodge at **Cannon Cay** (503/643-9224 in the U.S., www.goTarponFishing.com), is probably the most comfortable in the region and accommodates up to 12 guests. Screened-in cabins feature hot showers and electric lights. This is the only hotel on the island and is run by Dick Thomas, who began offering ecotourism trips around the area in spring of 1997, charging non-fisherfolk anywhere from $50 to $150 per day with a three-day minimum, depending on the nature of the services desired. A typical five-night package for anglers, aimed at those flying in to Honduras just to fish and including a night in La Ceiba, three days of fishing, and all domestic transportation, costs around $1,500. Seven days of fishing goes for $2,200. Prices include everything, even alcohol.

Puerto Lempira has a number of basic hotels, including the **Hotel Flores,** with 20 rooms and six hours of air conditioning per night; **Hospedaje Flores;** the **Hospedaje Modelo;** and the **Hospedaje Santa Teresita.**

APPENDIX A
TRAVEL BASICS

WHAT TO BRING

To state the obvious, bring your passport. Make a photocopy or two of the front pages and store those separately.

Traveler's checks. People are starting to use them less and less, bigger cities do accept credit cards, and you get a better exchange rate if you have cash. But they are also a good form of insurance.

Alarm clock. Rarely needed except for the early morning departure; make sure you test it before you leave!

Pocket knife. A Swiss Army–type knife with a bottle opener and tweezers is always handy. Leatherman tools are always useful.

Insect repellent/anti-itch gel. Communing with nature is pleasant as long as nature isn't biting. We're generally more concerned with pesky insects than large mammals, so bring along some repellent and, in case you are bit, something that will relieve the itch. Try Itch-X or cortisone cream.

Antibiotic ointment. Speeds up the recovery of cuts and wounds.

Flashlight. Signature trademark of both *The X-Files* and savvy travelers. Small, waterproof flashlights are handy for exploring caves.

Dental floss. Can be used as string for a multitude of purposes besides flossing—not that we've ever had to tie our shoes or close the backpack with it, but we could if we had to.

Spanish/English dictionary. Learn a foreign language one word at a time! Pick up newspapers and start "reading," dictionary in hand. Soon you'll find yourself with a brand-new vocabulary.

Plastic bags. They keep your shampoo from bubbling out over things in your luggage. Zip-locking bags are great.

Shoes. Good hiking boots for trekking, Teva-type sandals for the coasts and rivers, sneakers for the rest. Shoes that dry quickly are preferable.

An **umbrella** or **poncho** is valuable during the rainy season.

Think of other items. Bring gifts such as your favorite music or something from your home town (picture postcards, perhaps?).

Bring some good books and share them with the libraries or with the U.S. Peace Corps office on Avenida República de Chile (2 blocks up-hill from the Hotel Maya in Tegucigalpa).

Photography
Bring a camera and plenty of film! You'll see things in Honduras that you'll find nowhere else in the world. If you're not certain how many rolls of film to bring, don't worry. Unless you use a special brand, you'll find film in camera stores across the country. Specialty and professional film may be hard to find, and it's a good idea to bring a spare camera battery (or two).

ENTRY AND EXIT REQUIREMENTS

Entering Honduras is a straightforward process. If you're a citizen of Australia, Canada, New Zealand, the United States, the United Kingdom, Japan, or most other countries, you not need a visa or a tourist card, just a valid passport. Citizens of other countries should check with the local Honduran consulate or embassy. You are generally permitted a 30-day stay. If you need to stay in the country longer, an extension of an extra 30 days is easy to arrange at any immigration office within the country.

If you are coming to do business, contact the Foundation for Investment and Development of Exports (FIDE) office before you come: Condominio Lomas 4th floor, Col. Lomas del Guijarro Tegucigalpa, M.D.C. Honduras, C.A;. P.O. Box 2029, 232-9345, fax: 239-0766; e-mail: fide@hondutel.hn; http://www.hondurasinfo.hn/.

Immunization and Health Issues
Specific immunizations are not required for travel in Honduras. Especially if you're traveling to rural areas, it makes sense to get the appropriate shots to avoid tetanus, typhoid, and polio.

Listen to the far-off voice of your parents and wash your hands with soap often and before meals. As with any travel in the developing world, your body will be dealing with exotic microbes and bacteria. Though most bigger cities chlorinate their water, never trust water that is not either professionally bottled, boiled for 20 minutes, or otherwise purified. If you'll be traveling in rural areas it's a good idea to bring a sturdy water filter (I use a Katadyn), iodine tablets, or any other system to kill the bugs without poisoning yourself. Coffee and tea are generally fine, and you won't get sick from bottled sodas *(refrescos)* or beer *(cerveza)*.

The number-one source of traveler's diarrhea (known in Honduras as *turista)* is impure water. This includes ice made from impure water. Don't be afraid to ask if the ice in your drink is made from *agua purificada.* The second source is raw vegetables. In general, skip salads unless you are at a high-end restaurant and have asked the waiter whether the lettuce has been sterilized with chlorinated water solution. Tomatoes and carrots are generally safer than lettuce.

Air pollution in Tegucigalpa is typical of a Third World Capital. The most affected are children and the elderly. If you have asthma, you might want to stay away from the entire region around Easter, when the burning season begins and farmers burn their fields (and often forests) before planting.

When diving or snorkeling, a light Lycra "skin" will protect you from the sun and reduce the risk of being stung by coral or jellyfish. To treat a coral scrape, clean the area with soap and water and then rinse the wound with a disinfectant or vinegar. Fire coral can be particularly painful. Its defense includes venom, which immediately stings and then produces a rash. Jellyfish stings are even more severe. To treat these wounds, rinse the area first with salt water, then with fresh water. Ammonia or even urine will neutralize the venom. Then dry the wound and apply hydrocortisone or Benadryl cream. If you are concerned about coral cuts, be sure to bring an analgesic/antihistamine cream. Coral cuts are particularly susceptible to infection.

You can get most medical essentials at any Honduran pharmacy, but be smart and bring aspirin, bandages, an extra pair of glasses, and an antibacterial ointment with you. It is likely that the worst thing that will happen to you is a bunch of mosquito, sand fly, or ant bites, which will hurt a bit, then itch, then go away. Bring along some cortisone, Afterbite, calamine, or your favorite anti-itch remedy.

For more practical suggestions, check out two excellent guides, especially for those travelers who will have extended stays in Honduras. *Staying Healthy in Asia, Africa and Latin America,* by Dirk Schroeder (Avalon Travel Publishing, March 2000) is a handy, pocket-sized book. *Where There is No Doctor,* by David Werner (The Hesperian Foundation), is a highly recommended handbook for anyone staying in remote villages.

The U.S. Centers for Disease Control and Prevention has a fax information system; dial 404/332-4565 and follow the instructions. Request the "Bulletin for Health Risks in Central America" and have your fax number ready for the center to send you this information.

Malaria

Malaria is carried by the female anopheles mosquito and affects people in coastal areas. It is characterized by high fever, headaches, chills, and fatigue. In most cases it can be easily cured with the application of appropriate medicines. The best way to avoid malaria is to avoid getting bitten, especially in the evening. Bring plenty of toxic repellent such as DEET, or mellow repellent such as Skin-so-Soft, or both. Avoiding the bites will also ward off other mosquito-borne diseases such as dengue. I have never taken malaria prophylactics in Honduras and have never had a problem, but consult your doctor about taking a mild prophylactic such as chloriquine or a stronger one such as Lariam.

The drop in malaria in southern Honduras and its recent rise in Northern Honduras is an excellent case study of the often unintended side effects that accompany changes in the relationship between natural systems and economic systems. Southern Honduras, once a land of mangroves and forests, used to have a significant problem with malaria. The people of the south, those who survived childhood malaria, naturally developed a relatively high resistance to the disease. With the development of large-scale agro-industry growing cotton and sugar, and the simultaneous expansion of cattle grazing into former wetlands and forests, the land dried up and the average ambient temperature increased. The region became inhospitable to the anopheles mosquito that carries the disease, and consequently the incidence of malaria was radically reduced in Southern Honduras—and the people lost their resistance.

The same man-made climatic trends that forced out the mosquito also soon forced out the campesinos, who could grow no more crops in the exhausted soil and had no more virgin forests to cut down for slash-and-burn agriculture. Unable to carry on in the south, campesinos began to migrate to still-forested areas of the north and east, areas still inhabited by the anopheles. The result? The incidence of malaria exploded from 20,000 cases in 1987 to an estimated 90,000 in 1993. Most of these new cases were attributed to migrating campesinos. A complicating factor is that many mosquitoes have become resistant to pesticides as a result of their overuse by agro-industry.

SAFETY

Safety concerns are familiar to anyone who has traveled in a developing country. Travelers have tremendous wealth compared to most local people. Follow common sense, and don't be ostentatious. A developing country is not the wisest place to display an expensive watch or a huge diamond ring. While it's great to be adventurous, don't put yourself in harm's way.

There have been many reports recently of robberies on the beaches near Tela and Trujillo, generally at night. Buses have been stopped by bandits on the back roads behind Yojoa and in Olancho. Big cities such as San Pedro and Tegucigalpa are not the best places to walk alone at night. On the other hand, most Hondurans are scrupulously honest, many Hondurans leave their cars and homes unlocked, and when all is said, Honduras is still a relatively safe place, especially when compared to, for example, Miami.

TRANSPORTATION TO HONDURAS

Airlines
Honduras is served by a number of direct flights from the United States, Mexico, Europe, and Central America. Schedules change regularly, but most flights are to San Pedro Sula via Miami, New Orleans, or Houston. There are nonstops to Roatán from Miami, Houston, New Orleans, and even Milan. While there are no direct flights to Tegucigalpa from Europe, you can make connections in Miami. In addition, Iberia Airlines of Spain (800/772-4642) has direct flights from Miami to San Pedro Sula several times a week.

American Airlines (800/433-7300) has direct flights to San Pedro Sula from Miami. Continental Airlines (800/231-0856) flies from Houston and New Orleans to San Pedro Sula and Tegucigalpa, as does TACA International Airlines (800/535-8780). TACA also flies into Honduras from its hub in El Salvador, and has weekly service from Miami to Roatán. You should be aware that TACA has a terrible reputation for temporarily losing baggage. Miamia Air and Honduras Air Tours operate weekly charters from Miami and Houston nonstop to Roatán. Call them at 800/599-0014 or 303/871-1992, or e-mail honduair@gate.net.

Airports

Honduras has four international airports: in Tegucigalpa, San Pedro Sula, La Ceiba, and Roatán. The busiest of these is San Pedro Sula's. Tegucigalpa's Toncontín International Airport is located in a residential neighborhood. Although this brings a certain amount of danger to the flight—and nearby residents—it means that taxi fare to downtown isn't as expensive as from San Pedro Sula's airport. Toncontín has recently been renovated, and you can now get excellent cappuccinos while you wait for your flight.

The airport of choice for international flights is San Pedro Sula's. The terminal is modern, filled with car-rental agencies, shops, fast-food restaurants such as Wendy's, and yes, cappuccino bars.

Roatán has a modern airport, and most of the resorts will arrange to send a van or minibus to pick you up. Otherwise, someone will help you to a taxi.

Tiny La Ceiba airport is in need of an overhaul but it does the job, and cold drinks and even pizza are available as you wait for your plane.

Ferry Service

Ferry service between Port Isabel, Texas, and Puerto Cortés, Honduras, offers a quick, inexpensive mode of transportation, especially if you'd like to bring a vehicle. This is no ordinary cargo boat. The ferry has a casino, two dining rooms, a nightclub, saunas, hot tubs, and very comfortable cabins. It departs from Port Isabel weekly on Sunday evening, arrives in Puerto Cortés on Wednesday, departs the same day, and returns to Texas on Saturday. For more information, contact Fred Drew at International Decision Support, Inc., 800/750-9102 or 210/544-4526; e-mail: fdrew@ids.vt.com.

TRANSPORTATION WITHIN HONDURAS

Bus Service
First- and second-class buses serve the entire country. The best news for car-less travelers who have sat next to enough wet chickens is that new, luxury express buses serve the major cities. It's like flying first class, just closer to the ground. Unlike Mexico, Honduras does not have central bus terminals. In this aspect, it's very much like Guatemala.

Private stations in Comayagüela (near Tegucigalpa's airport) offer transport to the various corners of the country. The bus stations include the following:

Calle Real, Frente Parque La Libertad, Comayagüela, Honduras; 222-7572. Morning departures to Costa Rica, El Salvador, and Nicaragua.

Discua Litnea, near the Jacaleapa market, Comayagüela, Honduras; 232-7939.

Empresa Aurora, 6a Calle, 6a Avenida, Comayagüela, Honduras. Service to Juticalpa and Olancho.

Empresa El Rey, 6a Avenida y 9a Calle, Comayagüela, Honduras; 233-3010. Service to Comayagüela and San Pedro Sula.

Hedman Alas, 13a-14a Calle y 11a Avenida, Comayagüela, Honduras; 237-7143. Luxury service.

Driving in Honduras
Driving in Honduras is more challenging than in the United States. And the gasoline is more expensive. You can enter the country with your own car, or rent one here from local agencies or international agencies such as Hertz and Avis. If it's just a day trip you're planning, consider renting a taxi instead. But if you want to explore the country in a limited period of time, driving offers the greatest amount of flexibility. For experienced four-wheel-drivers, the network of dirt roads heading through the mountains seems like heaven.

The best advice is: Don't drive at night. While the highways are reputed to be the best in Central America, they are not without their potholes, sleeping black cows, kids on bikes, passed-out drunks, etc. At least in the day, you have a better response time to impending changes in road conditions.

On the plus side, unleaded gasoline was introduced in Honduras in recent years. This lessens environmental damage.

Rental companies include Avis, Budget, Hertz, National Car Rental, and Toyota Rent A Car. It's a good idea to rent a tough vehicle such as a "combi, " a four-door pickup truck with an extended cab.

If you're traveling through Honduras to regions farther south, take along the Driving Packet from the South American Explorer's Club (SAEC). Packed with hand-drawn maps, travel reports, recent South American fuel prices, good advice, and a panoply of resources, this a wanderlust mosaic of practical hints and suggestions—and a terrible temptation for those who are not sure if they're heading south or not. The cost is $25 for SAEC members, $30 for nonmembers, plus postage and handling. Contact the U.S. office at 607/277-0488, e-mail: explorer@samexplo.org; www. samexplo.org.

COMMUNICATIONS

Honduras's major newspapers are owned by politicians and offer a glimpse into the political debates. Major papers in San Pedro Sula are *El Tiempo, El Nuevo Día,* and *La Prensa.* In Tegucigalpa, the papers are *El Heraldo, La Tribuna,* and *El Periódico.* The English-language weekly *Honduras This Week* synopsizes major news and provides up-to-date tourism information, and is generally available at tourist hotels and restaurants. For more details, see Magazines, Newspapers, and Other Publications in Appendix B.

Telephone Service
The international country code for making telephone calls from the United States Honduras is 504. Be aware that some phone cards won't work for calls to Honduras due to a fraudulent system developed by U.S.-resident Hondureños calling home for free.

Hondutel, the Honduran telephone monopoly, has telephones available for use at its offices in just about all cities and towns in

Honduras. Domestic and international services are available in these offices. To place a call, give the receptionist the number you wish to call. You will be directed to a particular phone booth when the connection is made. Payment is expected after the call is completed.

If you are phoning the United States it is often easier to use "direct" calls that route you from a Honduran pay phone directly to a U.S.-based operator who will charge the call to your home account. Many airports and Hondutel offices have special phones for ATT Direct, MCI, etc. Check with your long-distance provider for the Honduran access number.

MONEY MATTERS

Currency
Honduran currency is the lempira (L), named after the Lencan chief who rebelled against the Spaniards. There are approximately 15L to US$1.

Banking
Banks are safe bets for exchanging money, but Honduras does have a black market that might give a marginally better rate. You can often change money in front of airports and at the Parque Central of each city. ATM cards can be used at Banco Atlántidas throughout the country and at machines found in Choluteca, Comayagua, Danlí, El Progreso, Juticalpa, La Lima, Puerto Cortés, Santa Rosa De Copán, and Tela.

Credit Cards
Visa and MasterCard are accepted in major hotels and restaurants in the larger cities. In smaller towns, you'll have to pay with cash. Cash advances are available from Bancahsa and Credomatic.

Tipping
Leave some small notes, up to 10 percent of the bill. Don't be afraid to reward those who take good care of you, from maids to waiters to boat captains. The money will make a difference to them. Think of bringing small gifts from home you can use as additional tips.

Business Hours

Business hours are from 9 a.m.–noon, Monday–Friday. An hour or two lunch break is normal, and business resumes from 2–6 p.m.

TIME ZONE

Honduras uses Central Standard Time, or Greenwich Mean Time minus six hours, the same as Houston, Texas.

METRIC SYSTEM

1 mile = 1.609 kilometers	1 kilometer = .62 mile
1 foot = .3048 meters	1 meter = 39.37 inches
1 pound = .45 kilogram	1 kilogram = 2.2 pounds
1 gallon = 3.78 liters	1 liter = .9 quart

VOLTAGE

Electricity is supplied at 110 volts. Most electrical outlets use a two-pronged, flat-pin plug. exactly the same as in the United States, though generally without the third, grounded prong. Remember that Honduras is an electricity-poor country, so be resourceful and turn off lights when they aren't needed. Don't leave your computer or other sensitive equipment plugged in when you don't need them, to minimize the risk of damage from power surges.

ENVIRONMENTAL VOCABULARY

Animals

    cocodrilo—crocodile
    danto—tapir
    lapa—scarlet macaw
    loro—parrot
    mapachín—raccoon

mariposa—butterfly
mono—monkey
mono congo—howler monkey
mono colorado, mono araña—spider monkey
murciélago—bat
pájaro, ave—bird
puma—cougar/mountain lion
rana—frog
sapo—toad
serpiente, culebra—snake
tepezcuintle—paca
tortuga—turtle
trucha—trout
venado—deer
venado coliblanco—white-tailed deer
zorillo—skunk
zorro—fox

The Environment
árbol—tree
arroyo—stream
bahía—bay
barranca—ravine
campesino—farmer
cueva—cave
encina—oak
gruta—grotto
laguna—lagoon
liquidambar—sweet gum
milpa—cornfield
palapa—thatched hut or shelter
río—river
roble—oak
selva—forest
sendero—path
tierra alta—highland
tierra baja—lowland
zona nucleo/zona de amortiguamiento—nuclear zone/ buffer zone.

APPENDIX B
ADDITIONAL RESOURCES

TOURIST INFORMATION

Honduras Institute of Tourism
P.O. Box 140458, Coral Gables, FL 33114-0458, 305/461-1601, 800/410-9608, domestic tourist information 800/222-TOUR (8687); fax: 305/461-1602; E-mail: 104202.3433@compuserve.com. Colonia San Carlos, Edif Europa, Tegucigalpa, Honduras 222-2124, fax: 222-6621; E-mail:tourism_info@mail.hodudata.com; www .hondurastips.honduras.com.

Foundation for Investment and Development of Exports (FIDE)
FIDE Miami Office: 2100 Ponce de Leon Blvd., Ste. 1175, Coral Gables, FL 33134, 305/444-3060, fax: 305/444-1610; e-mail: dghonduras@aol.com.
Tegucigalpa Office: Condominio Lomas 4th floor, Col. Lomas del Guijarro Tegucigalpa, M.D.C. Honduras, C.A;. P.O. Box 2029, Tel: (504) 232-9345, Fax: (504) 239-0766;e-mail: fide@hondutel.hn; www.hondurasinfo.hn/

Consulates and Embassies
If you need to visit your home-country embassy or to arrange for a visa for onward travel, be sure to phone ahead; consular office hours are often somewhat irregular.
Argentina
Colonia Rubén Darío #417, Tegucigalpa, 232-3376. 8 a.m.–1 p.m.
Belize
Lower level of the Hotel Honduras Maya, Tegucigalpa, 239-0134 8:30 a.m.–1 p.m.
Brazil
Colonia Remorma No. 1309 Calle La Salle, Tegucigalpa, 232–2021 8 a.m.–2 p.m.

Canada
Edificio Los Castaños, 6th Floor, Boulevard Morazán, Tegucigalpa, 231-4538 or 231-4545. 8 a.m.–noon.

Chile
Edificio Interamericana 6th Floor, Boulevard Morazán,Tegucigalpa, 231-3703 or 232-2114. Mon.–Fri. 8 a.m.–2 p.m.

Colombia
Edificio Palmira 4th Floor, Tegucigalpa, 232-9709. Mon.–Fri. 8 a.m.–2 p.m.

Costa Rica
Colonia El Triángulo, Tegucigalpa, 232-1768. Mon.–Fri. 8 a.m.–4 p.m.

Ecuador
Colonia Palmira, Avenida Juan Lindo #122, Tegucigalpa, 236-5980. Mon.–Fri. 8:30 a.m.–1:30 p.m.

El Salvador
Colonia San Carlos 205-2a Avenida, Tegucigalpa, 236-8045 or 36-7344. Mon.–Fri. 8:30 a.m.–noon and 1–3 p.m.

France
Colonia Palmira, Avenida Juan Lindo, Tegucigalpa, 236-6800. Mon.–Fri. 8 a.m.–noon and 1–6:30 p.m.

Germany
Edificio Paysen 3rd Floor, Boulevard Morazán, Tegucigalpa, 232-3161 or 232-3162. Mon.–Fri. 9 a.m.–noon.

Guatemala
Colonia Las Minitas 4a Calle, Avenida Juan Lindo #2421, Tegucigalpa, 232-9704 or 231-1543. Mon.–Fri. 9 a.m.–4 p.m.

Italy
Colonia Reforma, Avenida Principal #109, Tegucigalpa, 236-6391 or 236-6810. Mon.–Fri. 9 a.m.–1 p.m.

Japan
Colonia San Carlos, Tegucigalpa, 236-6825 or 236-5511. Mon.–Fri. 8:30 a.m.–noon and 2–5:30 p.m.

Mexico
Colonia Palmira, Avendia República de Mexico #2402,Tegucigalpa, 232-6471 or 232-0138. Mon.–Fri. 8–11 a.m.

Nicaragua
Colonia Lomas del Tepeyac, Bloque M-1 Calle 11a, Tegucigalpa, 232-4290. Mon.–Fri. 8:30 a.m.–noon.

Panama
Colonia Palmira, Edificio Palmira No. 200, Tegucigalpa, 231-5441.
Mon.–Fri. 8 a.m.–1 p.m.

Peru
Colonia Alemeda, Calle Ruben Diario No. 1902, Tegucigalpa, 231-5261 or 231-5272, Mon.–Fri. 8:30 a.m.–1:30 p.m.

Spain
Colonia Matamoros #103, Tegucigalpa, 236-6875 or 236-6589.
Mon.–Fri. 9 a.m.–1 p.m.

Sweden
Colonia Miramontes No. 2758, Tegucigalpa, 232-4935. Mon.–Fri. 8:30 a.m.–4:30 p.m.

Switzerland
Edificio Galería 2nd Floor, Boulevard Morazán, Tegucigalpa, 232-6239. Mon.–Fri. 8 a.m.–3 p.m.

United Kingdom
Colonia Palmira, Edificio Palmira, Tegucigalpa, 232-5429.
Mon.–Thurs. 8 a.m.–noon and 1–5 p.m.

United States
Avenida La Paz, Tegucigalpa, 236-9320. Mon.–Fri. 8 a.m.–5 p.m.

Venezuela
Colonia Rubén Darío, Calle Arturo Lopez Rodezno, Tegucigalpa, 232-2628. Mon.–Fri. 8:30 a.m.–3:30 p.m.

MAPS

Treaty Oak
P.O. Box 50295
Austin, TX 78763-0295
512/326-4141, fax: 512/443-0973
E-mail: maps@treatyoak.com
www.treatyoak.com

Wide World Books and Maps
1911 N. 45th
Seattle, WA 98103
206/634-3453

World of Maps
118 Holland Avenue
Ottawa, ON, Canada K1Y 0X6
613/ 724-6776, fax: 613/724-7776
E-mail: maps@magi.com
www.magi.com/~maps/
Contact: Brad Green
Has a new map of Honduras hot off the press, published by ITMB of Vancouver. Scale is 1:750,000, and it's full color with a detailed index on the reverse listing all the communities that appear on the map. "Elevations are clearly shown with hypsometric tints of colour." There are indexed city maps of Tegucigalpa and Comayagüela as well as a plan of Copán. All of the wildlife refuges, biological reserves, marine parks, and national parks are clearly shown. The map costs $7.95 plus a few dollars extra for postage and handling.

RECOMMENDED READING

Travel Guidebooks

Adventuring in Central America, David Rains Wallace. San Francisco: Sierra Club Books, 1995. Nature guide to the land of the panther, partially funded by USAID.

Backpacking in Central America, Tim Burford. Old Saybrook, Conn.: Globe Pequot Press, 1996. A good overall guide to hiking throughout the isthmus.

Cheap Thrills in Honduras, U.S. Peace Corps. Tegucigalpa: Enlace Travel Guide, 1996. Available only at the Peace Corps headquarters in Teguz, a great compilation of volunteers' favorite places to hang out or check out lakes on top of steep mountains.

Honduras: The Undiscovered Country, Andrew Hubbard. 1996. White-water River Guide available from the author for $15 at 1191 Sunnycrest Ave., Ventura, CA 93003; 805/654-1294.

La Mosquitia: A Guide to the Land of Savannas, Rain Forests and Turtle Hunters, Derek Parent. New York: Intrepid Traveler. Publications, 1995. The must-have guide for anyone considering a walkabout in this region of Honduras. Available from the author (e-mail: derekp@generation.net) or from Intrepid Traveler Publications (ITP), 116 Consumer Square, Suite 387, Plattsburgh, NY12901; 514/698-2288. Also see author's website for updates on travel in the region: www.generation.net/~derekp/.

Live Well in Honduras: How to Relocate, Retire, and Increase Your Standard of Living, Frank Ford. Santa Fe: John Muir Publications, 1998. A guide for those thinking of settling in Honduras, with photos by none other than James D. Gollin.

Mexico and Central American Handbook, Ben Box. Chicago: Passport Books, 1996. The classic text for travelers hopping through more than one country at a time. This guidebook has been known to stop bullets (in Nicaragua, at least).

Moon Handbooks: Honduras, Chris Humphrey. Emeryville, Calif.: Avalon Travel Publishing, 2000.

The Environment

Enduring Crises: The Political Ecology of Poverty and Environmental Destruction in Honduras, Susan Stonich. Boulder, Colo.: Westview Press, 1993. Disturbing reflections on environmental destruction in Honduras.

High Jungles and Low, Archie Carr, Gainesville, Fla.: University Press of Florida, 1992. Classic tale of the man who founded the Caribbean Conservation Corporation, which fights for the survival of sea turtles.

Ley General del Ambiente y su Reglamento General, Secretaria del Ambiente (SEDA), Tegucigalpa: Editorial Guaymuras, 1996. Spanish-language review of environmental law in Honduras.

Rethinking Tourism and Ecotravel: The Paving of Paradise and What You Can Do to Stop It, Deborah McLaren. West Hartford, Conn.: Kumarian Press, 1997.

Culture

America's First Cuisines, Sophie D. Coe. Austin: University of Texas Press, 1994. Which foods are native to the Americas? The author serves up the juicy story behind maize, beans, and cacao.

Blue Pariah: Inside Honduras, Guillermo Yuscaran. Tegucigalpa: Nuevo Sol, 1994. The author recounts his travels with his favorite canine. A must-read!

Don't Be Afraid, Gringo: A Honduras Woman Speaks From the Heart: The Story of Elvia Alvarado, Elvia Alvarado. San Francisco: Institute of Food and Development Policy, 1987. A telling tale of development and human rights.

History Carved in Stone: A Guide to Copan, William Fasch and Ricardo Agarcia, 1992. Locally published text. Excellent review of the city's history.

Inside Honduras, Kent Norsworthy and Tom Barry. Albuquerque, New Mexico.: Inter-Hemispheric Resource Center, 1994. Part of a regional series by the excellent Resource Center.

Maya Explorer: John Lloyd Stephens and the Lost Cities of Central America and the Yucatan, Victor Wolfgang von Hagen. San Francisco: Chronicle Books, 1990 re-issue of 1947 text. A colorful and well told story. We hope it never goes out of print!

Northcoast Honduras: Tropical Karma and Other Stories, Guillermo Yuscaran. Tegucigalpa: Nuevo Sol, 1993. More delightful stories from a master storyteller. Did we say "must-read"?

Pueblos Indigenas y Garífuna de Honduras, Ramón Rivas. Tegucigalpa: Editorial Guaymuras, 1993. Spanish-language review of indigenous groups.

Field Guides

A Guide to the Birds of Mexico and Northern Central America, Steve Howell and Sophie Webb. Oxford: Oxford University Press, 1995. Incredible field guide used by birders throughout the region.

A Neotropical Companion: An Introduction to the Animals, Plants and Ecosystems of the New World Tropics, John Kricher. Princeton, N.J.: Princeton University Press, 1989. Illustrated and highly useful guide.

Latin American Insects and Entomology, Charles Hogue. Berkeley: University of California Press, 1993.

Venomous Reptiles of Latin America, Jonathan Campbell and William Lamar. Ithaca, N.Y.: Comstock Publishing, 1989.

The Maya

Breath on the Mirror: Mythic Voices of the Living Maya, Dennis Tedlock. San Francisco: Harper Collins, 1993.

Maya Cosmos: Three Thousand Years on the Shaman's Path, David Friedel, Linda Schele, and Joy Parker. New York: William Morrow, 1993. Mind-bogglingly good.

The Ancient Maya, Sylvanius Morley, George Brainerd, and revised by Robert Sharer. Palo Alto, Calif.: Stanford University Press, 1983.

The Forest of Kings: The Untold Story of the Ancient Maya, Linda Schele and David Freidel. New York: William Morrow, 1990.

The Maya, Michael Coe. New York: Praeger, 1966.

Magazines, Newspapers, and Other Publications

Connection to the Americas
Resource Center of the Americas
317 17th Avenue, SE
Minneapolis, MN 55414-2077
612/627-9445, fax: 612/ 627-9450
E-mail: rctamn@igc.apc.org

Hombres de Maiz
Apartado Postal 317-1002
Paseo de Estudiantes
San Jose, Costa Rica
Central American Spanish-language magazine focusing on agr-culture, human rights, and development; U.S. subscriptions are $75/year.

Honduras This Week
Apartado Postal 1312
Tegucigalpa, M.D.C., Honduras
31-5821 or 32-0832, fax: 32-2300

E-mail: hontweek@hondutel.hn
www.marrder.com/htw/
Weekly English-language newspaper

Honduras Tips
Apartado Postal 2699
San Pedro Sula, Honduras
56-8567, fax: 56-7762
www.hondurastips.hn
Contact: John Dupis, Editor
Up-to-date information on cities, hotels, and restaurants in Honduras. U.S. subscriptions are $20/year; individual copies $6.

Latin Trade
First Union Financial Center
200 S. Biscayne Blvd., Suite 1150
Miami, FL 33131
E-mail: lattrade@aol.com
Formerly known as U.S./Latin Trade, this magazine is a glossy monthly focusing on business issues in the Americas.

NACLA Report on the Americas
475 Riverside Drive, Suite 454
New York, NY 10115
212/870-3146
E-mail: nacla@igc.apc.org
Published bimonthly by the North American Congress on Latin America (NACLA); U.S. subscriptions are $27/year for individuals; foreign subscriptions are $37/year for individuals.

Transitions Abroad
18 Hulst Road
P.O. Box 1300
Amherst, MA 01004
E-mail: trabroad@aol.com
Publishes a highly recommended bimonthly magazine as well as the comprehensive *Alternative Travel Directory* book.

Vientos Tropicales
P.O. Box 16176
Chapel Hill, NC 27516-6176

919/361-0997, fax: 919/361-2597

E-mail: vientos@vnet.net

Provides general reference materials on Central America to libraries and individuals. Request a copy of their catalog of Honduran publications.

ONLINE RESOURCES

Note that the addresses (or URLs) of the following websites are subject to change. If you receive a message that the website does not exist, do a search for the title to see if it has merely changed its home. Also, an updated list will appear for the next decade or so online at the Eco Travels website (www.planeta.com).

Honduras-Related Websites

Newspapers

El Tiempo
206.48.104.140/dtiempo/index.html

Honduras This Week
www.marrder.com/htw/

La Prensa
www.hondurasinfo.hn/

La Tribuna
www.latribuna.hn/

More Specific Information

Butterfly/Insect Museum
www.gbm.hn/museo

Catrachos
www.marrder.com/catrachos/

Catrachos Online!
www.nortropic.com/catrachos

Coconut Telegraph
www.bayislands.com

Committee for the Defense of the Gulf of Fonseca
http://members.aol.com/coddegolf/index.html

Coral Reef Alliance
www.coral.org

Destination Honduras Peace Corps
www.peacecorps.gov/www/dp/honduras1.html

Embassy of Honduras
pw2.netcom.com/~embhondu/index.htm

Escape Artists–Honduras
www.escapeartist.com/elhondo2/elhondo2.htm

Friends of Celaque Mountain National Park
www.generation.net/~derekp/celaque.html

Garífuna World
www.garifuna-world.com

Green Arrow Guide to Honduras
www.greenarrow.com/honduras/honduras.htm

Honduras Geology
www.wolfenet.com/~krautara

Honduras Information Project
www.orion.uci.edu/~cweber/html

Honduras on Shortwave
www.mcrest.edu/%7Emoore/central/honduras.html

Honduras Resources Alejandro Hernandez
www.owlnet.rice.edu/%7Ealexh/hresources.html

Honduras Web Explorer
www.hondurasweb.com

Walkabout in the Honduran Mosquitia
www.generation.net/~derekp/

General Interest Websites

Eco Travels in Latin America
www.planeta.com
Maintained by Ron Mader (an original co-author of this book), this site includes updates on environmental contacts, travel providers, Spanish language schools, and an inclusive list of information on parks and protected areas in Honduras.

Environment and Latin America Network
csf.colorado.edu/elan/index.html
Scholarly archive and discussion.

Green Arrow Guide
www.greenarrow.com
Travel information and conservation projects throughout Central America.

Institute for Agriculture and Trade Policy
www.igc.apc.org/iatp/
Publishes updated information on environment and trade policies.

Latin American Trade Council of Oregon (LATCO)
www.latco.org
Forum for business-related activities and announcements.

Resource Center for the Americas
www.americas.org/rcta/
Minnesota-based center that assists teachers and students in understanding the region.

CALENDAR

Honduras al Natural, EcoArte, Apartado Postal 4420, Tegucigalpa, Honduras; 237-8621. This annual calendar or agenda is produced by acclaimed environmental photographer Vicente Murphy. The handsome calendar is released each fall and is widely available in Tegucigalpa bookstores.

INDEX

ABOUT THE AUTHOR

James D. Gollin, a former investment banker, now serves on the board of or advises a number of activist and philanthropic organizations, including the Rainforest Action Netwouk, the Sierra Madre Alliance, Threshold Foundation, and Angelica Foundation. A writer and award-winning photographer, Gollins work has appeared in The Christian Science Monitor, The New York Times, Eco Traveler, Rodale's Scuba Diving, Continental Profiles, and other publications. Gollin lives in Santa Fe, New Mexico, and travels regularly to Honduras for both work and pleasure.

AVALON
TRAVEL
p u b l i s h i n g

BECAUSE TRAVEL MATTERS.

AVALON TRAVEL PUBLISHING knows that travel is more than coming and going—travel is taking part in new experiences, new ideas, and a new outlook. Our goal is to bring you complete and up-to-date information to help you make informed travel decisions.

AVALON TRAVEL GUIDES feature a combination of practicality and spirit, offering a unique traveler-to-traveler perspective perfect for an afternoon hike, around-the-world journey, or anything in between.

WWW.TRAVELMATTERS.COM

Avalon Travel Publishing guides are available
at your favorite book or travel store.

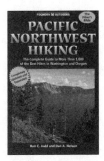

FOR TRAVELERS WITH SPECIAL INTERESTS

GUIDES

The 100 Best Small Art Towns in America • Asia in New York City
The Big Book of Adventure Travel • Cities to Go
Cross-Country Ski Vacations • Gene Kilgore's Ranch Vacations
Great American Motorcycle Tours • Healing Centers and Retreats
Indian America • Into the Heart of Jerusalem
The People's Guide to Mexico • The Practical Nomad
Saddle Up! • Staying Healthy in Asia, Africa, and Latin America
Steppin' Out • Travel Unlimited • Understanding Europeans
Watch It Made in the U.S.A. • The Way of the Traveler
Work Worldwide • The World Awaits
The Top Retirement Havens • Yoga Vacations

SERIES

Adventures in Nature
The Dog Lover's Companion
Kidding Around
Live Well

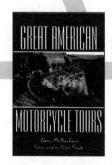

MOON HANDBOOKS provide comprehensive

coverage of a region's arts, history, land, people, and social issues in addition to detailed practical listings for accommodations, food, outdoor recreation, and entertainment. Moon Handbooks allow complete immersion in a region's culture—ideal for travelers who want to combine sightseeing with insight for an extraordinary travel experience.

USA

Alaska-Yukon • Arizona • Big Island of Hawaii • Boston
Coastal California • Colorado • Connecticut • Georgia
Grand Canyon • Hawaii • Honolulu-Waikiki • Idaho
Kauai • Los Angeles • Maine • Massachusetts • Maui
Michigan • Montana • Nevada • New Hampshire
New Mexico • New York City • New York State
North Carolina • Northern California • Ohio • Oregon
Pennsylvania • San Francisco • Santa Fe-Taos • Silicon Valley
South Carolina • Southern California • Tahoe • Tennessee
Texas • Utah • Virginia • Washington • Wisconsin
Wyoming • Yellowstone-Grand Teton

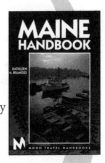

INTERNATIONAL

Alberta and the Northwest Territories • Archaeological Mexico
Atlantic Canada • Australia • Baja • Bangkok • Bali • Belize
British Columbia • Cabo • Canadian Rockies • Cancún
Caribbean Vacations • Colonial Mexico • Costa Rica • Cuba
Dominican Republic • Ecuador • Fiji • Havana • Honduras
Hong Kong • Indonesia • Jamaica • Mexico City • Mexico
Micronesia • The Moon • Nepal • New Zealand
Northern Mexico • Oaxaca • Pacific Mexico • Pakistan
Philippines • Puerto Vallarta • Singapore • South Korea
South Pacific • Southeast Asia • Tahiti
Thailand • Tonga-Samoa • Vancouver
Vietnam, Cambodia and Laos
Virgin Islands • Yucatán Peninsula

www.moon.com

Rick Steves shows you where to travel and how to travel—all while getting the most value for your dollar. His Back Door travel philosophy is about making friends, having fun, and avoiding tourist rip-offs.

Rick's been traveling to Europe for more than 25 years and is the author of 20 guidebooks, which have sold more than a million copies. He also hosts the award-winning public television series *Travels in Europe with Rick Steves*.

RICK STEVES' COUNTRY & CITY GUIDES
Best of Europe
France, Belgium & the Netherlands
Germany, Austria & Switzerland
Great Britain & Ireland
Italy • London • Paris • Rome • Scandinavia • Spain & Portugal

RICK STEVES' PHRASE BOOKS
French • German • Italian • French, Italian & German
Spanish & Portuguese

MORE EUROPE FROM RICK STEVES
Rick Steves' Europe 101
Europe Through the Back Door
Mona Winks
Postcards from Europe

WWW.RICKSTEVES.COM

ROAD TRIP USA

Getting there is half the fun, and Road Trip USA guides are your ticket to driving adventure. Taking you off the interstates and onto less-traveled, two-lane highways, each guide is filled with fascinating trivia, historical information, photographs, facts about regional writers, and details on where to sleep and eat—all contributing to your exploration of the American road.

*"Books so full of the pleasures of the American road,
you can smell the upholstery."*
~ **BBC radio**

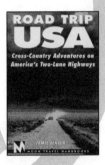

THE ORIGINAL CLASSIC GUIDE
Road Trip USA

ROAD TRIP USA REGIONAL GUIDE
Road Trip USA: California and the Southwest

ROAD TRIP USA GETAWAYS
Road Trip USA Getaways: Chicago
Road Trip USA Getaways: New Orleans
Road Trip USA Getaways: San Francisco
Road Trip USA Getaways: Seattle

www.roadtripusa.com

TRAVEL ✦ SMART®

guidebooks are accessible, route-based driving guides. Special interest tours provide the most practical routes for family fun, outdoor activities, or regional history for a trip of anywhere from two to 22 days. Travel Smarts take the guesswork out of planning a trip by recommending only the most interesting places to eat, stay, and visit.

"One of the few travel series that rates sightseeing attractions. That's a handy feature. It helps to have some guidance so that every minute counts."

~ San Diego Union-Tribune

TRAVEL SMART REGIONS

DEEP SOUTH
TRAVEL ✦ SMART®

A different kind of guidebook!
Takes the guesswork out of your travels—local
authors list only the best places to eat, stay, and visit

Alaska
American
Southwest
Arizona
Carolinas
Colorado
Deep South
Eastern
Canada
Florida Gulf
Coast
Florida
Georgia
Hawaii
Illinois/Indiana
Iowa/Nebraska
Kentucky/Tennessee
Maryland/Delaware
Michigan
Minnesota/Wisconsin
Montana/Wyoming/Idaho
Nevada

New England
New Mexico
New York State
Northern California
Ohio
Oregon
Pacific Northwest
Pennsylvania/New Jersey
South Florida and the Keys
Southern California
Texas
Utah
Virginias
Western Canada

PACIFIC NORTHWEST
TRAVEL ✦ SMART®

A different kind of guidebook!
Takes the guesswork out of your travels—a local
author lists only the best places to eat, stay, and visit

Foghorn Outdoors

guides are for campers, hikers, boaters, anglers, bikers, and golfers of all levels of daring and skill. Each guide contains site descriptions and ratings, driving directions, facilities and fees information, and easy-to-read maps that leave only the task of deciding where to go.

"Foghorn Outdoors has established an ecological conservation standard unmatched by any other publisher."
~ **Sierra Club**

CAMPING Arizona and New Mexico Camping
Baja Camping • California Camping
Camper's Companion • Colorado Camping
Easy Camping in Northern California
Easy Camping in Southern California
Florida Camping • New England Camping
Pacific Northwest Camping
Utah and Nevada Camping

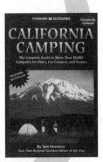

HIKING 101 Great Hikes of the San Francisco Bay Area
California Hiking • Day-Hiking California's National Parks
Easy Hiking in Northern California
Easy Hiking in Southern California
New England Hiking
Pacific Northwest Hiking • Utah Hiking

FISHING Alaska Fishing • California Fishing
Washington Fishing

BOATING California Recreational Lakes and Rivers
Washington Boating and Water Sports

OTHER OUTDOOR RECREATION California Beaches
California Golf • California Waterfalls
California Wildlife • Easy Biking in Northern California
Florida Beaches
The Outdoor Getaway Guide For Southern California
Tom Stienstra's Outdoor Getaway Guide: Northern California

WWW.FOGHORN.COM

CiTY·SMaRT™

The best way to enjoy a city is to get advice from someone who lives there—and that's exactly what City Smart guidebooks offer. City Smarts are written by local authors with hometown perspectives who have personally selected the best places to eat, shop, sightsee, and simply hang out. The honest, lively, and opinionated advice is perfect for business travelers looking to relax with the locals or for longtime residents looking for something new to do Saturday night.

*A portion of sales from each title
benefits a non-profit literacy organization in that city.*

CITY SMART CITIES

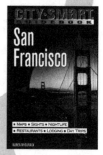

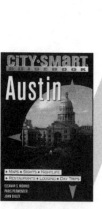

Albuquerque	Anchorage
Austin	Baltimore
Berkeley/Oakland	Boston
Calgary	Charlotte
Chicago	Cincinnati
Cleveland	Dallas/Ft. Worth
Denver	Indianapolis
Kansas City	Memphis
Milwaukee	Minneapolis/St. Paul
Nashville	Pittsburgh
Portland	Richmond
San Francisco	Sacramento
St. Louis	Salt Lake City
San Antonio	San Diego
Tampa/St. Petersburg	Toronto
Tucson	Vancouver

www.travelmatters.com

User-friendly, informative, and fun:
Because travel *matters*.

Visit our newly launched web site and explore the variety of titles and travel information available online, featuring an interactive *Road Trip USA* exhibit.

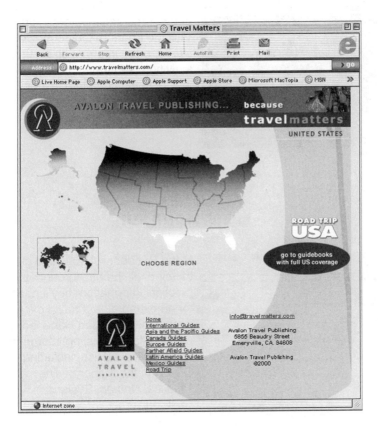

www.ricksteves.com

The Rick Steves web site is bursting with information to boost your travel I.Q. and liven up your European adventure. Including:

- The latest from Rick on what's hot in Europe
- Excerpts from Rick's books
- Rick's comprehensive Guide to European Railpasses

www.foghorn.com

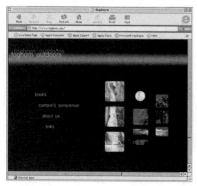

Foghorn Outdoors guides are the premier source for United States outdoor recreation information. Visit the Foghorn Outdoors web site for more information on these activity-based travel guides, including the complete text of the handy *Foghorn Outdoors: Camper's Companion*.

www.moon.com

Moon Handbooks' goal is to give travelers all the background and practical information they'll need for an extraordinary travel experience. Visit the Moon Handbooks web site for interesting information and practical advice, including Q&A with the author of *The Practical Nomad*, Edward Hasbrouck.